CASEBOOK SERIES

JANE AUSTEN: *Emma* (Revised) David Lodge
JANE AUSTEN: *'Northanger Abbey'* & *'Persuasion'* B. C. South~
JANE AUSTEN: *'Sense and Sensibility'*, *'Pride and Pr~*   *' Park'*

                     .. ĸ. Jones & W. Tydeman
            _ ʌder Western Eyes'* C. B. Cox
          ʌan Watt
DICKENS: *Bleak House* A. E. Dyson
DICKENS: *'Hard Times'*, *'Great Expectations'* & *'Our Mutual Friend'* Norman Page
DICKENS: *'Dombey and Son'* & *'Little Dorrit'* Alan Shelston
DONNE: *Songs and Sonets* Julian Lovelock
GEORGE ELIOT: *Middlemarch* Patrick Swinden
GEORGE ELIOT: *'The Mill on the Floss'* & *'Silas Marner'* R. P. Draper
T. S. ELIOT: *'Prufrock'*, *'Gerontion'* & *'Ash Wednesday'* B. C. Southam
T. S. ELIOT: *The Waste Land* C. B. Cox & Arnold P. Hinchliffe
T. S. ELIOT: *Plays* Arnold P. Hinchliffe
HENRY FIELDING: *Tom Jones* Neil Compton
E.M. FORSTER: *A Passage to India* Malcolm Bradbury
WILLIAM GOLDING: *Novels 1954–64* Norman Page
HARDY: *The Tragic Novels* (Revised) R. P. Draper
HARDY: *Poems* James Gibson & Trevor Johnson
HARDY: *Three Pastoral Novels* R. P. Draper
GERARD MANLEY HOPKINS: *Poems* Margaret Bottrall
HENRY JAMES: *'Washington Square'* & *'The Portrait of a Lady'* Alan Shelton
JONSON: *Volpone* Jonas A. Barish
JONSON: *'Every Man in his Humour'* & *'The Alchemist'* R. V. Holdsworth
JAMES JOYCE: *'Dubliners'* & *'A Portrait of the Artist as a Young Man'* Morris Beja
KEATS: *Odes* G.S. Fraser
KEATS: *Narrative Poems* John Spencer Hill
D.H. LAWRENCE: *Sons and Lovers* Gamini Salgado
D.H. LAWRENCE: *'The Rainbow'* & *'Women in Love'* Colin Clarke
LOWRY: *Under the Volcano* Gordon Bowker
MARLOWE: *Doctor Faustus* John Jump
MARLOWE: *'Tamburlaine the Great'*, *'Edward II'* & *'The Jew of Malta'* J. R. Brown
MARLOWE: *Poems* Arthur Pollard
MAUPASSANT: *In the Hall of Mirrors* T. Harris
MILTON: *Paradise Lost* A. E. Dyson & Julian Lovelock
O'CASEY: *'Juno and the Paycock'*, *'The Plough and the Stars'* & *'The Shadow of a Gunman'* Ronald Ayling
EUGENE O'NEILL: *Three Plays* Normand Berlin
JOHN OSBORNE: *Look Back in Anger* John Russell Taylor
PINTER: *'The Birthday Party'* & *Other Plays* Michael Scott
POPE: *The Rape of the Lock* John Dixon Hunt
SHAKESPEARE: *A Midsummer Night's Dream* Antony Price
SHAKESPEARE: *Antony and Cleopatra* (Revised) John Russell Brown
SHAKESPEARE: *Coriolanus* B. A. Brockman

SHAKESPEARE: *Early Tragedies* Neil Taylor & Bryan Loughrey
SHAKESPEARE: *Hamlet* John Jump
SHAKESPEARE: *Henry IV Parts I and II* G.K. Hunter
SHAKESPEARE: *Henry V* Michael Quinn
SHAKESPEARE: *Julius Caesar* Peter Ure
SHAKESPEARE: *King Lear* (Revised) Frank Kermode
SHAKESPEARE: *Macbeth* (Revised) John Wain
SHAKESPEARE: *Measure for Measure* C. K. Stead
SHAKESPEARE: *The Merchant of Venice* John Wilders
SHAKESPEARE: *'Much Ado About Nothing'* & *'As You Like It'* John Russell Brown
SHAKESPEARE: *Othello* (Revised) John Wain
SHAKESPEARE: *Richard II* Nicholas Brooke
SHAKESPEARE: *The Sonnets* Peter Jones
SHAKESPEARE: *The Tempest* (Revised) D. J. Palmer
SHAKESPEARE: *Troilus and Cressida* Priscilla Martin
SHAKESPEARE: *Twelfth Night* D. J. Palmer
SHAKESPEARE: *The Winter's Tale* Kenneth Muir
SPENSER: *The Faerie Queene* Peter Bayley
SHERIDAN: *Comedies* Peter Davison
STOPPARD: *'Rosencrantz and Guildenstern are Dead'*, *'Jumpers'* & *'Travesties'*
T. Bareham
SWIFT: *Gulliver's Travels* Richard Gravil
SYNGE: *Four Plays* Ronald Ayling
TENNYSON: *In Memoriam* John Dixon Hunt
THACKERAY: *Vanity Fair* Arthur Pollard
TROLLOPE: *The Barsetshire Novels* T. Bareham
WEBSTER: *'The White Devil'* & *'The Duchess of Malfi'* R. V. Holdsworth
WILDE: *Comedies* William Tydeman
VIRGINIA WOOLF: *To the Lighthouse* Morris Beja
WORDSWORTH: *Lyrical Ballads* Alun R. Jones & William Tydeman
WORDSWORTH: *The 1807 Poems* Alun R. Jones
WORDSWORTH: *The Prelude* W. J. Harvey & Richard Gravil
YEATS: *Poems 1919–35* Elizabeth Cullingford
YEATS: *Last Poems* Jon Stallworthy

Issues in Contemporary Critical Theory Peter Barry
Thirties Poets: 'The Auden Group' Ronald Carter
Tragedy: Developments in Criticism R.P. Draper
The Epic Ronald Draper
Poetry Criticism and Practice: Developments since the Symbolists A.E. Dyson
Three Contemporary Poets: Gunn, Hughes, Thomas A.E. Dyson
Elizabethan Poetry: Lyrical & Narrative Gerald Hammond
The Metaphysical Poets Gerald Hammond
Medieval English Drama Peter Happé
The English Novel: Developments in Criticism since Henry James Stephen Hazell
Poetry of the First World War Dominic Hibberd
The Romantic Imagination John Spencer Hill
Drama Criticism: Developments since Ibsen Arnold P. Hinchliffe
Three Jacobean Revenge Tragedies R.V. Holdsworth
The Pastoral Mode Bryan Loughrey
The Language of Literature Norman Page
Comedy: Developments in Criticism D.J. Palmer
Studying Shakespeare John Russell Brown
The Gothic Novel Victor Sage
Pre-Romantic Poetry J.R. Watson

Shakespeare

Richard II

A CASEBOOK

EDITED BY

NICHOLAS BROOKE

MACMILLAN

First published 1973 by
MACMILLAN PRESS LTD
Houndmills, Basingstoke, Hampshire RG21 2XS
and London
Companies and representatives
throughout the world

ISBN 0-333-03937-8

A catalogue record for this book is available
from the British Library.

13 12 11 10 9
99 98 97 96 95

Printed in Hong Kong

CONTENTS

ACKNOWLEDGEMENTS

Edward Arnold Ltd for chapter VIII from *Shakespeare's Plays in Performance* by John Russell Brown; Chatto & Windus Ltd for the extract from *Shakespeare and Elizabethan Poetry* by M. C. Bradbrook; Chatto & Windus Ltd and Barnes & Noble Inc., New York, for the extract from *Shakespeare's History Plays* by E. M. W. Tillyard; Columbia University Press for the extract from *Unity in Shakespearean Tragedy* by Brents Stirling; J. M. Dent & Sons Ltd for the extracts from 'Characters of Shakespeare's Plays' and 'A View of the English Stage' from *The Complete Works of W. Hazlitt* edited by P. P. Howe; J. M. Dent & Sons Ltd and E. P. Dutton & Co. Inc. for the extracts from *Of Dramatic Poesy* by John Dryden, edited with an introduction by George Watson, vol. I. Everyman's Library edition, and *Shakespearean Criticism* by S. T. Coleridge, edited by T. M. Raysor, vol. I. Everyman's Library edition; the Folio Society for *Introduction to King Richard II* as revised in *Stage Directions* by John Gielgud; the *Guardian* for the Review of F. R. Benson's Richard II by C. E. Montague, *The Manchester Guardian*; Hill & Wang Inc. for the extract from *Samuel Johnson* edited by W. K. Wimsatt; extract from *Angel with Horns* by A. P. Rossiter, edited by Graham Storey, © Longmans Green & Co. Ltd, 1961, with the permission of the publishers, Theatre Arts Books, New York; Methuen & Co. Ltd for the extract from *Shakespeare's Wordplay* by M. M. Mahood; Methuen & Co. Ltd for extracts from 'Richard II' in Nicholas Brooke's *Shakespeare's Early Tragedies*; The Modern Language Association of America for the extract from 'Symphonic Imagery in Richard II' by Richard D. Altick, PMLA 62

(1947); Princeton University Press for the extract from 'Shakespeare: *King Richard II*' in Ernst H. Kantorowicz *The King's Two Bodies: A Study in Mediaeval Theology* (© 1957 by Princeton University Press); 'The Linked Analogies of Richard II' by J. A. Bryant Jr, first published in *The Sewanee Review*, LXV, 3 (Summer 1957), © 1957 by The University of the South: appears in Mr Bryant's *Hippolyta's View* (University of Kentucky Press, 1961) reprinted with the permission of the author and the publishers; A. P. Watt & Son and The Macmillan Company (New York) for the extract from *Essays and Introductions* by W. B. Yeats, by permission of Mr Michael B. Yeats and Mrs W. B. Yeats.

GENERAL EDITOR'S PREFACE

Each of this series of Casebooks concerns either one well-known and influential work of literature or two or three closely linked works. The main section consists of critical readings, mostly modern, brought together from journals and books. A selection of reviews and comments by the author's contemporaries is also included, and sometimes comments from the author himself. The Editor's Introduction charts the reputation of the work from its first appearance until the present time.

The critical forum is a place of vigorous conflict and disagreement, but there is nothing in this to cause dismay. What is attested is the complexity of human experience and the richness of literature, not any chaos or relativity of taste. A critic is better seen, no doubt, as an explorer than as an 'authority'; but explorers ought to be, and usually are, well equipped. The effect of good criticism is to convince us of what C. S. Lewis called 'the enormous extension of our being which we owe to authors'. This Casebook will be justified only if it helps to promote the same end.

A single volume can represent no more than a small selection of critical opinions. Some critics have been excluded for reasons of space, and it is hoped that readers will follow up the further suggestions in the Select Bibliography. Other contributors have been severed from their original context, to which some readers may wish to return. Indeed, if they take a hint from the critics represented here, they certainly will.

A. E. DYSON

INTRODUCTION

It is often assumed that Shakespeare's reputation has been as consistent in kind as it has been constant in elevation. The truth is quite otherwise. The plays especially admired have varied very much, and some have see-sawed from total neglect to the highest esteem. Those few (primarily *Hamlet*) which have consistently held the stage and the attention of critics have been valued at different times for such remotely different qualities that they almost seem to have become different plays. We can only read critical accounts, whether of performance or of the text, and no doubt accounts are more selective than an actual performance can ever be. Even so, the variety and the contradictions are extraordinary, and cannot wholly be accounted for by the richness of Shakespeare's work. *Richard II* is particularly interesting in this respect, which is why this collection has an unusually high proportion of earlier critics. When the play first appeared in the mid-1590s it was both popular and highly controversial; politically, it was regarded as subversive, if not positively revolutionary. A hundred and fifty years later it had disappeared from the stage, and Samuel Johnson found no live interest in it. In the later nineteenth century it was controversial again, but this time in dispute on the nature of masculinity, with virtually no political reference at all. By the 1940s it rated as one of the most popular of the plays, and then once more the stress shifted to its political themes, but they were turned upside-down into a pattern of medieval orthodoxy.

In December 1595 Sir Edward Hoby invited a party, including Robert Cecil, to a private showing of *Richard II* at his house. It is probable, but not certain, that it was Shakespeare's play; it is also likely that his interest in it was political. What is certain is that when the first printed edition appeared in 1597 most of Act IV was omitted; all, in fact, that shows the 'voluntary' abdication of a King. Clearly a censor had intervened; but censorship of books and stage was by different authorities, and the scene appears to have been shown on the stage. When, later, it was included in print, it first appeared in a very scrappy form which must derive from memory of performance. In 1601 Queen Elizabeth said to the Keeper of the Tower : 'I am Richard the Second, know ye not that?' She also said that 'this tragedy was played forty times in open streets and houses'. Whether this was actually Shakespeare's play or some briefer exemplary representation of Richard's fall we do not know; but to have such significance it must have included the deposition. Shakespeare, deliberately or not, invoked this association, which became emblematic of the pressure on Elizabeth in her last years to abdicate. It is curious (but not necessarily significant) that the self-division he portrays, that Richard 'looks like a King' but has not the spirit of one, is the opposite of Elizabeth's claim to have a man's spirit in the body of a woman. The link became crucial in February 1601 when the play was revived as a prelude to Essex's abortive rebellion; the players were charged with incitement, but claimed that the performance had been paid for by Essex's supporters. Other History plays ran into censorship trouble : substantial cuts were made in 2 *Henry IV*; and though Shakespeare completed his series with the more discreet (though often equivocal) *Henry V*, after 1599 he, like Jonson and Chapman, turned to Roman history for political drama.

Richard II retained its political significance throughout the seventeenth century. Dryden supplemented his sympathy for the King with revulsion from the 'fortunate usurper'. But his primary concern was with qualities of language : so much of Shakespeare's verse sounded bombastic to Restoration ears, that most of his plays appeared in drastically rewritten versions. That is what Nahum Tate claimed as his motive in this case, and he does have interesting things to say about the play on its own account, chiefly (like Dryden) admiring its pathos. But Tate's 'improved' version appeared in 1681 when the exclusion question was moving towards its crisis; it was not allowed on the stage at all, and when he attempted to evade the censor by redressing it in Sicilian costume (apparently without corresponding changes in the text) the play was suppressed after its second performance. It was printed as *The Sicilian Usurper*, but there is no attempt to main-

tain the disguise in Tate's Dedicatory Epistle. His political sym-
pathies were the opposite of Dryden's, and his disclaimer in the
Epistle is clearly disingenuous. His assertion that he has outdone
Shakespeare and Holinshed in distorting history by dignifying
Richard's character as a compliment to Charles II is specious,
since the better the King who is shown abdicating, the more obvious the hint that Charles should retire; and it is blatant when he
describes Richard's abdication as 'magnanimity'. In several passages his discussion of the King seems to propose Charles, often
ironically; he claims to have so improved Richard that he appears
'Preferring the Good of his Subjects to his own private Pleasure'.

The play reappeared early in the eighteenth century in a version by Theobald which seems to have avoided political concern;
but in 1738 a new adaptation was put on at Covent Garden by
John Rich, which certainly excited political attention though it
avoided suppression. It was repeated in 1739, but not thereafter.
Garrick contemplated a revival, but never put it on, and the
play seems to have disappeared from the English stage until the
nineteenth century. Its only surviving fame was in the passage
Dryden quoted which was often printed in miscellanies. Johnson
shows no sign of suppressing political interest : he seems merely
unaware of it, and found no substitute. For him the play had
become merely a staging of Holinshed's *Chronicle*, with several
passages almost verbatim.

The nineteenth century revived it in a quite new form.
Macready first played Richard at Newcastle in 1813, but success
depended on Kean's performances from 1815 onwards. The
centre of interest shifted (as with most of Shakespeare) on to the
character of the hero; but with Richard, more than others, the
character proved controversial and by the end of the century became the centre of violent antagonisms. Coleridge identified a
quality of 'feminine friendism' which he found sympathetic, and
not (for once) a subject for moral reflection. Hazlitt was more
moralistic, stressing the weakness of Richard, but his view emerges
in interesting counterpoint with his account of Kean's performance, which he said showed the King as 'a character of *passion*,
that is, of feeling combined with energy; whereas it is a character of *pathos*, that is to say, of feeling combined with weakness'.
Hazlitt's view has become so dominant that it requires a strong

effort of imagination to recognise the possibility of Kean's interpretation; yet it clearly worked since Hazlitt attests that it had
been supposed his finest part. It is very well worth imagining
since other witnesses attest that in his own terms Kean made
the elegiac speeches of Act III very moving, and most modern
Richards have moved so far in the other direction that they look
ridiculous every time it is remarked how much he *looks* like his
father, the Black Prince.

Hazlitt's other idea, that the play could be a satire on the effete
aristocracy of his time, seems to have been abortive. Coleridge
was more immediately influential in suggesting that 'the great
object of the historic drama . . . [is] of familiarising the people
to the great names of their country, and thereby of exciting a
steady patriotism, a love of just liberty, and a respect for all those
fundamental institutions, which bind men together'. Coleridge
does not specify how the play would achieve all these ends, but
he does naturally quote Gaunt's dying speech which thereafter
came to replace Dryden's choice in the anthologies. When Kean's
son Charles revived the play in the middle of the century he
elaborated historical pageantry, making the play a live museum
with archaeologically detailed sets, hundred of extras, and
dummy horses. At the beginning of the twentieth century Beer-
bohm Tree went further : his horses were alive.

But Tree was out of date : Benson had been playing Richard
since 1895, and in 1899 Montague's review of his performance
in Manchester finally shifted the centre of gravity to the equivocal
hero himself. Twenty years earlier Dowden had given elaborate
definition to a Victorian moralistic view of Richard. He treated
all the history plays as a single document, moving back and
forth without any reference to their separate structures. His prime
objective would seem to have derived from Coleridge's patriotic
observation : to write a history of the Kings of England using
Shakespeare as the primary source. Richard lacked the moral
fibre to grasp reality, whether of religion or of rule; his only edu-
cational value could be as a bad example. Dowden's ideas were
those of the public school movement; his aim was the extension
and government of the British Empire. His influence was felt for
more than fifty years, but the last vivid expression of it was in
Swinburne's rambling, wildly ill-informed, but characteristically

exuberant essay of 1909 (the year of his death after a long and sad senility). Pater's essay in 1889 was of an entirely different kind, and quality. He was very conscious of the play's autonomous structure, even more of its distinctive unity of poetic tone. In these respects, as in his sympathy for Richard, he doubtless owed a lot to the best of Coleridge's criticism. But'he also had a much more precise grasp of history, for which Shakespeare was clearly not his primary source. He recognised, as very few have done before or since, that the image of divine monarch projected in Richard was new in Shakespeare's day, and by no means simply a traditional orthodoxy. The divine right of Kings was James I's theme; le Roi Soleil was Louis XIV. Pater's is the fullest, and by far the best, of the essays on the play. Indeed much of the diversity apparent in the recent essays reprinted here can be seen as deriving from different aspects of his work; they needed fuller demonstration, but have never been represented in better balance.

Balance is not remarkable in either Montague or Yeats, and they generated excitement from their single-mindedness. Both were in violent, explicit, and welcome reaction against Dowden, and both derived the idea of the artist-king from Pater. Montague's review of F. R. Benson's performance appeared in 1899, and elaborated an idea of Richard's poetic mode of apprehension which projects a Pre-Raphaelite hero. It is perhaps not surprising that when James Agate read the review to Benson in his dressing room, the actor repudiated any intention of playing the aesthete. Yeats saw Benson two years later at Stratford-on-Avon, and though less detailed, is considerably sharper than Montague. He had long known Dowden in Dublin, and took the occasion for a radical attack on his values. Richard, attacked by Dowden on behalf of the public school ethic, was pressed by Yeats into the service of the *fin-de-siècle* in an ardent defence of the sensitive individual against the worship of team games.

The image of Richard as a poet-king with a flower-like beauty persisted until very recently; but it was joined by E. M. W. Tillyard to a new concern with the play as part of a political epic. The wheel may seem to have gone full circle, but the political image has been reversed : Tillyard responded to an imaginative concept of Order closely akin to many of Yeats' later poems, or, perhaps more pertinently, to all T. S. Eliot's work. Poetry between the wars was redirected towards political commitment, and critical attention to *Richard II* changed in that tradition. Whether that now seems 'modern' is questionable; the process traced in this introduction is continuous, and it is only for convenience that a break is made at this point in the contents of this volume. The later essays may be left to speak for themselves, with the proviso that the distinction between 'production' and 'criticism' is fortunately becoming once more meaningless as it was in the earlier section. Many recent essays can be seen as developing lines from Pater, but they are far from producing a current orthodoxy about the play. The history of what it has meant to earlier interpreters makes clear how diverse its possibilities are, and it is wholly proper that it is once more becoming open to experiment in the theatre and to imaginative re-vision.

NICHOLAS BROOKE

PART ONE

Earlier Critics of *Richard II*

John Dryden

Bombast is commonly the delight of that audience which loves poetry, but understands it not: and as commonly has been the practice of those writers who, not being able to infuse a natural passion into the mind, have made it their business to ply the ears and to stun their judges by the noise. But Shakespeare does not often thus; for the passions in his scene between Brutus and Cassius are extremely natural, the thoughts are such as arise from the matter, the expression of 'em not viciously figurative. I cannot leave this subject, before I do justice to that divine poet by giving you one of his passionate descriptions: 'tis of Richard the Second when he was deposed, and led in triumph through the streets of London by Henry of Bullingbrook: the painting of it is so lively, and the words so moving, that I have scarce read any thing comparable to it in any other language. Suppose you have seen already the fortunate usurper passing through the crowd, and followed by the shouts and acclamations of the people; and now behold King Richard entering upon the scene: consider the wretchedness of his condition, and his carriage in it; and refrain from pity if you can:

> As in a theatre, the eyes of men,
> After a well-graced actor leaves the stage,
> Are idly bent on him that enters next,
> Thinking his prattle to be tedious:
> Even so, or with much more contempt, men's eyes
> Did scowl on Richard: no man cried, God save him:
> No joyful tongue gave him his welcome home,
> But dust was thrown upon his sacred head,
> Which with such gentle sorrow he shook off,
> His face still combating with tears and smiles
> (The badges of his grief and patience),
> That had not God (for some strong purpose) steel'd
> The hearts of men, they must perforce have melted,
> And barbarism itself have pitied him.[1]

To speak justly of this whole matter : 'tis neither height of thought that is discommended, nor pathetic vehemence, nor any nobleness of expression in its proper place; but 'tis a false measure of all these, something which is like 'em, and is not them; 'tis the Bristol-stone,[2] which appears like a diamond; 'tis an extravagant thought, instead of a sublime one; 'tis roaring madness, instead of vehemence; and a sound of words, instead of sense. If Shakespeare were stripped of all the bombast in his passions, and dressed in the most vulgar words, we should find the beauties of his thoughts remaining . . .

SOURCE : 'The Grounds of Criticism in Tragedy',
Preface to *Troilus and Cressida* (1679).

NOTES

1. *Richard II*, v, ii, 23–36.
2. i.e. rock-crystal.

Nahum Tate

The Buisiness of this Epistle is more Vindication than Complement; and when we are to tell our Grievances 'tis most natural to betake our selves to a Friend. 'Twas thought perhaps that this unfortunate Offspring having been stifled on the *Stage*, shou'd have been buried in Oblivion; and so it might have happened had it drawn its Being from me Alone, but it still retains the immortal Spirit of its first-Father, and will survive in Print, though forbid to tread the *Stage*. They that have not seen it Acted, by its being silenc't, must suspect me to have Compil'd a Disloyal or Reflecting *Play*. But how far distant this was from my Design and Conduct in the Story will appear to him that reads with half an Eye. To form any Resemblance between the Times here written of, and the Present, had been unpardonable Presumption in Me. If the Prohibiters conceive any such Notion I am not accountable for That. I fell upon the new-modelling of this Tragedy, (as I had just before done on the *History of King Lear*) charm'd with the many Beauties I discover'd in it, which I knew wou'd become the *Stage*; with as little design of Satyr on present Transactions, as *Shakespear* himself that wrote this Story before this Age began. I am not ignorant of the posture of Affairs in King *Richard* the Second's Reign, how dissolute then the Age, and how corrupt the Court; a Season that beheld *Ignorance* and *Infamy* preferr'd to *Office* and *Pow'r*, exercis'd in Oppressing, Learning and Merit; but why a History of those Times shou'd be supprest as a Libel upon Ours, is past my Understanding. 'Tis sure the worst *Complement* that ever was made to a Prince.

> O Rem ridiculam, Cato, & jocosam,
> Dignámque Auribus, & tuo Cachinno.
> Ride, quicquid amas, Cato, Catullum
> Res est Ridicula, &c.

Our *Shakespear* in this Tragedy, bated none of his Characters an Ace of the Chronicle; he took care to shew 'em no worse Men than They were, but represents them never a jot better. His *Duke of York* after all his buisy pretended Loyalty, is found false to his Kinsman and Sovereign, and joyn'd with the *Conspirators*. His King *Richard* Himself is painted in the worst Colours of History. Dissolute, Unadviseable, devoted to Ease and Luxury. You find old *Gaunt* speaking of him in this Language

> Then there are found
> Lascivious Meeters, to whose Venom sound
> The open Ear of Youth do's always Listen.
> Where doth the World thrust forth a Vanity,
> (So it be New, there's no respect how Vile)
> That is not quickly buzz'd into his Ear?
> That all too late comes Counsel to be heard.

without the least palliating of his Miscarriages, which I have done in the new Draft, with such words as These.

> Your Sycophants bred from your Child-hood with you,
> Have such Advantage had to work upon you,
> That scarce your Failings can be call'd your Faults.

His Reply in *Shakespear* to the blunt honest Adviser runs thus.

> And Thou a Lunatick Lean-witted-fool, &c.
> Now by my Seat's right Royal Majesty,
> Wer't Thou not Brother to great *Edward*'s Son
> The Tongue that runs thus roundly in thy Head
> Shou'd run thy Head from thy unreverent Shoulders.

On the contrary (though I have made him express some Resentment) yet he is neither enrag'd with the good Advice, nor deaf to it. He answers Thus—

> Gentle Unkle;
> Excuse the Sally's of my Youthfull Blood.
> We shall not be unmindfull to redress
> (However difficult) our States Corruptions,
> And purge the Vanities that crowd our Court.

I have every where given him the Language of an Active, Prudent Prince. Preferring the Good of his Subjects to his own private Pleasure. On his *Irish* Expedition, you find him thus bespeak his Queen—

> Though never vacant Swain in silent Bow'rs
> Cou'd boast a Passion so sincere as Mine,
> Yet where the Int'rest of the Subject calls
> We wave the dearest Transports of our Love,
> Flying from Beauties Arms to rugged War, &c.

Nor cou'd it suffice me to make him speak like a King (who as Mr *Rhymer* says in his *Tragedies of the last Age considered*, are always in Poëtry presum'd Heroes) but to *Act so too*, viz. with *Resolution* and *Justice*. Resolute enough our *Shakespear* (copying the History) has made him, for concerning his seizing old *Gaunt*'s Revennues, he tells the wise Diswaders,

> Say what ye will, we seize into our Hands
> His Plate, his Goods, his Money and his Lands.

But where was the Justice of this Action? This Passage I confess was so material a Part of the Chronicle (being the very Basis of *Bullingbrook*'s Usurpation) that I cou'd not in this new Model so far transgress Truth as to make no mention of it; yet for the honour of my Heroe I suppose the foresaid Revennues to be *Borrow'd* onely for the present Exigence, not *Extorted*.

> Be Heav'n our Judge, we mean him fair,
> And shortly will with Interest restore
> The Loan our suddain Streights make necessary.

My Design was to engage the pitty of the Audience for him in his Distresses, which I cou'd never have compass'd had I not before shewn him a Wise, Active and Just Prince. Detracting Language (if any where) had been excusable in the Mouths of the Conspirators: part of whose Dialogue runs thus in *Shakespear*:

NORTHUMBERLAND   Now afore Heav'n 'tis shame such Wrongs are
    born
In him a Royal Prince and many more
Of noble Blood in this Declining Land :

The King is not Himself, but basely led
By Flatterers, &c.

ROSS   The Commons He has pil'd with grievous Taxes
And lost their Hearts, &c.

WILLOUGHBY   And daily new Exactions are devis'd
As Blanks, Benevolences, and I wot not what;
But what o' Gods Name doth become of This?

NORTHUMBERLAND   War hath not wasted it, for warr'd he has not;
But basely yielded upon Comprimize.
That which his Ancestours atchiev'd with Blows
More has He spent in Peace than they in War, &c.

with much more villifying Talk; but I wou'd not allow even Traytors and Conspirators thus to bespatter the Person whom I design'd to place in the Love and Compassion of the Audience. Ev'n this very Scene (as I have manag'd it) though it shew the Confederates to be Villains, yet it flings no Aspersion on my Prince.

Further, to Vindicate ev'n his *Magnanimity* in Regard of his Resigning the Crown, I have on purpose inserted an intirely new Scene between him and his Queen, wherein his Conduct is sufficiently excus'd by the Malignancy of his Fortune, which argues indeed Extremity of Distress, but Nothing of Weakness.

After this account it will be askt why this Play shou'd be supprest, first in its own Name, and after in Disguise? All that I can answer to this, is, That it was *Silenc'd on the Third Day.* I confess, I expected it wou'd have found Protection from whence it receiv'd Prohibition; and so questionless it wou'd, cou'd I have obtain'd my Petition to have it perus'd and dealt with according as the Contents Deserv'd, but a positive Doom of Suppression *without Examination* was all that I cou'd procure.

The Arbitrary Courtiers of the Reign here written, scarcely did more Violence to the Subjects of their Time, then I have done to *Truth*, in disguising their foul Practices. Take ev'n the *Richard* of *Shakespear* and History, you will find him Dissolute, Careless, and Unadvisable : peruse my Picture of him and you will say, as *Æneas* did of *Hector*, (though the Figure there was alter'd for the Worse and here for the Better) *Quantum mutatus ab illo!* And likewise for his chief Ministers of State, I have laid Vertues to their Charge of which they were not Guilty. Every Scene is full of Respect to Majesty and the dignity of Courts, not one alter'd Page but what breaths Loyalty, yet had this Play the hard fortune to receive its Prohibition from Court.

For the two days in which it was Acted, the Change of the Scene, Names of Persons, &c. was a great Disadvantage : many things were by this means render'd obscure and incoherent that in their native Dress had appear'd not only proper but gracefull. I call'd my Persons *Sicilians* but might as well have made 'em Inhabitants of the *Isle of Pines*, or, World in the *Moon*, for whom an Audience are like to have small Concern. Yet I took care from the Beginning to adorn my Prince with such heroick Vertues, as afterwards made his distrest Scenes of force to draw Tears from the Spectators; which, how much more touching they would have been had the Scene been laid at Home, let the Reader judge. The additional Comedy I judg'd necessary to help off the heaviness of the Tale, which Design, Sir, you will not only Pardon, but Approve. I have heard you commend this Method in Stage writing, though less agreeable to stricktness of Rule; and I find your Choice confirm'd by our *Laureat*'s last Piece, who confesses himself to have broken a Rule for the Pleasure of Variety.[1] *The Audience* (says he) *are grown weary of melancholly Scenes, and I dare prophesie that few Tragedies (except those in Verse) shall succeed in this Age if they are not lightned with a course of Mirth.*

SOURCE : 'The Epistle Dedicatory (to George Raynsford) to *The History of King Richard II*' (1681).

NOTE

1. Dryden, Epistle Dedicatory to *The Spanish Fryar*.

Samuel Johnson

This play is extracted from the *Chronicle of Holinshed*, in which many passages may be found which Shakespeare has, with very little alteration, transplanted into his scenes; particularly a speech of the bishop of Carlisle in defence of King Richard's unalienable right and immunity from human jurisdiction.

Jonson, who in his *Catiline* and *Sejanus* has inserted many speeches from the Roman historians, was perhaps induced to that practice by the example of Shakespeare, who had condescended sometimes to copy more ignoble writers. But Shakespeare had more of his own than Jonson and, if he sometimes was willing to spare his labour, showed by what he performed at other times that his extracts were made by choice or idleness rather than necessity.

This play is one of those which Shakespeare has apparently revised; but as success in works of invention is not always proportionate to labour, it is not finished at last with the happy force of some other of his tragedies nor can be said much to affect the passions or enlarge the understanding.

SOURCE : 'General observations on *Richard II*'
in Johnson's *Shakespeare* (1765).

S. T. Coleridge

The transitional state between the epic and the drama is the historic drama. In the epic a pre-announced fate gradually adjusts and employs the will and the incidents as its instruments (ἕπομαι, *sequor*[1]), while the drama places fate and will in opposition[2] [and is] then most perfect when the victory of fate is obtained in consequence of imperfections in the opposing will, so as to leave the final impression that the fate itself is but a higher and more intelligent Will.

From the length of the speeches, the number of long speeches, and that (with one exception) the events are all *historical*, presented in their *results*, not produced by acts seen, or that take place before the audience, this tragedy is ill-suited to our present large theatres. But in itself, and for the closet, I feel no hesitation in placing it the first and most admirable of all Shakespeare's *purely* historical plays. For the two parts of *Henry IV* form a species of themselves, which may be named the *mixt* drama. The distinction does not depend on the quantity of historical events compared with the fictions, for there is as much *history* in *Macbeth* as in *Richard*, but in the relation of the history to the plot. In the purely historical plays, the history *informs* the plot; in the mixt it *directs* it; in the rest, as *Macbeth, Hamlet, Cymbeline, Lear*, it subserves it.

But this Richard II. O God forbid that however unsuited for the stage yet even there it should fall dead on the hearts of jacobinized Englishmen. Then indeed *praeteriit gloria mundi*. The spirit of patriotic reminiscence is the all-permeating spirit of this drama.

It is, perhaps, the most purely historical of Shakspeare's dramas. There are not in it, as in the others, characters introduced merely for the purpose of giving a greater individuality and realness, as in the comic parts of *Henry IV*, by presenting, as it were, our very selves. Shakspeare avails himself of every opportunity to effect the great object of the historic drama, that, namely, of familiarizing the people to the great names of their country, and thereby of exciting a steady patriotism, a love of just liberty, and a respect for all those fundamental institutions of social life, which bind men together :

> This royal throne of kings, this scepter'd isle,
> This earth of majesty, this seat of Mars,
> This other Eden, demi-paradise;
> This fortress, built by nature for herself,
> Against infection, and the hand of war;
> This happy breed of men, this little world;
> This precious stone set in the silver sea,
> Which serves it in the office of a wall,
> Or as a moat defensive to a home,[a]
> Against the envy of less happier lands;
> This blessed plot, this earth, this realm, this England,
> This nurse, this teeming womb of royal kings,
> Fear'd by their breed, and famous by their birth, &c.
>
> (ii, i, 40–52)

Add the famous passage in *King John* –

> This England never did, nor ever[b] shall,
> Lie at the proud foot of a conqueror,
> But when it first did help to wound itself.
> Now these her princes are come home again,
> Come the three corners of the world in arms,
> And we shall shock them : nought shall make us rue,
> If England to itself do rest but true. (v, vii, 112–18)

And it certainly seems that Shakspeare's historic dramas produced a very deep effect on the minds of the English people, and in earlier times they were familiar even to the least informed of all ranks, according to the relation of Bishop Corbett.[3] Marlborough, we know, was not ashamed to confess that his principal acquaintance with English history was derived from them;[4] and I believe that a large part of the information as to our old names and achievements even now abroad is due, directly or indirectly, to Shakspeare.

In the very beginning, also, is displayed that feature in Richard's character, which is never forgotten throughout the

---

[a] Read 'house'.   [b] Read 'never'.

play—his attention to decorum, and high feeling of the kingly dignity. These anticipations show with what judgement Shakspeare wrote, and illustrate his care to connect the past and future, and unify them with the present by forecast and reminiscence. . . .

> (i, i, 150–1   Mowbray's speech.
> In haste whereof, most heartily I pray
> Your highness to assign our trial day.)

Query. The occasional interspersion of rhymes and the more frequent winding up of a speech therewith—what purpose was this to answer? In the earnest drama, I mean. Deliberateness! An attempt as in Mowbray to collect himself and *be cool* at the close? I can see that in the following speeches the rhyme answers the purposes of the Greek chorus, and distinguish[es] the *general* truths from the passions of the dialogue; but this is not exactly to *justify* the practice, which is infrequent in proportion to the excellence of Shakespeare's plays. One thing, however, is to be observed : they are *historical, known,* and so far *formal* characters, the reality of which is already a *fact.*

This [historical reality should be] dwelt upon as predominant in *Richard* [*II*], the purest historic play—indeed, *John* and *Henry VIII* excepted, the only *pure*.

This should be borne in mind. The whole of this scene of the quarrel between Mowbray and Bolingbroke seems introduced for the purpose of showing by anticipation the characters of Richard and Bolingbroke. In the latter there is observable a decorous and courtly checking of his anger in subservience to a predetermined plan, especially in his calm speech after receiving sentence of banishment compared with Mowbray's unaffected lamentation. In the one, all is ambitious hope of something yet to come; in the other it is desolation and a looking backward of the heart.

> (i, ii, 37–41
> GAUNT   God's is the quarrel; for God's substitute,
> His deputy anointed in His sight,
> Hath caused his death : the which, if wrongfully,
> Let heaven revenge; for I may never lift
> An angry arm against His minister.)

Without the hollow extravagance of Beaumont and Fletcher's ultra-royalism, how carefully does Shakespeare acknowledge and reverence the eternal distinction between the mere individual and the symbolic or representative, on which all genial law, no less than patriotism, depends.

This second scene quite commencing, and anticipative of, the tone and character of the play at large. . . .

I, iv. A striking conclusion of a first act—letting the reader into the secret [of Richard's weakness], having before impressed the dignified and kingly manners of Richard, yet by well managed anticipations leading to the full gratification of the auditor's pleasure in his own penetration.

In this scene a new light is thrown on Richard's character. Until now he has appeared in all the beauty of royalty; but here, as soon as he is left to himself, the inherent weakness of his character is immediately shown. It is a weakness, however, of a peculiar kind, not arising from want of personal courage, or any specific defect of faculty, but rather an intellectual feminineness which feels a necessity of ever leaning on the breast of others, and of reclining on those who are all the while known to be inferiors. To this must be attributed as its consequences all Richard's vices, his tendency to concealment, and his cunning, the whole operation of which is directed to the getting rid of present difficulties. Richard is not meant to be a debauchee; but we see in him that sophistry which is common to man, by which we can deceive our own hearts, and at one and the same time apologize for, and yet commit, the error. Shakspeare has represented this character in a very peculiar manner. He has not made him amiable with counterbalancing faults; but has openly and broadly drawn those faults without reserve, relying on Richard's disproportionate sufferings and gradually emergent good qualities for our sympathy; and this was possible, because his faults are not positive vices, but spring entirely from defect of character.

(II, i, 84   Gaunt's punning on his death-bed.[5]
RICHARD   Can sick men play so nicely with their names?)

The passion that carries off its excess by play on words, as naturally and, therefore, as appropriately to drama, as by gesticulations, looks, or tones. This belonging to human nature as *human*, independent of associations and habits from any particular rank of life or mode of employment; and in this consists Shakespeare's vulgarisms, as in *Macbeth*,

> The devil damn thee black, thou cream-faced loon! etc.

It is (to play on Dante's words) in truth the NOBILE *volgare eloquenza*.
And here the death-bed feeling in which all things appear but as *puns* and equivocations.
No doubt, something of Shakspeare's punning must be attributed to his age, in which direct and formal combats of wit were a favourite pastime of the courtly and accomplished. It was an age more favourable, upon the whole, to vigour of intellect than the present, in which a dread of being thought pedantic dispirits and flattens the energies of original minds. But independently of this, I have no hesitation in saying that a pun, if it be congruous with the feeling of the scene, is not only allowable in the dramatic dialogue, but oftentimes one of the most effectual intensives of passion. . . .

(II, ii, 5–13

> QUEEN To please the king I did; to please myself
> I cannot do it; yet I know no cause
> Why I should welcome such a guest as grief,
> Save bidding farewell to so sweet a guest
> As my sweet Richard : yet again, methinks,
> Some unborn sorrow, ripe in fortune's womb,
> Is coming towards me, and my inward soul
> With nothing trembles : at some thing it grieves,
> More than with parting from my lord the king.)

It is clear that Shakespeare never meant to represent Richard II as a vulgar debauchee, but merely [as a man with] a wantonness in feminine shew, feminine *friendism*, intensely woman-like love of those immediately about him, mistaking the delight of being loved by him for a love for him.
Tender superstitions [are] encouraged by Shakespeare. *Terra*

incognita of the human mind : and how sharp a line of distinction he commonly draws between these obscure forecastings of general experience in each individual, and the vulgar errors of mere tradition.

SOURCE : 'Marginalia and Notebooks' in T. M. Raysor (ed.) *S. T. Coleridge* : Shakespearean Criticism, vol. 1 (1960).

NOTES

1. It scarcely seems probable that Coleridge cites these words to connect with them 'epic' etymologically, but if this is not the case his purpose seems rather obscure.

2. Schlegel makes the same remark (*Werke*, v, 72), but probably no one would press this fact as an evidence of his influence.

3. This is the poet, Richard Corbet (1582–1635), bishop successively of Oxford and Norwich. The allusion is most conveniently found in the *Shakespeare Allusion Book*, i, 271. Or see Corbet's *Poems* (London, 1807), pp. 193–4.

4. For this story, see Ferdinando Warner's *Remarks on the History of Fingal* (1762), p. 26. (Cf. ii, 229.)

5. Schlegel also defends Gaunt's punning (*Werke*, vi, 194), but merely by reference to a similar occurrence in the *Ajax* of Sophocles. As Coleridge was always interested in puns and would probably have discussed this instance in a favourite play without the suggestion of Schlegel, the slight parallelism may surely be set down as due to coincidence.

W. C. Hazlitt

1. MR KEAN'S RICHARD II

The Examiner   *March* 19, 1815

We are not in the number of those who are anxious in recommend-
ing the getting-up of Shakespear's plays in general, as a duty
which our stage-managers owe equally to the author, and the
reader of those wonderful compositions. The representing the
very finest of them on the stage, even by the best actors, is, we
apprehend, an abuse of the genius of the poet, and even in those
of a second-rate class, the quantity of sentiment and imagery
greatly outweighs the immediate impression of the situation and
story. Not only are the more refined poetical beauties and minu-
ter strokes of character lost to the audience, but the most striking
and impressive passages, those which having once read we can
never forget, fail comparatively of their effect, except in one
or two rare instances indeed. It is only the *pantomime* part of
tragedy, the exhibition of immediate and physical distress, that
which gives the greatest opportunity for 'inexpressible dumb-
show and noise', which is sure to tell, and tell completely on the
stage. All the rest, all that appeals to our profounder feelings,
to reflection and imagination, all that affects us most deeply in
our closets, and in fact constitutes the glory of Shakespear, is little
else than an interruption and a drag on the business of the stage.
Segnius per aures demissa, &c. Those parts of the play on which
the reader dwells the longest, and with the highest relish in the
perusal, are hurried through in the performance, while the most
trifling and exceptionable are obtruded on his notice, and occupy
as much time as the most important. We do not mean to say that
there is less knowledge or display of mere stage-effect in Shakespear than in other writers, but that there is a much greater knowledge and display of other things, which divide the attention with
it, and to which it is not possible to give an equal force in the

representation. Hence it is, that the reader of the plays of Shakespear is almost always disappointed in seeing them acted; and,
for our own parts, we should never go to see them acted, if we
could help it.

Shakespear has embodied his characters so very distinctly, that
he stands in no need of the actor's assistance to make them more
distinct; and the representation of the character on the stage
almost uniformly interferes with our conception of the character
itself. The only exceptions we can recollect to this observation,
are Mrs Siddons and Mr Kean—the former of whom in one or
two characters, and the latter, not certainly in any one character,
but in very many passages, have raised our imagination of the
part they acted. It may be asked then, why all great actors chuse
characters from Shakespear to come out in; and again, why these
become their favourite parts? First, it is not that they are able to
exhibit their author, but that he enables them to shew themselves
off. The only way in which Shakespear appears to greater advantage on the stage than common writers is, that he stimulates the
faculties of the actor more. If he is a sensible man, he perceives
how much he has to do, the inequalities he has to contend with,
and he exerts himself accordingly; he puts himself at full speed,
and lays all his resources under contribution; he attempts more,
and makes a greater number of brilliant failures; he plays off all
the tricks of his art to mimic the poet; he does all he can, and bad
is often the best. We have before said that there are some few
exceptions. If the genius of Shakespear does not shine out un-
diminished in the actor, we perceive certain effects and refrac-
tions of it in him. If the oracle does not speak quite intelligibly,
yet we perceive that the priest at the altar is inspired with the
god, or possessed with a demon. To speak our minds at once, we
believe that in acting Shakespear there is a greater number of good
things marred than in acting any other author. In fact, in going
to see the plays of Shakespear, it would be ridiculous to suppose
that any one ever went to see Hamlet or Othello represented by
Kean or Kemble; we go to see Kean or Kemble in Hamlet or
Othello. On the contrary, Miss O'Neill and Mrs Beverley are,
we take it, one and the same person. As to the second point, viz.
that Shakespear's characters are decidedly favourites on the stage
in the same proportion as they are in the closet, we deny it alto-

gether. They either do not tell so much, or very little more than many others. Mrs Siddons was quite as great in Mrs Beverley and Isabella as in Lady Macbeth or Queen Katherine : yet no one, we apprehend, will say that the poetry is equal. It appears, therefore, not that the most intellectual characters excite most interest on the stage, but that they are objects of greater curiosity; they are nicer tests of the skill of the actor, and afford greater scope for controversy, how far the sentiment is 'overdone or come tardy off'. There is more in this circumstance than people in general are aware of. We have no hesitation in saying, for instance, that Miss O'Neill has more popularity *in the house* than Mr Kean. It is quite as certain, that he is more thought of *out of it*. The reason is, that she is not 'food for the critics', whereas Mr Kean notoriously is; there is no end of the topics he affords for discussion—for praise and blame.

All that we have said of acting in general applies to his Richard II. It has been supposed that this is his finest part : this is, however, a total misrepresentation. There are only one or two electrical shocks given in it; and in many of his characters he gives a much greater number.—The excellence of his acting is in proportion to the number of hits, for he has not equal truth or purity of style. Richard II was hardly given correctly as to the general outline. Mr Kean made it a character of *passion*, that is, of feeling combined with energy; whereas it is a character of *pathos*, that is to say, of feeling combined with weakness. This, we conceive, is the general fault of Mr Kean's acting, that it is always energetic or nothing. He is always on full stretch—never relaxed. He expresses all the violence, the extravagance, and fierceness of the passions, but not their misgivings, their helplessness, and sinkings into despair. He has too much of that strong nerve and fibre that is always equally elastic. We might instance to the present purpose, his dashing the glass down with all his might, in the scene with Hereford, instead of letting it fall out of his hands, as from an infant's; also, his manner of expostulating with Bolingbroke, 'Why on thy knee, thus low, &c.' which was altogether fierce and heroic, instead of being sad, thoughtful, and melancholy. If Mr Kean would look into some passages in this play, into that in particular, 'Oh that I were a mockery king of snow, to melt away before the sun of Bolingbroke', he would find a clue to this character, and to human nature in general, which he seems to have missed—how far feeling is connected with the sense of weakness as well as of strength, or the power of imbecility, and the force of passiveness. We never saw Mr Kean look better than when we saw him in *Richard II* and his voice appeared to us to be stronger. We saw him near, which is always in his favour; and we think one reason why the Editor of this Paper was disappointed in first seeing this celebrated actor, was his being at a considerable distance from the stage. We feel persuaded that on a nearer and more frequent view of him, he will agree that he is a perfectly original, and sometimes a perfectly natural actor; that if his conception is not always just or profound, his execution is masterly; that where he is not the very character he assumes, he makes a most brilliant rehearsal of it : that he never wants energy, ingenuity, and animation, though he is often deficient in dignity, grace, and tenderness; that if he frequently disappoints us in those parts where we expect him to do most, he as frequently surprises us by striking out unexpected beauties of his own; and that the objectionable parts of his acting arise chiefly from the physical impediments he has to overcome.

Of the other characters of the play, it is needless to say much. Mr Pope was respectable in John of Gaunt. Mr Holland was lamentable in the Duke of York, and Mr Elliston indifferent in Bolingbroke. This alteration of *Richard II* is the best that has been attempted; for it consists entirely of omissions, except one or two scenes which are idly tacked on to the conclusion.

SOURCE : *A View of the English Stage* (1818).

2. THE CHARACTER OF RICHARD II

Richard II is a play little known compared with *Richard III* which last is a play that every unfledged candidate for theatrical fame chuses to strut and fret his hour upon the stage in; yet we confess that we prefer the nature and feeling of the one to the noise and bustle of the other; at least, as we are so often forced to see it acted. In *Richard II* the weakness of the king leaves us leisure to take a greater interest in the misfortunes of the man. After the first act, in which the arbitrariness of his behaviour only proves his want of resolution, we see him staggering under the unlooked-for blows of fortune, bewailing his loss of kingly power, not preventing it, sinking under the aspiring genius of Bolingbroke, his authority trampled on, his hopes failing him, and his pride crushed and broken down under insults and injuries, which his own misconduct had provoked, but which he has not courage or manliness to resent. The change of tone and behaviour in the two competitors for the throne according to their change of fortune, from the capricious sentence of banishment passed by Richard upon Bolingbroke, the suppliant offers and modest pretensions of the latter on his return to the high and haughty tone with which he accepts Richard's resignation of the crown after the loss of all his power, the use which he makes of the deposed king to grace his triumphal progress through the streets of London, and the final intimation of his wish for his death, which immediately finds a servile executioner, is marked throughout with complete effect and without the slightest appearance of effort. The steps by which Bolingbroke mounts the throne are those by which Richard sinks into the grave. We feel neither respect nor love for the deposed monarch; for he is as wanting in energy as in principle: but we pity him, for he pities himself. His heart is by no means hardened against himself, but bleeds afresh at every new stroke of mischance, and his sensibility, absorbed in his own person, and unused to misfortune, is not only tenderly alive to its own sufferings, but without the fortitude to bear them. He is, however, human in his distresses; for to feel pain, and sorrow, weakness, disappointment, remorse and anguish, is the lot of humanity, and we sympathize with him accordingly. The sufferings of the man make us forget that he ever was a king.

The right assumed by sovereign power to trifle at its will with the happiness of others as a matter of course, or to remit its exercise as a matter of favour, is strikingly shewn in the sentence of banishment so unjustly pronounced on Bolingbroke and Mowbray, and in what Bolingbroke says when four years of his banishment are taken off, with as little reason.

> How long a time lies in one little word!
> Four lagging winters and four wanton springs
> End in a word : such is the breath of kings.

A more affecting image of the loneliness of a state of exile can hardly be given than by what Bolingbroke afterwards observes of his having 'sighed his English breath in foreign clouds'; or than that conveyed in Mowbray's complaint at being banished for life.

> The language I have learned these forty years,
> My native English, now I must forego;
> And now my tongue's use is to me no more
> Than an unstringed viol or a harp,
> Or like a cunning instrument cas'd up,
> Or being open, put into his hands
> That knows no touch to tune the harmony.
> I am too old to fawn upon a nurse,
> Too far in years to be a pupil now.—

How very beautiful is all this, and at the same time how very *English* too!

Richard II may be considered as the first of that series of English historical plays, in which 'is hung armour of the invincible knights of old', in which their hearts seem to strike against their coats of mail, where their blood tingles for the fight, and words are but the harbingers of blows. Of this state of accomplished barbarism the appeal of Bolingbroke and Mowbray is an admirable specimen. Another of these 'keen encounters of their wits', which serve to whet the talkers' swords, is where Aumerle answers in the presence of Bolingbroke to the charge which Bagot brings against him of being an accessory in Gloster's death. . . .

The truth is, that there is neither truth nor honour in all these noble persons : they answer words with words, as they do blows with blows, in mere self defence : nor have they any principle whatever but that of courage in maintaining any wrong they dare commit, or any falsehood which they find it useful to assert. How different were these noble knights and 'barons bold' from their more refined descendants in the present day, who, instead of deciding questions of right by brute force, refer everything to convenience, fashion, and good breeding! In point of any abstract love of truth or justice, they are just the same now that they were then.

The characters of old John of Gaunt and of his brother York, uncles to the King, the one stern and foreboding, the other honest, good-natured, doing all for the best, and therefore doing nothing, are well kept up. The speech of the former, in praise of England, is one of the most eloquent that ever was penned. We should perhaps hardly be disposed to feed the pampered egotism of all countrymen by quoting this description, were it not that the conclusion of it (which looks prophetic) may qualify any improper degree of exultation. . . .

The character of Bolingbroke, afterwards Henry IV is drawn with a masterly hand :—patient for occasion, and the steadily availing himself of it, seeing his advantage afar off, but only seizing on it when he has it within his reach, humble, crafty, bold, and aspiring, encroaching by regular but slow degrees, building power on opinion, and cementing opinion by power. His disposition is first unfolded by Richard himself, who however is too self-willed and secure to make a proper use of his knowledge.

> Ourself and Bushy, Bagot here and Green,
> Observed his courtship of the common people :
> How he did seem to dive into their hearts,
> With humble and familiar courtesy,
> What reverence he did throw away on slaves;
> Wooing poor craftsmen with the craft of smiles,
> And patient under-bearing of his fortune,
> As 'twere to banish their affections with him.

> Off goes his bonnet to an oyster-wench;
> A brace of draymen bid God speed him well,
> And had the tribute of his supple knee,
> With thanks my countrymen, my loving friends;
> As were our England in reversion his,
> And he our subjects' next degree in hope.

Afterwards, he gives his own character to Percy, in these words:

> I thank thee, gentle Percy, and be sure
> I count myself in nothing else so happy,
> As in a soul rememb'ring my good friends;
> And as my fortune ripens with thy love,
> It shall be still thy true love's recompense.

We know how he afterwards kept his promise. His bold assertion of his own rights, his pretended submission to the king, and the ascendancy which he tacitly assumes over him without openly claiming it, as soon as he has him in his power, are characteristic traits of this ambitious and politic usurper. But the part of Richard himself gives the chief interest to the play. His folly, his vices, his misfortunes, his reluctance to part with the crown, his fear to keep it, his weak and womanish regrets, his starting tears, his fits of hectic passion, his smothered majesty, pass in succession before us, and make a picture as natural as it is affecting. Among the most striking touches of pathos are his wish 'O that I were a mockery king of snow to melt away before the sun of Bolingbroke', and the incident of the poor groom who comes to visit him in prison, and tells him how 'it yearned his heart that Bolingbroke upon his coronation-day rode on roan Barbary'. We shall have occasion to return hereafter to the character of Richard II in speaking of Henry VI. There is only one passage more, the description of his entrance into London with Bolingbroke, which we should like to quote here, if it had not been so used and worn out, so thumbed and got by rote, so praised and painted, but its beauty surmounts all these considerations. . . .

SOURCE: *Characters of Shakespear's Plays* (1817).

Edward Dowden

The play of *King Richard II* possesses none of the titanic stormy force which breathes through *King Richard III*, but in delicate cunning in the rendering of character it excels the more popular play. The two principal figures in *King Richard II*, that of the king who fell, and that of the king who rose—the usurping Bolingbroke—grow before us insensibly through a series of fine and characteristic strokes. They do not, like the figures in *King Richard III*, forcibly possess themselves of our imagination, but engage it before it is aware, and by degrees advance stronger claims upon us, and make good those claims. It will be worth while to try to ascertain what Shakspere looked upon as most significant in the character of these two royal persons,—the weak king who could not rule, and the strong king who pressed him from his place.

There is a condition of the intellect which we describe by the word 'boyishness'. The mind in the boyish stage of growth 'has no discriminating convictions, and no grasp of consequences'. It has not as yet got hold of realities; it is 'merely dazzled by phenomena instead of perceiving things as they are'. The talk of a person who remains in this sense boyish is often clever, but it is unreal; now he will say brilliant things upon this side of a question, and now upon the opposite side. He has no consistency of view. He is wanting as yet in seriousness of intellect; in the adult mind.[1] Now if we extend this characteristic of boyishness, from the intellect to the entire character, we may understand much of what Shakspere meant to represent in the person of Richard II. Not alone his intellect, but his feelings, live in the world of phenomena, and altogether fail to lay hold of things as they are; they have no consistency and no continuity. His will is entirely unformed; it possesses no authority and no executive power; he is at the mercy of every chance impulse and transitory mood. He has a kind of artistic relation to life, without being an artist. An artist in life seizes upon the stuff of circumstance, and with strenuous will, and strong creative power, shapes some new and noble form of human existence.

Richard, to whom all things are unreal, has a fine feeling for 'situations'. Without true kingly strength or dignity, he has a fine feeling for the royal situation. Without any making real to himself what God or what death is, he can put himself, if need be, in the appropriate attitude towards God and towards death. Instead of comprehending things as they are, and achieving heroic deeds, he satiates his heart with the grace, the tenderness, the beauty, or the pathos of situations. Life is to Richard a show, a succession of images; and to put himself into accord with the aesthetic requirements of his position is Richard's first necessity. He is equal to playing any part gracefully which he is called upon by circumstances to enact. But when he has exhausted the aesthetic satisfaction to be derived from the situations of his life, he is left with nothing further to do. He is an amateur in living; not an artist.

Nothing had disturbed the graceful dream of Richard's adolescence. The son of the Black Prince, beautiful in face and form, though now past his youth, a king since boyhood, he has known no antagonism of men or circumstance which might arouse the will. He has an indescribable charm of person and presence; Hotspur remembers him as 'Richard, that sweet, lovely rose'. But a king who rules a discontented people and turbulent nobles needs to be something more than a beautiful blossoming flower. Richard has abandoned his nature to self-indulgence, and therefore the world becomes to him more unreal than ever. He has been surrounded by flatterers, who helped to make his atmosphere a luminous mist, through which the facts of life appeared with all their ragged outlines smoothed away. In the first scene of the play he enacts the part of a king with a fine show of dignity; his bearing is splendid and irreproachable. Mowbray is obstinate, and will not throw down the gage of Bolingbroke; Richard exclaims :

> Rage must be withstood :
> Give me his gage : lions make leopards tame.

But Mowbray retains the gage. 'We were not born to sue, but to command,' declares Richard with royal majesty; yet he admits that to command exceeds his power. What of that? Has not Richard borne himself splendidly, and uttered himself in a royal metaphor : 'Lions make leopards tame'?

At this very moment Bolingbroke, with eye set upon his purpose afar off, has resolutely taken the first step towards attaining it. The challenge of Mowbray conceals a deeper purpose. So little does Bolingbroke really feel of hostility to his antagonist, that one of his first acts, as soon as he is in a position to act with authority, is to declare Mowbray's repeal.[2] But to stand forward as champion of the wrongs of England, to make himself the eminent justiciary by right of nature, this is the initial step towards future kingship; and Bolingbroke perceives clearly that the fact of Gloster's death may serve as fulcrum for the lever which is to shake the throne of England. Nor is the King quite insensible of the tendency of his cousin's action. Already he begins to quail before his bold antagonist :

How high a pitch his resolution soars.

Richard tries gracefully to conceal his discomposure, and to deceive Bolingbroke; but he is not, like Richard the hunchback, a daring and efficient hypocrite. He betrays his weakness and his distrust, administering to the two men decreed to exile an oath which pledges them never to reconcile themselves in their banishment, and never to plot against the king.

Bolingbroke accepts his exile, parts from the English crowd with an air of gracious, condescending familiarity, which flatters (whereas Richard's undignified familiarity only displeases),[3] and bids farewell to his country as a son bids farewell to the mother with whom his natural loyalty remains, and whom, in due time, he will see again. John of Gaunt is lying on his death-bed. The last of the great race of the time of Edward III, no English spirit will breathe such patriotism as his until the days of Agincourt. With the prophetic inspiration of a dying man he dares to warn his grand-nephew, and to rebuke him for his treason against the ancient honour of England. Richard, who, with his characteristic sensibility of a superficial kind, turns pale as he listens, recovers himself by a transition from overawed alarm to boyish insolence. The white-haired warrior, now a prophet, who lies dying before him, is

> A lunatic, lean-witted fool,
> Presuming on an ague's privilege.

who dares with a frozen admonition to make pale the royal cheek of Richard. The facts are very disagreeable, and why should a king admit into his consciousness an ugly or disagreeable fact? By and by, being informed that John of Gaunt is dead, Richard has the most graceful and appropriate word ready for so solemn an occasion :

> The ripest fruit first falls, and so doth he;
> His time is spent, our pilgrimage must be.

In which pilgrimage the first step is to seize upon

> The plate, coin, revenues, and moveables,
> Whereof our uncle Gaunt did stand possessed.

Even York, the temporising York, who would fain be all things to all men if by any means he might save himself, is amazed and ventures to remonstrate against the criminal folly of this act. But Richard, like all self-indulgent natures, has only a half belief in any possible future; he chooses to make the present time easy, and let the future provide for itself; he has been living upon chances too long; he has too long been mortgaging the health of to-morrow for the pleasure of to-day :

> Think what you will, we seize into our hands
> His plate, his goods, his money, and his lands.

But now the tempest begins to sing. Bolingbroke (before he can possibly have heard of his father's death and the seizure by Richard of his own rights and royalties) has equipped an expedition, and is about to land upon the English coast. The King makes a hasty return from his 'military promenade' in Ireland.[4] The first words of each, as he touches his native soil, are characteristic, and were, doubtless, placed by Shakspere in designed contrast. *'How far is it, my lord, to Berkeley now?'* The banished

man has no tender phrases to bestow upon English earth, now
that he sets foot upon it once more. All his faculties are firm set,
and bent upon achievement. But Richard, who has been absent
for a few days in Ireland, enters with all possible zeal into the
sentiment of his situation :

> I weep for joy
> To stand upon my kingdom once again.
> Dear earth, I do salute thee with my hand,
> Though rebels wound thee with their horses' hoofs;
> As a long-parted mother with her child
> Plays fondly with her tears and smiles in meeting,
> So weeping, smiling, greet I thee, my earth,
> And do thee favours with my royal hands.

Which sentimental favours form a graceful incident in the play
of Richard's life, but can hardly compensate the want of true
and manly patriotism. This same earth which Richard caressed
with extravagant sensibility was the England which John of
Gaunt with strong enthusiasm had apostrophised :

> This blessed plot, this earth, this realm, this England,
> This nurse, this teeming womb of royal kings,
> Fear'd by their breed, and famous for their birth,
> Renowned for their deeds.

It was the England which Richard had alienated from himself
and leased out 'like to a tenement or pelting farm'. What of that,
however? Did not Richard address his England with phrases
full of tender sensibility, and render her mockery favours with his
royal hands?

Bolingbroke has already gained the support of the Welsh.
Richard has upon his side powers higher than natural flesh and
blood. Shall he not rise like the sun in the eastern sky, and with
the majesty of his royal apparition scare away the treasons of the
night? Is he not the anointed deputy of God?

> Not all the water in the rough rude sea
> Can wash the balm from an anointed king :
> The breath of worldly men cannot depose
> The deputy elected by the Lord.

Yes; he will rely on God; it is devout; it is not laborious. For every armed man who fights for Bolingbroke,

> God for his Richard hath in heavenly pay
> A glorious angel.

And at this moment Salisbury enters to announce the revolt of Wales. Richard has been slack in action, and arrived a day too late. Remorseless comment upon the rhetorical piety of the King! A company of angels fight upon his side; true, but the sturdy Welshmen stand for Bolingbroke! He is the deputy elected by the Lord; but the Lord's deputy has arrived a day too late!

And now Richard alternates between abject despondency (relieved by accepting all the aesthetic satisfaction derivable from the situation of vanquished king) and an airy, unreal confidence. There is in Richard, as Coleridge has finely observed, 'a constant overflow of emotions from a total incapability of controlling them, and thence a waste of that energy, which should have been reserved for actions, in the passion and effort of mere resolves and menaces. The consequence is moral exhaustion and rapid alternations of unmanly despair and ungrounded hope, every feeling being abandoned for its direct opposite upon the pressure of external accident.'[5] A certain unreality infects every motion of Richard; his feelings are but the shadows of true feeling. Now he will be great and a king; now what matters it to lose a kingdom? If Bolingbroke and he alike serve God, Bolingbroke can be no more than his fellow-servant. Now he plays the wanton with his pride, and now with his misery :

> Of comfort no man speak :
> Let's talk of graves, of worms and epitaphs;
>
> For God's sake, let us sit upon the ground
> And tell sad stories of the death of kings.

At one moment he pictures God mustering armies of pestilence in his clouds to strike the usurper and his descendants; in the next he yields to Bolingbroke's demands, and welcomes his 'right noble cousin'. He is proud, and he is pious; he is courageous and cowardly; and pride and piety, cowardice and courage, are all the passions of a dream.

Yet Shakspere has thrown over the figure of Richard a certain atmosphere of charm. If only the world were not a real world, to which serious hearts are due, we could find in Richard some wavering, vague attraction. There is a certain wistfulness about him; without any genuine kingly power, he has a feeling for what kingly power must be; without any veritable religion, he has a pale shadow of religiosity. And few of us have ourselves wholly escaped from unreality. 'It takes a long time really to feel and understand things as they are; we learn to do so only gradually.'[6] Into what glimmering limbo will such a soul as that of Richard pass when the breath leaves the body? The pains of hell and the joys of heaven belong to those who have serious hearts. Richard has been a graceful phantom. Is there some tenuous, unsubstantial world of spirits reserved for the sentimentalist, the dreamer, and the dilettante? Richard is, as it were, fading out of existence. Bolingbroke seems not only to have robbed him of his authority, but to have encroached upon his very personality, and to have usurped his understanding and his will. Richard is discovering that he is no more than a shadow; but the discovery itself has something unreal and shadowy about it. Is not some such fact as this symbolised by the incident of the mirror? Before he quite ceases to be king, Richard, with his taste for 'pseudo-poetic pathos',[7] would once more look upon the image of his face, and see what wrinkles have been traced upon it by sorrow. And Bolingbroke, suppressing his inward feeling of disdain, directs that the mirror be brought. Richard gazes against it, and finds that sorrow has wrought no change upon the beautiful lips and forehead. And then exclaiming,

> A brittle glory shineth in this face,
> As brittle as the glory is the face,

he dashes the glass against the ground.

> For there it is crack'd in a hundred shivers.
> Mark, silent King, the moral of this sport,
> How soon my sorrow hath destroy'd my face.
> BOLINGBROKE   The shadow of your sorrow hath destroy'd
> The shadow of your face.
> RICHARD   Say that again.
> The shadow of my sorrow ! ha ! let's see.

Does Richard, as Professor Flathe (contemptuously dismissing the criticisms of Gervinus and of Kreyssig) maintains, rise morally from his humiliation as a king? Is he heartily sorry for his misdoings? While drinking the wine and eating the bread of sorrow, does he truly and earnestly repent, and intend to lead a new life? The habit of his nature is not so quickly unlearnt. Richard in prison remains the same person as Richard on the throne. Calamity is no more real to him now than prosperity had been in brighter days. The soliloquy of Richard in Pomfret Castle (*Act* v, *Scene* v) might almost be transferred, as far as tone and manner are concerned, to one other personage in Shakspere's plays—to Jacques. The curious intellect of Jacques gives him his distinction. He plays his parts for the sake of understanding the world in his way of superficial fool's-wisdom. Richard plays his parts to possess himself of the aesthetic satisfaction of an amateur in life, with a fine feeling for situations. But each lives in the world of shadow, in the world of mockery wisdom, or the world of mockery passion. Mr Hudson is right when he says, 'Richard is so steeped in voluptuous habits that he must needs be a voluptuary even in his sorrow, and make a luxury of woe itself; pleasure has so thoroughly mastered his spirit, that he cannot think of bearing pain as a duty or an honour, but merely as a license for the pleasure of maudlin self-compassion; so he hangs over his griefs, hugs them, nurses them, buries himself in them, as if the sweet agony thereof were to him a glad refuge from the stings of self-reproach, or a dear release from the exercise of manly thought.'[8]

Yet to the last a little of real love is reserved by one heart or two for the shadowy, attractive Richard; the love of a wife who is filled with a piteous sense of her husband's mental and moral effacement, seeing her 'fair rose wither', and the love of a groom whose loyalty to his master is associated with loyalty to his master's horse, roan Barbary. This incident of roan Barbary is an invention of the poet. Did Shakspere intend only a little bit of helpless pathos? Or is there a touch of hidden irony here? A poor spark of affection remains for Richard, but it has been kindled half by Richard, and half by Richard's horse. The fancy of the fallen king disports itself for the last time, and hangs its latest wreath around this incident. Then suddenly comes the darkness. Suddenly the hectic passion of Richard flares; he snatches an

axe from a servant, and deals about him deadly blows. In another moment he is extinct; the graceful futile existence has
ceased.

SOURCE : *Shakspere—His Mind and Art* (1875).

NOTES

1. John Henry Newman, *Idea of a University*, preface.
2. Kreyssig suggests that this piece of magnanimity was really a
piece of fine hypocrisy; Bolingbroke was perhaps aware of Norfolk's
death at the time that he gave order for his repeal.

3.   The skipping King, he ambled up and down
          With shallow jesters and rash bavin wits,
          Soon kindled and soon burnt; carded his state,
          Mingled his royalty with capering fools,

                  .   .   .   .

          Grew a companion to the common streets.

Thus Henry IV describes his predecessor as a lesson to Prince Henry,
whose familiarity with his future subjects is neither in his father's
manner, nor in that of Richard II.

4. Fr. Kreyssig, *Vorlesungen über Shakespeare*, vol. i, p. 191.
5. *Lectures upon Shakespeare* (ed. 1849), vol. i, p. 178.
6. J. H. Newman, 'Unreal Words', *Parochial and Plain Sermons*,
vol. v, p. 43.
7. Kreyssig.
8. *Shakespeare: his Life, Art and Character*, vol. ii, p. 55.

Walter Pater

SHAKESPEARE'S ENGLISH KINGS

> A brittle glory shineth in this face :
> As brittle as the glory is the face.

The English plays of Shakespeare needed but the completion of
one unimportant interval to possess the unity of a popular chronicle from Richard the Second to Henry the Eighth, and possess,
as they actually stand, the unity of a common motive in the handling of the various events and persons which they bring before us.
Certain of his historic dramas, not English, display Shakespeare's
mastery in the development of the heroic nature amid heroic circumstances; and had he chosen, from English history, to deal
with Cœur-de-Lion or Edward the First, the innate quality of
his subject would doubtless have called into play something of
that profound and sombre power which in *Julius Caesar* and
Macbeth has sounded the depths of mighty character. True, on
the whole, to fact, it is another side of kingship which he has
made prominent in his English histories. The irony of kingship—
average human nature, flung with a wonderfully pathetic effect
into the vortex of great events; tragedy of everyday quality
heightened in degree only by the conspicuous scene which does
but make those who play their parts there conspicuously unfortunate; the utterance of common humanity straight from the
heart, but refined like other common things for kingly uses by
Shakespeare's unfailing eloquence : such, unconsciously for the
most part, though palpably enough to the careful reader, is the
conception under which Shakespeare has arranged the lights and
shadows of the story of the English kings, emphasising merely
the light and shadow inherent in it, and keeping very close to the
original authorities, not simply in the general outline of these dramatic histories but sometimes in their very expression. Certainly
the history itself, as he found it in Hall, Holinshed, and Stowe,
those somewhat picturesque old chroniclers who had themselves
an eye for the dramatic 'effects' of human life, has much of this

sentiment already about it. What he did not find there was the natural prerogative—such justification, in kingly, that is to say, in exceptional, qualities, of the exceptional position, as makes it practicable in the result. It is no *Henriade* he writes, and no history of the English people, but the sad fortunes of some English kings as conspicuous examples of the ordinary human condition. As in a children's story, all princes are in extremes. Delightful in the sunshine above the wall into which chance lifts the flower for a season, they can but plead somewhat more touchingly than others their everyday weakness in the storm. Such is the motive that gives unity to these unequal and intermittent contributions toward a slowly evolved dramatic chronicle, which it would have taken many days to rehearse; a not distant story from real life still well remembered in its general course, to which people might listen now and again, as long as they cared, finding human nature at least wherever their attention struck ground in it.

He begins with John, and allows indeed to the first of these English kings a kind of greatness, making the development of the play centre in the counteraction of his natural gifts—that something of heroic force about him—by a madness which takes the shape of reckless impiety, forced especially on men's attention by the terrible circumstances of his end, in the delineation of which Shakespeare triumphs, setting, with true poetic tact, this incident of the king's death, in all the horror of a violent one, amid a scene delicately suggestive of what is perennially peaceful and genial in the outward world. Like the sensual humours of Falstaff in another play, the presence of the bastard Faulconbridge, with his physical energy and his unmistakable family likeness—'those limbs which Sir Robert never holp to make'[1]—contributes to an almost coarse assertion of the force of nature, of the somewhat ironic preponderance of nature and circumstance over men's artificial arrangements, to the recognition of a certain potent natural aristocracy, which is far from being always identical with that more formal, heraldic one. And what is a coarse fact in the case of Faulconbridge becomes a motive of pathetic appeal in the wan and babyish Arthur. The magic with which nature models tiny and delicate children to the likeness of their rough fathers is nowhere more justly expressed than in the words of King Philip—

Look here upon thy brother Geoffrey's face !
These eyes, these brows were moulded out of his :
This little abstract doth contain that large
Which died in Geoffrey ; and the hand of time
Shall draw this brief into as huge a volume.

It was perhaps something of a boyish memory of the shocking
end of his father that had distorted the piety of Henry the Third
into superstitious terror. A frightened soul, himself touched with
the contrary sort of religious madness, doting on all that was alien
from his father's huge ferocity, on the genialities, the soft gilding,
of life, on the genuine interests of art and poetry, to be credited
more than any other person with the deep religious expression of
Westminster Abbey, Henry the Third, picturesque though useless, but certainly touching, might have furnished Shakespeare,
had he filled up this interval in his series, with precisely the kind
of effect he tends towards in his English plays. But he found it
completer still in the person and story of Richard the Second, a
figure—'that sweet lovely rose'—which haunts Shakespeare's
mind, as it seems long to have haunted the minds of the English
people, as the most touching of all examples of the irony of kingship.

Henry the Fourth—to look for a moment beyond our immediate subject, in pursuit of Shakespeare's thought—is presented, of
course, in general outline, as an impersonation of 'surviving force' :
he has a certain amount of kingcraft also, a real fitness for great
opportunity. But still true to his leading motive, Shakespeare, in
King Henry the Fourth, has left the high-water mark of his poetry
in the soliloquy which represents royalty longing vainly for the
toiler's sleep; while the popularity, the showy heroism, of Henry
the Fifth, is used to give emphatic point to the old earthy commonplace about 'wild oats'. The wealth of homely humour in
these plays, the fun coming straight home to all the world, of
Fluellen especially in his unconscious interview with the king,
the boisterous earthiness of Falstaff and his companions, contribute to the same effect. The keynote of Shakespeare's treatment
is indeed expressed by Henry the Fifth himself, the *greatest* of
Shakespeare's kings.—'Though I speak it to you,' he says *incog-
nito*, under cover of night, to a common soldier on the field, 'I

think the king is but a man, as I am : the violet smells to him as it doth to me : all his senses have but human conditions; and though his affections be higher mounted than ours yet when they stoop they stoop with like wing.' And, in truth, the really kingly speeches which Shakespeare assigns to him, as to other kings weak enough in all but speech, are but a kind of flowers, worn for, and effective only as personal embellishment. They combine to one result with the merely outward and ceremonial ornaments of royalty, its pageantries, flaunting so naively, so credulously, in Shakespeare, as in that old medieval time. And then, the force of Hotspur is but transient youth, the common heat of youth, in him. The character of Henry the Sixth again, *roi fainéant*, with La Pucelle[2] for his counterfoil, lay in the direct course of Shakespeare's design : he has done much to fix the sentiment of the 'holy Henry'. Richard the Third, touched, like John, with an effect of real heroism, is spoiled like him by something of criminal madness, and reaches his highest level of tragic expression when circumstances reduce him to terms of mere human nature :

> A horse !   A horse !   My kingdom for a horse !

The Princes in the Tower recall to mind the lot of young Arthur :

> I'll go with thee,
> And find the inheritance of this poor child,
> His little kingdom of a forced grave.

And when Shakespeare comes to Henry the Eighth, it is not the superficial though very English splendour of the king himself, but the really potent and ascendant nature of the butcher's son on the one hand, and Katharine's subdued reproduction of the sad fortunes of Richard the Second on the other, that define his central interest.[3]

With a prescience of the Wars of the Roses, of which his errors were the original cause, it is Richard who best exposes Shakespeare's own constant sentiment concerning war, and especially that sort of civil war which was then recent in English memories. The soul of Shakespeare, certainly, was not wanting in a sense of the magnanimity of warriors. The grandiose aspects of war, its magnificent apparelling, he records monumentally

enough—the 'dressing of the lists', the lion's heart, its unfaltering
haste thither in all the freshness of youth and morning :

> Not sick although I have to do with death—
> The sun doth gild our armour : Up, my Lords !—
> I saw young Harry with his beaver on,
> His cuisses on his thighs, gallantly arm'd,
> Rise from the ground like feather'd Mercury.

Only, with Shakespeare, the afterthought is immediate :

> They come like sacrifices in their trim.

—Will it never be to-day? I will trot to-morrow a mile, and my
way shall be paved with English faces.

This sentiment Richard reiterates very plaintively, in association
with the delicate sweetness of the English fields, still sweet and
fresh, like London and her other fair towns in that England of
Chaucer, for whose soil the exiled Bolingbroke is made to long so
dangerously, while Richard on his return from Ireland salutes it :

> That pale, that white-fac'd shore,—
> As a long-parted mother with her child.—
> So, weeping, smiling, greet I thee, my earth !
> And do thee favour with my royal hands.

Then (of Bolingbroke)

> Ere the crown he looks for live in peace,
> Ten thousand bloody crowns of mothers' sons
> Shall ill become the flower of England's face ;
> Change the complexion of her maid-pale peace
> To scarlet indignation, and bedew
> My pastures' grass with faithful English blood.

> Why have they dared to march?

asks York,

> So many miles upon her peaceful bosom,
> Frighting her pale-fac'd visages with war?

waking, according to Richard,

> Our peace, which in our country's cradle,
> Draws the sweet infant breath of gentle sleep :

bedrenching 'with crimson tempest'

> The fresh green lap of fair king Richard's land :

frighting 'fair peace' from 'our quiet confines', laying

> The summer's dust with showers of blood,
> Rained from the wounds of slaughter'd Englishmen :

bruising

> Her flowerets with the armed hoofs
> Of hostile paces.

Perhaps it is not too fanciful to note in this play a peculiar recoil from the mere instruments of warfare, the contact of the 'rude ribs', the 'flint bosom', of Barkloughly Castle or Pomfret or

> Julius Cæsar's ill-erected tower :

the

> Boisterous untun'd drums
> With harsh-resounding trumpets' dreadful bray
> And grating shock of wrathful iron arms.

It is as if the lax, soft beauty of the king took effect, at least by contrast, on everything beside.

One gracious prerogative, certainly, Shakespeare's English kings possess : they are a very eloquent company, and Richard is the most sweet-tongued of them all. In no other play perhaps is there such a flush of those gay, fresh, variegated flowers of speech —colour and figure, not lightly attached to, but fused into, the very phrase itself—which Shakespeare cannot help dispensing to his characters, as in this 'play of the Deposing of King Richard the Second', an exquisite poet if he is nothing else, from first to last, in light and gloom alike, able to see all things poetically, to give a poetic turn to his conduct of them, and refreshing with his golden language the tritest aspects of that ironic contrast between the pretensions of a king and the actual necessities of his destiny.

What a garden of words! With him, blank verse, infinitely
graceful, deliberate, musical in inflexion, becomes indeed a true
'verse royal', that rhyming lapse, which to the Shakespearian
ear, at least in youth, came as the last touch of refinement on it,
being here doubly appropriate. His eloquence blends with that
fatal beauty, of which he was so frankly aware, so amiable to his
friends, to his wife, of the effects of which on the people his enemies were so much afraid, on which Shakespeare himself dwells so
attentively as the 'royal blood' comes and goes in the face with his
rapid changes of temper. As happens with sensitive natures, it
attunes him to a congruous suavity of manners, by which anger
itself became flattering : it blends with his merely youthful hope-
fulness and high spirits, his sympathetic love for gay people,
things, apparel—'his cote of gold and stone, valued at thirty thousand marks', the novel Italian fashions he preferred, as also with
those real amiabilities that made people forget the darker touches
of his character, but never tire of the pathetic rehearsal of his
fall, the meekness of which would have seemed merely abject in
a less graceful performer.

Yet it is only fair to say that in the painstaking 'revival' of
King Richard the Second, by the late Charles Kean, those who
were very young thirty years ago were afforded much more than
Shakespeare's play could ever have been before—the very person
of the king based on the stately old portrait in Westminster Abbey,
'the earliest extant contemporary likeness of any English sovereign', the grace, the winning pathos, the sympathetic voice of
the player, the tasteful archaeology confronting vulgar modern
London with a scenic reproduction, for once really agreeable, of
the London of Chaucer. In the hands of Kean the play became
like an exquisite performance on the violin.

The long agony of one so gaily painted by nature's self, from
his 'tragic abdication' till the hour in which he

> Sluiced out his innocent soul thro' streams of blood,

was for playwrights a subject ready to hand, and became early
the theme of a popular drama, of which some have fancied surviving favourite fragments in the rhymed parts of Shakespeare's
work.

> The king Richard of Yngland
> Was in his flowris then regnand :
> But his flowris efter sone
> Fadyt, and ware all undone

says the old chronicle. Strangely enough, Shakespeare supposes him an over-confident believer in that divine right of kings, of which people in Shakespeare's time were coming to hear so much; a general right, sealed to him (so Richard is made to think) as an ineradicable personal gift by the touch—stream rather, over head and breast and shoulders—of the 'holy oil' of his consecration at Westminster; not, however, through some oversight, the genuine balm used at the coronation of his successor, given, according to legend, by the Blessed Virgin to Saint Thomas of Canterbury. Richard himself found that, it was said, among other forgotten treasures, at the crisis of his changing fortunes, and vainly sought reconsecration therewith—understood, wistfully, that it was reserved for his happier rival. And yet his coronation, by the pageantry, the amplitude, the learned care, of its order, so lengthy that the king, then only eleven years of age, and fasting, as a communicant at the ceremony, was carried away in a faint, fixed the type under which it has ever since continued. And nowhere is there so emphatic a reiteration as in *Richard the Second* of the sentiment which those singular rites were calculated to produce.

> Not all the water in the rough rude sea
> Can wash the balm from an anointed king,

as supplementing another, almost supernatural, right.— 'Edward's seven sons,' of whom Richard's father was one,

> Were as seven phials of his sacred blood.

But this, too, in the hands of Shakespeare, becomes for him, like any other of those fantastic, ineffectual, easily discredited, personal graces, as capricious in its operation on men's wills as merely physical beauty, kindling himself to eloquence indeed, but only giving double pathos to insults which 'barbarism itself' might have pitied—the dust in his face, as he returns, through the streets of London, a prisoner in the train of his victorious enemy.

> How soon my sorrow hath destroyed my face!

he cries, in that most poetic invention of the mirror scene, which does but reinforce again that physical charm which all confessed. The sense of 'divine right' in kings is found to act not so much as a secret of power over others, as of infatuation to themselves. And of all those personal gifts the one which alone never altogether fails him is just that royal utterance, his appreciation of the poetry of his own hapless lot, an eloquent self-pity, infecting others in spite of themselves, till they too become irresistibly eloquent about him.

In the Roman Pontifical, of which the order of Coronation is really a part, there is no form for the inverse process, no rite of 'degradation', such as that by which an offending priest or bishop may be deprived, if not of the essential quality of 'orders', yet, one by one, of its outward dignities. It is as if Shakespeare had had in mind some such inverted rite, like those old ecclesiastical or military ones, by which human hardness, or human justice, adds the last touch of unkindness to the execution of its sentences, in the scene where Richard 'deposes' himself, as in some long, agonising ceremony, reflectively drawn out, with an extraordinary refinement of intelligence and variety of piteous appeal, but also with a felicity of poetic invention, which puts these pages into a very select class, with the finest 'vermeil and ivory' work of Chatterton or Keats.

> Fetch hither Richard that in common view
> He may surrender!

And Richard more than concurs: he throws himself into the part, realises a type, falls gracefully as on the world's stage.— Why is he sent for?

> To do that office of thine own good will
> Which tired majesty did make thee offer.
>
> Now mark me! how I will undo myself.

'Hath Bolingbroke deposed thine intellect?' the Queen asks him, on his way to the Tower:

> Hath Bolingbroke
> Deposed thine intellect? hath he been in thy heart?

And in truth, but for that adventitious poetic gold, it would be only 'plume-plucked Richard'.

> I find myself a traitor with the rest,
> For I have given here my soul's consent
> To undeck the pompous body of a king.

He is duly reminded, indeed, how

> That which in mean men we entitle patience
> Is pale cold cowardice in noble breasts.

Yet at least within the poetic bounds of Shakespeare's play, through Shakespeare's bountiful gifts, his desire seems fulfilled.

> O! that I were as great
> As is my grief.

And his grief becomes nothing less than a central expression of all that in the revolutions of Fortune's wheel goes *down* in the world.

No! Shakespeare's kings are not, nor are meant to be, great men: rather, little or quite ordinary humanity, thrust upon greatness, with those pathetic results, the natural self-pity of the weak heightened in them into irresistible appeal to others as the net result of their royal prerogative. One after another, they seem to lie composed in Shakespeare's embalming pages, with just that touch of nature about them, making the whole world akin, which has infused into their tombs at Westminster a rare poetic grace. It is that irony of kingship, the sense that it is in its happiness child's play, in its sorrows, after all, but children's grief, which gives its finer accent to all the changeful feeling of these wonderful speeches: the great meekness of the graceful, wild creatures tamed at last.

> Give Richard leave to live till Richard die!

his somewhat abject fear of death, turning to acquiescence at
moments of extreme weariness :

> My large kingdom for a little grave !
> A little little grave, an obscure grave !

his religious appeal in the last reserve, with its bold reference to
the judgment of Pilate, as he thinks once more of his 'anointing'.

And as happens with children he attains contentment finally
in the merely passive recognition of superior strength, in the nat-
uralness of the result of the great battle as a matter of course,
and experiences something of the royal prerogative of poetry to
obscure, or at least to attune and soften men's griefs. As in some
sweet anthem of Handel, the sufferer, who put finger to the organ
under the utmost pressure of mental conflict, extracts a kind of
peace at last from the mere skill with which he sets his distress to
music.

> Beshrew thee, Cousin, that didst lead me forth
> Of that sweet way I was in to despair !

'With Cain go wander through the shades of night !' cries the
new king to the gaoler Exton, dissimulating his share in the murder he is thought to have suggested; and in truth there is something of the murdered Abel about Shakespeare's Richard. The
fact seems to be that he died of 'waste and a broken heart' : it
was by way of proof that his end had been a natural one that,
stifling a real fear of the face, the face of Richard, on men's minds,
with the added pleading now of all dead faces, Henry exposed
the corpse to general view; and Shakespeare, in bringing it on
the stage, in the last scene of his play, does but follow out the
motive with which he has emphasised Richard's physical beauty
all through it—that 'most beauteous inn', as the Queen says
quaintly, meeting him on the way to death—residence, then soon
to be deserted, of that wayward, frenzied, but withal so affection-
ate soul. Though the body did not go to Westminster immediately,
his tomb,

> That small model of the barren earth
> Which serves as paste and cover to our bones,[4]

the effigy clasping the hand of his youthful consort, was already prepared there, with 'rich gilding and ornaments', monument of poetic regret, for Queen Anne of Bohemia, not of course the 'Queen' of Shakespeare, who however seems to have transferred to this second wife something of Richard's wildly proclaimed affection for the first. In this way, through the connecting link of that sacred spot, our thoughts once more associate Richard's two fallacious prerogatives, his personal beauty and his 'anointing'.

According to Johnson, *Richard the Second* is one of those plays which Shakespeare has 'apparently revised'; and how doubly delightful Shakespeare is where he seems to have revised! 'Would that he had blotted a thousand'—a thousand hasty phrases, we may venture once more to say with his earlier critic, now that the tiresome German superstition has passed away which challenged us to a dogmatic faith in the plenary verbal inspiration of every one of Shakespeare's clowns. Like some melodiously contending anthem of Handel's, I said, of Richard's meek 'undoing' of himself in the mirror-scene; and, in fact, the play of *Richard the Second* does, like a musical composition, possess a certain concentration of all its parts, a simple continuity, an evenness in execution, which are rare in the great dramatist. With *Romeo and Juliet*, that perfect symphony (symphony of three independent poetic forms set in a grander one[5] which it is the merit of German criticism to have detected) it belongs to a small group of plays, where, by happy birth and consistent evolution, dramatic form approaches to something like the unity of a lyrical ballad, a lyric, a song, a single strain of music. Which sort of poetry we are to account the highest, is perhaps a barren question. Yet if, in art generally, unity of impression is a note of what is perfect, then lyric poetry, which in spite of complex structure often preserves the unity of a single passionate ejaculation, would rank higher than dramatic poetry, where, especially to the reader, as distinguished from the spectator assisting at a theatrical performance, there must always be a sense of the effort necessary to keep the various parts from flying asunder, a sense of imperfect continuity, such as the older criticism vainly sought to obviate by the rule of the dramatic 'unities'. It follows that a play attains artistic perfection just in proportion as it approaches that unity of lyrical effect, as if a song or ballad were still lying at the root of it, all the various expression of the conflict of character and circumstance falling at last into the compass of a single melody, or musical theme. As, historically, the earliest classic drama arose out of the chorus, from which this or that person, this or that episode, detached itself, so, into the unity of a choric song the perfect drama ever tends to return, its intellectual scope deepened, complicated, enlarged, but still with an unmistakable singleness, or identity, in its impression on the mind. Just there, in that vivid single impression left on the mind when all is over, not in any mechanical limitation of time and place, is the secret of the 'unities'—the true imaginative unity—of the drama.

SOURCE : *Appreciations* (1889).

NOTES

1. ELINOR   Do you not read some tokens of my son [Cœur-de-Lion]
            In the large composition of this man?
2. Perhaps the one person of *genius* in these English plays.
      The spirit of deep prophecy she hath,
      Exceeding the nine Sibyls of old Rome :
      What's past and what's to come she can descry.
3. Proposing in this paper to trace the leading sentiment in Shakespeare's English Plays as a sort of *popular dramatic chronicle*, I have left untouched the question how much (or, in the case of *Henry the Sixth* and *Henry the Eighth*, how little) of them may be really his : how far inferior hands have contributed to a result, true on the whole to the greater, that is to say, the Shakespearian, elements in them.
4. Perhaps a *double entendre* : of any ordinary grave, as comprising, in effect, the whole small earth now left to its occupant : or, of such a tomb as Richard's in particular, with its actual model, or effigy, of the clay of him. Both senses are so characteristic that it would be a pity to lose either.
5. The Sonnet : the Aubade : the Epithalamium.

C. E. Montague

F. R. BENSON'S RICHARD II

Mr Benson, whom nothing seems to tire, played Richard II on Saturday afternoon and Petruchio in the evening. Of the latter one need not at this time of day say much. Like his Hamlet—of which by a misprint we were made to say the other day that it was one of his 'least known' instead of one of his 'best known' pieces of acting—it is familiar to every Manchester playgoer. It is unconventional, and in that sense contentious; when it was seen in London ten years ago those of the critics who hold a brief for the conventions of the moment were scandalised at the notion that anything Shaksperean or partly Shaksperean should be played in a vein so boisterous. By this time one would hope that Mr Benson must have brought it home to everybody that the play is itself a roaring extravaganza, only to be carried off at all upon the stage by a sustained rush of high spirits that leaves no time to think. It is full of legible notices to this effect—the burlesque bidding for Bianca, for instance, and the 'my horse, my ox, my ass' speech, and endless others. Mr Benson's gusty and tearing Petruchio, with a lyrical touch of romance in the voice and look here and there in his delivery of lines like

> Such wind as scatters young men through the world,
> To seek their fortunes further than at home,
> Where small experience grows,

strikes us as not only the best Petruchio we have seen but the only reading of the part that will hold water. The play, too, furnishes Mrs Benson with, we think, her best part in Katharine and Mr Weir with a very good one in Grumio, both played in the same key of vehement and fantastical humour as Mr Benson's Petruchio. It does one good to see a play so well understood and

so courageously and consistently played on that understanding.
It was played with infinite zest and spirit on Saturday night to a
very full house, which it kept in almost continuous laughter.

The chief interest of the day, however, attached to Mr Benson's Richard II, a piece of acting which is much less known here,
and to whose chief interest we do not think that critical justice
has ever been done. An actor faulty in some other ways, but
always picturesque, romantic, and inventive, with a fine sensibility to beauty in words and situations and a voice that gives this
sensibility its due, Mr Benson brings out admirably that half of
the character which criticism seems almost always to have taken
pains to obscure—the capable and faithful artist in the same skin
as the incapable and unfaithful King. With a quite choice and
pointed infelicity, Professor Dowden has called Shakspere's
Richard II 'an amateur in living, not an artist'; Mr Boas, generally one of the most suggestive of recent writers on Shakspere, has
called his grace of fancy 'puerile' and its products 'pseudo-poetic'.
The general judgment on the play reads as if the critics felt they
would be 'only encouraging' kings like the Richard of this play
if they did not assure him throughout the ages that his poetry was
sad stuff at the best. 'It's no excuse', one seems to hear them say,
and 'Serve you right, you and your poetry.' It is our critical way
to fall thus upon the wicked or weak in books and leave him half-
dead, after taking from him even the good side that he hath.
Still it is well to see what Shakspere meant us to, and we wonder
whether any one who hears Mr Benson in this part with an open
mind can doubt that Shakspere meant to draw in Richard not
only a rake and muff on a throne and falling off it but, in the
same person, an exquisite poet: to show with one hand how kingdoms are lost and with the other how the creative imagination
goes about its work; to fill the same man with the attributes of a
feckless wastrel in high place and with the quite distinct but not
incompatible attributes of a typical, a consummate artist.

'But', it will be asked by persons justly tired of sloppy talk about
art, 'What is an artist; what, exactly, is it in a man that makes an
artist of him?' Well, first a proneness in his mind to revel and
bask in its own sense of fact; not in the use of fact—that is for the
men of affairs, the Bolingbrokes; nor in the explanation of fact—
that is for the men of science; but simply in his own quick and

glowing apprehension of what is about him, of all that is done on the earth or goes on in the sky, of dying and being born, of the sun, clouds, and storms, of great deeds and failures, the changes of the seasons, and the strange events of men's lives. To mix with the day's diet of gifts and sounds the man of this type seems to bring a wine of his own that lights a fire in his blood while he takes the meal. What the finest minds of other types eschew he does, and takes pains to do. To shun the dry light, to drench all he sees with himself, his own temperament, the humours of his own moods— this is not his dread but his wish, as well as his bent. 'The eye sees what the eye brings the means of seeing.' 'A fool sees not the same tree that a wise man sees.' 'You shall see the world in a grain of sand and heaven in a wild flower.' This heightened and delighted personal sense of fact, a knack of seeing visions at the instance of seen things, is the basis of art.

Only the basis, though. For that art may come a man must add to it a veritable passion for arresting and defining in words or lines and colours or notes of music, not each or any thing that he sees, nor anybody else's sense of that thing, nor yet the greatest common measure of many trained or untrained minds' senses of it, but his own unique sense of it, the precise quality and degree of emotion that the spectacle of it breeds in him and nobody else, the net result of its contact with whatever in his own tempera-ment he has not in common with other men. That is the truth of art, to be true less to facts without you than to yourself as stirred by facts. And truth it must be with a vengeance. To find a glove-fit of words for your sense of 'the glory and the freshness of a dream', to model the very form and pressure of an inward vision to the millionth of a hair's breadth—the vocabulary of mensura-tion ludicrously fails to describe those infinitesimal niceties of ad-justment between the inward feeling and the means of its present-ment. And indeed it is only half true to speak as if feeling and its expression were separable at all. In a sense the former implies the latter. The simplest feeling is itself changed by issuing in a cry. Attaining a kind of completeness, given, as it were, its rights, it is not the same feeling after the cry that it was before. It has become not merely feeling interpreted by something outside it and separ-able from it, but fuller feeling, a feeling with more in it, feeling pushed one stage further in definiteness and intensity, an arch of feeling crowned at last. So, too, all artistic expression, if one thinks the matter out, is seen to be not merely a transcription of the artist's sense of fact but a perfecting of that sense itself; and the experience which never attains expression, the experience which is loosely said to be unexpressed, is really an unfinished, imperfect experience and one which, in the mind of an artist, passionately craves for its own completion through adequate expression. 'There are no beautiful thoughts', a fastidious artist has said, 'without beautiful forms.' The perfect expression *is* the completed emotion. So the artist is incessantly preoccupied in leading his sense of fact up to the point at which it achieves not merely expression but its own completion in the one word, phrase, line, stanza that can make it, simply as a feeling of his own, all that it has in it to be. He may be said to write or paint because there is a point beyond which the joy of tasting the world about him cannot go unless he does so; and his life passes in a series of moments at which thought and expression, the sense of fact and the consummate presentation of that sense, rush together like Blake's 'soul and body united', to be indistinguishably fused together in a whole in which, alone, each can attain its own perfection.

We have drawn out this tedious description of the typical artist because the further it goes the more close a description does it become of the Richard whom Mr Benson shows us in the last three acts. In him every other feeling is mastered, except at a few passing moments, by a passion of interest in the exercise of his gift of exquisite responsiveness to the appeal made to his artistic sensibility by whatever life throws for the moment in his way. Lamb said it was worth while to have been cheated of the legacy so as not to miss 'the idea of' the rogue who did it. That, on a little scale, is the kind of aesthetic disinterestedness which in Shakspere's Richard, rightly presented by Mr Benson, passes all bounds. The 'idea of' a King's fall, the 'idea of' a wife and husband torn apart, the 'idea of' a very crucifixion of indignities—as each new idea comes he revels in his own warmed and lighted apprehension of it as freely as in his apprehension of the majesty and mystery of the idea of a kingship by divine right. He runs out to meet the thought of a lower fall or a new shame as a man might go to his door to see a sunset or a storm. It has been called the aim of artistic culture to witness things with appropriate emotions. That is this

Richard's aim. Good news or bad news, the first thing with him is to put himself in the right vein for getting the fullest and most poignant sense of its contents. Is ruin the word—his mind runs to steep itself in relevant pathos with which in turn to saturate the object put before it; he will 'talk of graves and epitaphs', 'talk of wills', 'tell sad stories of the death of kings'. Once in the vein, he rejoices like a good artist who has caught the spirit of his subject. The very sense of the loss of hope becomes 'that sweet way I was in to despair'. To his wife at their last meeting he bequeaths, as one imaginative writer might bequeath to another some treasure of possibilities of tragic effect, 'the lamentable tale of me'. And to this intoxicating sense of the beauty or poignancy of what is next him he joins the true passion of concern for its perfect expression. At the height of that preoccupation enmities, fears, mortifications, the very presence of onlookers are as if they were not. At the climax of the agony of the abdication scene Shakspere, with a magnificent boldness of truth, makes the artist's mind, in travail with the lovely poetical figure of the mirror, snatch at the possibility of help at the birth of the beautiful thing, even from the bitterest enemy,—

> say that again;
> The shadows of my sorrow; ha, let's see.

And nothing in Mr Benson's performance was finer than the King's air, during the mirror soliloquy, as of a man going about his mind's engrossing business in a solitude of its own making. He gave their full value, again, to all those passages, so enigmatic, if not ludicrous, to strictly prosaic minds, in which Richard's craving for finished expression issues in a joining of words with figurative action to point and eke them out; as where he gives away the crown in the simile of the well, inviting his enemy, with the same artistic neutrality as in the passage of the mirror, to collaborate manually in an effort to give perfect expression to the situation. With Aumerle Richard is full of these little symbolic inventions, turning them over lovingly as a writer fondles a phrase that tells. 'Would not this ill do well', he says of one of them, like a poet showing a threnody to a friend.

There was just one point—perhaps it was a mere slip—at which

Mr Benson seemed to us to fail. In the beginning of the scene at Pomfret what one may call the artistic heroism of this man, so craven in everything but art, reaches its climax. Ruined, weary, with death waiting in the next room, he is shown still toiling at the attainment of a perfect, because perfectly expressed, apprehension of such sad dregs as are left him of life, still following passionately on the old quest of the ideal word, the unique image, the one perfect way of saying the one thing.

> I cannot do it; yet I'll hammer it out.

Everybody knows that cry of the artist wrestling with the angel in the dark for the word it will not give, of Balzac 'plying the pick for dear life, like an entombed miner', of our own Stevenson, of Flaubert 'sick, irritated, the prey a thousand times a day of cruel pain' but 'continuing my labour like a true working man, who, with sleeves turned up, in the sweat of his brow, beats away at his anvil, whether it rain or blow, hail or thunder'. That 'yet I'll hammer it out' is the gem of the whole passage, yet on Saturday Mr Benson, by some strange mischance, left the words clean out. He made amends with a beautiful little piece of insight at the close, where, after the lines

> Mount, mount, my soul! Thy seat is up on high,
> Whilst my gross flesh sinks downward, here to die,

uttered much as any other man might utter them under the first shock of the imminence of death, he half rises from the ground with a brightened face and repeats the two last words with a sudden return of animation and interest, the eager spirit leaping up, with a last flicker before it goes quite out, to seize on this new 'idea of' the death of the body. Greater love of art could no man have than this, and it was a brilliant thought of Mr Benson's to end on such a note. But indeed the whole performance, but for the slip we have mentioned, was brilliant in its equal grasp of the two sides of the character, the one which everybody sees well enough and the one which nearly everybody seems to shun seeing, and in the value which it rendered to the almost continuous flow of genuine and magnificent poetry from Richard, to the descant on mortality in kings, for instance, and the exquisite greeting to English soil and the gorgeous rhetoric of the speeches on divine right in kings. Of Mr Benson's achievements as an actor his Richard II strikes us as decidedly the most memorable.

SOURCE : *The Manchester Guardian* (4 December 1899).

W. B. Yeats

AT STRATFORD-ON-AVON (1901)

In *La Peau de chagrin* Balzac spends many pages in describing a coquette, who seems the image of heartlessness, and then invents an improbable incident that her chief victim may discover how beautifully she can sing. Nobody had ever heard her sing, and yet in her singing, and in her chatter with her maid, Balzac tells us, was her true self. He would have us understand that behind the momentary self, which acts and lives in the world, and is subject to the judgment of the world, there is that which cannot be called before any mortal judgment seat, even though a great poet, or novelist, or philosopher be sitting upon it. Great literature has always been written in a like spirit, and is, indeed, the Forgiveness of Sin, and when we find it becoming the Accusation of Sin, as in George Eliot, who plucks her Tito in pieces with as much assurance as if he had been clockwork, literature has begun to change into something else. George Eliot had a fierceness hardly to be found but in a woman turned argumentative, but the habit of mind her fierceness gave its life to was characteristic of her century, and is the habit of mind of the Shakespearian critics. They and she grew up in a century of utilitarianism, when nothing about a man seemed important except his utility to the State, and nothing so useful to the State as the actions whose effect can be weighed by reason. The deeds of Coriolanus, Hamlet, Timon, Richard II had no obvious use, were, indeed, no more than the expression of their personalities, and so it was thought Shakespeare was accusing them, and telling us to be careful lest we deserve the like accusations. It did not occur to the critics that you cannot know a man from his actions because you cannot watch him in every kind of circumstance, and that men are made useless to the State as often by abundance as by emptiness, and that a man's business may at times be revelation, and not reformation. Fortinbras was, it is likely enough, a better king than Hamlet

would have been, Aufidius was a more reasonable man than Coriolanus, Henry V was a better man-at-arms than Richard II,
but, after all, were not those others who changed nothing for the
better and many things for the worse greater in the Divine Hierarchies? Blake has said that 'the roaring of lions, the howling of
wolves, the raging of the stormy sea, and the destructive sword
are portions of Eternity, too great for the eye of man', but Blake
belonged by right to the ages of Faith, and thought the State of
less moment than the Divine Hierarchies. Because reason can
only discover completely the use of those obvious actions which
everybody admires, and because every character was to be judged
by efficiency in action, Shakespearian criticism became a vulgar
worshipper of success. I have turned over many books in the library at Stratford-on-Avon, and I have found in nearly all an
antithesis, which grew in clearness and violence as the century
grew older, between two types, whose representatives were
Richard II, 'sentimental', 'weak', 'selfish', 'insincere', and Henry
V, 'Shakespeare's only hero'. These books took the same delight
in abasing Richard II that schoolboys do in persecuting some
boy of fine temperament, who has weak muscles and a distaste
for school games. And they had the admiration for Henry V
that schoolboys have for the sailor or soldier hero of a romance
in some boys' paper. I cannot claim any minute knowledge of
these books, but I think that these emotions began among the
German critics, who perhaps saw something French and Latin
in Richard II, and I know that Professor Dowden, whose book
I once read carefully, first made these emotions eloquent and
plausible. He lived in Ireland, where everything has failed, and
he meditated frequently upon the perfection of character which
had, he thought, made England successful, for, as we say, 'cows
beyond the water have long horns'. He forgot that England, as
Gordon has said, was made by her adventurers, by her people
of wildness and imagination and eccentricity; and thought that
Henry V, who only seemed to be these things because he had
some commonplace vices, was not only the typical Anglo-Saxon,
but the model Shakespeare held up before England; and he even
thought it worth while pointing out that Shakespeare himself
was making a large fortune while he was writing about Henry's
victories. In Professor Dowden's successors this apotheosis went

further; and it reached its height at a moment of imperialistic enthusiasm, of ever-deepening conviction that the commonplace shall inherit the earth, when somebody of reputation, whose name I cannot remember, wrote that Shakespeare admired this one character alone out of all his characters. The Accusation of Sin produced its necessary fruit, hatred of all that was abundant, extravagant, exuberant, of all that sets a sail for shipwreck, and flattery of the commonplace emotions and conventional ideals of the mob, the chief Paymaster of accusation.

I cannot believe that Shakespeare looked on his Richard II with any but sympathetic eyes, understanding indeed how ill-fitted he was to be king, at a certain moment of history, but understanding that he was lovable and full of capricious fancy, 'a wild creature' as Pater has called him. The man on whom Shakespeare modelled him had been full of French elegances as he knew from Holinshed, and had given life a new luxury, a new splendour, and been 'too friendly' to his friends, 'too favourable' to his enemies. And certainly Shakespeare had these things in his head when he made his king fail, a little because he lacked some qualities that were doubtless common among his scullions, but more because he had certain qualities that are uncommon in all ages. To suppose that Shakespeare preferred the men who deposed his king is to suppose that Shakespeare judged men with the eyes of a Municipal Councillor weighing the merits of a Town Clerk; and that had he been by when Verlaine cried out from his bed, 'Sir, you have been made by the stroke of a pen, but I have been made by the breath of God', he would have thought the Hospital Superintendent the better man. He saw indeed, as I think, in Richard II the defeat that awaits all, whether they be artist or saint, who find themselves where men ask of them a rough energy and have nothing to give but some contemplative virtue, whether lyrical fantasy, or sweetness of temper, or dreamy dignity, or love of God, or love of His creatures. He saw that such a man through sheer bewilderment and impatience can become as unjust or as violent as any common man, any Bolingbroke or Prince John, and yet remain 'that sweet lovely rose'. The courtly and saintly ideals of the Middle Ages were fading, and the practical ideals of the modern age had begun to threaten the unuseful dome of the sky; Merry England was fading, and yet it was not so faded that the poets could not watch the procession of the world with that untroubled sympathy for men as they are, as apart from all they do and seem, which is the substance of tragic irony.

Shakespeare cared little for the State, the source of all our judgments, apart from its shows and splendours, its turmoils and battles, its flamings-out of the uncivilised heart. He did indeed think it wrong to overturn a king, and thereby to swamp peace in civil war, and the historical plays from *Henry IV* to *Richard III*, that monstrous birth and last sign of the wrath of Heaven, are a fulfilment of the prophecy of the Bishop of Carlisle, who was 'raised up by God' to make it; but he had no nice sense of utilities, no ready balance to measure deeds, like that fine instrument, with all the latest improvements, Gervinus and Professor Dowden handle so skilfully. He meditated as Solomon, not as Bentham meditated, upon blind ambitions, untoward accidents, and capricious passions, and the world was almost as empty in his eyes as it must be in the eyes of God.

> Tired with all these, for restful death I cry;—
> As, to behold desert a beggar born,
> And needy nothing trimm'd in jollity,
> And purest faith unhappily forsworn,
> And gilded honour shamefully misplaced,
> And maiden virtue rudely strumpeted,
> And right perfection wrongfully disgraced,
> And strength by limping sway disabled,
> And art made tongue-tied by authority,
> And folly, doctor-like, controlling skill,
> And simple truth miscall'd simplicity,
> And captive good attending captain ill :
> Tired with all these, from these would I be gone,
> Save that, to die, I leave my love alone. (*Sonnet 66*)

Source : *Ideas of Good and Evil* (1903), reprinted in
Essays and Introductions (1961).

A. C. Swinburne

Coleridge, whose ignorance of Shakespeare's predecessors was apparently as absolute as it is assuredly astonishing in the friend of Lamb, has attempted by super-subtle advocacy to explain and excuse, if not to justify and glorify, the crudities and incongruities of dramatic conception and poetic execution which signalize this play as unmistakably the author's first attempt at historic drama[1] : it would perhaps be more exactly accurate to say, at dramatic history. But they are almost as evident as the equally wonderful and youthful genius of the poet. The grasp of character is uncertain : the exposition of event is inadequate. . . .

The inspired effeminacy and the fanciful puerility which dunces attribute to the typical character of a representative poet never found such graceful utterance as the greatest of poets has given to the unmanliest of his creatures when Richard lands in Wales. Coleridge credits the poor wretch with 'an intense love of his country', intended to 'redeem him in the hearts of the audience' in spite of the fact that 'even in this love there is something feminine and personal'. There is nothing else in it : as anybody but Coleridge would have seen. It is exquisitely pretty and utterly unimaginable as the utterance of a man.

SOURCE : *Three Plays of Shakespeare* (1909).

NOTE

1. Swinburne was quite wrong. He sustained his exuberant tone for 26 pages, but there is only space for two short extracts. [Ed.]

PART TWO

Recent Comments
on Production

John Gielgud

KING RICHARD THE SECOND (1963)

Richard the Second is a ceremonial play. In spite of its long list of characters only a few are of the first importance, and most of these are very broadly treated, especially in the early scenes. The young King himself, though his personal beauty and the sub- servient manner in which he is treated, as he sits idly on his throne, must draw all eyes to him immediately, is only lightly sketched at first in a few rather enigmatic strokes. It is not until after his re- turn from Ireland, almost halfway through the play, that his inner character begins to be developed in a series of exquisite cadenzas and variations. In these later scenes, the subtleties of his speeches are capable of endless shades and nuances, but (as is nearly always the case in Shakespeare) the actor's vocal efforts must be con- trived within the framework of the verse, and not outside it. Too many pauses and striking variations of tempo will tend to hold up the action disastrously and so ruin the pattern and symmetry of the text. . . .

Richard is one of the rare parts in which the actor may indulge himself, luxuriating in the language he has to speak, and atti- tudinizing in consciously graceful poses. Yet the man must seem, too, to be ever physically on his guard, shielding himself, both in words and movement, from the dreaded impact of the unknown circumstances which, he feels, are always lying in wait to strike him down. He is torn between the intrinsic weakness of his nature and the pride and fastidiousness of his quality and breeding. He strives continually to retain his kingly dignity, to gain time by holding it up to the light before his enemies (as he will actually hold up the mirror later on in the deposition scene), while he prepares inwardly to face the shock of the next humiliation. Fin- ally, cast out into the empty darkness of his prison, he is forced to realize at last that neither his personal beauty nor the divine right of kingship can save him from inevitable horror, as he is forced to contemplate his private doom.

Thus the actor has a dual responsibility. He must present the external action as the King suffers his defeats—the news of his favourites' deaths, the surrender to Bolingbroke at Flint, the defiant shame of the deposition scene and the agonies of farewell to his Queen. Yet he must somehow contrive at the same time to execute the poetic intricacies of the text with a full appreciation of its musical intention, using a completely lucid (and possibly stylized) method of vocal and plastic interpretation. The speaking of blank verse can only be projected, so as to hold an audience, by artificial and technical means—tone, emphasis and modulation. The task may seem an impossibly difficult one—to play, as it were, in two different styles at once, just as a singer has to do in opera. But this is actually a question of technique. A good actor experiences emotion at rehearsal—or imagines the experience of it vividly, which is not quite the same thing—and then selects, through trial and error, what he wishes to convey at each given moment of his performance. So he has always a double task—that of living in his role and at the same time judging his own effects in relation to his fellow players and the audience, so as to present an apparently spontaneous, living being, in a pattern carefully devised beforehand, but capable of infinite shades of colour and tempo, and bound to vary slightly at every performance. The actor is, after all, a kind of conjuror, and in a part like Richard he will find infinite opportunities to put his skill into practice, playing, as Richard himself plays, on the feelings of an audience until they are at one with the complicated nature of the character; then, even when they cannot condone his actions or sympathize with his misfortunes, they come at length to understand his intricate nature and can share in his unique experience. . . .

Unfortunately, throughout the tragedy, the verse seems to be too evenly distributed, and often with more music than sense of character. Everyone speaks in images, parentheses, and elaborate similes, whether gardeners, exquisites, or tough realistic nobles, and though this richness of metaphor gives, in reading, a beautiful, tapestried, somewhat Gothic effect (like an illuminated missal or a Book of Hours), the continually artificial style tends to become somewhat indigestible on the stage, and stands between the audience and their desire to get on more intimate terms with the characters and situations. It is therefore especially important to have actors for the chief parts who are strongly contrasted individual types as well as skilled speakers of verse.

The more simply the characters are played on broad, conventional (but not too melodramatic) lines, the scenes appearing to flow smoothly and swiftly with the correct stress and phrasing, but without too much elaboration, either of action, grouping, or pauses, the better will the beauty of the general pattern emerge and the interest of the audience be sustained. The actor of Richard may then be allowed, like the solo violin in a concerto, to take certain liberties with his cadenzas, developing their intricacies legitimately in an almost unlimited variety of pace and detail, in contrast to the more plodding ground bass of Bolingbroke, Northumberland and the other nobles.

Many of the shorter scenes in the play can produce an exquisite effect; especially the famous episode of the Queen with the gardeners at Langley, for example, and the little duologue between the Welsh captain and Salisbury (which has something of the same sensitive yet sinister effect as the little scene in *Macbeth* in which the murderers wait for Banquo on the lonely heath). These passages should have a romantic, simple expressiveness in contrast to the formality of the great scenes which precede and follow them.

There are several difficult links in the action. The scene between Ross, Willoughby and Northumberland after Gaunt's death, and the passage when the three favourites part for the last time on hearing of Bolingbroke's return, seem almost like choral exercises for three voices, and should, perhaps, be directed mainly from this point of view. The quarrel of the peers, before the entrance of Richard in the deposition scene, is difficult to stage without a dangerous risk of seeming ridiculous (the throwing down and picking up of gloves and so on), and it is advisable to make some discreet cuts to avoid bathos both here and in the Aumerle conspiracy scenes, if they are included. The character of York, used by Shakespeare as a kind of wavering chorus throughout the play, touching yet sometimes absurd, can be of great value, provided that the actor and director can contrive between them a tactful compromise between comedy and dramatic effect. To make him a purely farcical character (as has sometimes been attempted) weakens the play, and is quite opposed, it seems to me, to the intention of the dramatist. The women in the cast are very lightly drawn, and they are difficult parts for actresses to clothe with flesh and blood, though vocally and pictorially they can make a considerable effect—the two Duchesses old and proud, the little Queen so young and helpless —in the somewhat conventional episodes allotted to them.

Most of the characters, except Gaunt, York, Carlisle and the two Duchesses, seem to be young and full of life, and there should be something of the same impetuous brilliance that is so wonderfully vivid in *Romeo and Juliet* in the way they glitter and struggle and hurl themselves towards their fates. *Richard the Second* is a play, above all, which must in performance be finely orchestrated, melodious, youthful, headlong, violent and vivid. It must not be heavy or dragging, and the actors must know where they are going in their long speeches. Every effort must be made to contrast scene against scene. At first we must be made aware of the lightness of Richard's character, his fatal, obstinate frivolity, unchecked by the baleful warnings and implacable nobility of Gaunt. Then, as we reach the heart of the play, and the King's own heart and soul are gradually revealed to us by Shakespeare, we must see him forced, by the realization of his favourites' deaths and the desertion of his countrymen, reluctantly beginning to abandon his contemplative poetic fantasies, to face the brutal reality of Northumberland's hostility and the grim determination of the ruthless Bolingbroke.

The great problem, as in all Shakespearian plays, is to achieve a straightforward musical rendering of the verse, and yet to combine this with a sense of exciting actuality in the action. The events of the play must really seem to happen, and yet, as in an opera, the music of the lines must be neither slurred, dragged nor unduly hurried. In short, the technical brilliance of the poetic writing must be correctly balanced and simply executed, with the added colour of character and personality, while at the same time the shock of the actual events presented must appear to be spontaneous and realistically convincing. The poetry must be welded imperceptibly into the dramatic action to a point where the audience will accept the two together—and, if successfully managed, the two styles should support one another to create a complete harmony of effect.

SOURCE: 'King Richard the Second', *Stage Directions* (1963).

John Russell Brown

NARRATIVE AND FOCUS: *RICHARD II* (1966)

So far I have considered the actor's contribution to performance, but relationships between performances, shifts of interest from one character to another, the effects of movement and changing modes of illusion have already drawn our attention. Now the stage-picture must come to the forefront. As a play is performed, a dramatist is controlling the audience's view of its action, now towards a single character, now a group, now a dead body, or an empty throne, or nothing.

An audience is aware of the physical objects displayed before it, as well as the words it hears. Shape, size, colour; contrasts, numbers, distance; movement, organisation and lack of organisation are all influencing the audience's response. There are moments when a number of figures seem to stand within a realistic perspective in calculated relationship to each other, and moments when they form a two-dimensional frieze (no figure more important than another), or when a small eccentric detail dominates the whole, or when an empty space is more impressive than the rest of a crowded stage. We need to speak of the changing picture on the stage as of a composition, as we might speak of the formal characteristics of a painting. This deployment is part of the performed play and strongly affects what it does to an audience; it is part of the theatrical language which Shakespeare developed during the course of his career.

Two warnings are needed. First it will not be sufficient to list the contents of the stage-picture and their relationships. We must try to describe how the audience perceives that picture. In a picture gallery we recognise that there is an appropriate way of looking at any picture. It would be absurd to stand all the time within a foot or two of a French impressionist painting, a Monet or a Degas. That would be appropriate only if we were considering the painter's technique. In order to see the effect that his picture is able to transmit, we would automatically step back a few paces and so become aware of the relationship of the brush-strokes to each other, of the whole effect of light, colour, movement and space. The picture is made for such a wide focus. Other pictures —some Dutch realists for example—invite, and require, a minute scrutiny : one needs to step up close to the canvas. So it is in the theatre : the right focus, be it wide or intense, is necessary for seeing the masterpiece. Without this adaptation we may see only what appears to be incompetent brush-work, or an inability to give distinction or emphasis.

In watching a play in a theatre—any play, in any theatre—we sometimes sit forward in our chair, head forward and eyes intent on one particular point in the arena or picture which is the stage; this kind of dramatic focus is intense, concentrated. We observe or watch for the minutest action or word; we often see only one particular person or hear only one particular sound, even though the stage may be crowded or noisy, or disorderly. The opposite extreme is a wide dramatic focus. Instead of sitting forward we are sometimes relaxed, sitting back, and responsive to the whole picture. At such a time no one person or sound, or action dominates the impression we receive; we are sitting back and 'taking it all in'; we are conscious of the overall effect, of the interweaving of pattern and the range of colour. It is a wide focus. We can become aware of a changing dramatic focus by marking these two extremes.

We must also remember constantly that the play exists in time; the stage picture is always developing from one form to another and at varying speeds. One momentary grouping may gain emphasis or meaning because it echoes an earlier grouping, in a different setting or with another dominating figure. A single figure may be more eloquent of loneliness because just before the stage had been crowded and animated. The changing visual impressions are also modified by narrative. So a sudden liveliness may appear to be little more than a meaningless disturbance, because the audience is wholly unprepared for it and so it shocks rather than elucidates. When narrative expectation is thwarted by a movement to some other part of the fable, an apparently static, formal scene may lose its impression of stability, or a brief descriptive scene take on an unusual air of deliberation. The stage picture is always changing and the audience's reaction to it can be controlled by dramatic narrative and response to character and situation.

The stage picture cannot be assessed easily; but if we do not discover the appropriate focus for each moment we may misread the dramatic text—and that is done all too easily.

*   *   *

I shall consider first, *Richard II* : an early play, written, for the most part, in a particularly lucid style.

It begins with the stage set formally. Richard is enthroned and surrounded, as the Quarto edition of 1597 says, with *'nobles and attendants'*. Richard commands the centre of the stage, but he is seen as a king in relationship to his subjects, rather than as a person interesting in his own right. He speaks in set fashion to his uncle, John of Gaunt, and requires precise, official answer. When Gaunt's son, Henry Bolingbroke, and Thomas Mowbray, Duke of Norfolk, are called to the King's presence, they bitterly accuse each other of treason. Richard fails to reconcile their demands of honour and appoints a day for trial by combat at Coventry. The whole stage empties at once, and on the outcome of that future event the audience's attention will wait.

So the first scene would appear if it were played on its own merits, with each word spoken as simply as possible. But if the audience has some previous knowledge of Richard's history, or if the actors try to give consistent portrayals of their roles, there will be further and conflicting impressions. Richard's formal protestation of impartiality, his 'Forget, forgive; conclude and be agreed', and his comments on 'bold' Bolingbroke, may carry subtextual impressions of irony, apprehension or antagonism. Bolingbroke's accusations may seem aimed at the King rather than Mowbray, and Mowbray's confidence to stem from royal support rather than his own innocence. But even if these impressions are missed, the audience will be made to question the scene's textual and visual impressions by the simple duologue of the next scene. Mowbray has been accused of murdering Thomas, Duke of Gloucester, a son of Edward III and so Bolingbroke's uncle and the King's, but now, in contrast to the visual elaboration of the first formal picture, a quiet, still, intimate scene shows Thomas' widowed Duchess appealing for revenge, and his brother, John of Gaunt refusing because :

> correction lieth in those hands
> Which made the fault.

The King and judge of the first scene had been responsible for Mowbray murdering Gloucester, a fact to which no overt allusion has hitherto been made. Now the audience must question the earlier picture in retrospect, or find their unease strengthened. The new information is given unemphatically, for Gaunt does not have to persuade his hearer of its truth, but just before the audience's interest is redirected to the lists at Coventry, the Duchess is shown alone, believing that she goes to die.

For the third scene, at Coventry, the full stage is again 'set' (as the Quarto has it) formally. The King enters in procession to the sound of trumpets, and personal feelings are subdued within the larger gestures and more fluent responses of public ceremonial. But now the focus is changed, for the audience will watch both sides closely, and 'God's substitute' also, as he stands as judge on a higher level of the stage. The excitement of the duel itself is quenched before it begins, when Richard, with a simple movement of his hand, stops proceedings. This is unexpected and so draws all the alerted attention to the King who holds attention by wise words about civil strife and his own duties, and then pronounces the judgement which he and his council have agreed upon : Bolingbroke is to be banished for ten years and Mowbray for life. But this is not all : the newly watchful audience may discern a brief sign of complicity or shame as Richard with 'some unwillingness' passes sentence on Mowbray, and a covert accusation as the banished man claims a 'dearer merit' : a single hesitation can now sharpen the audience's perception of signs of subtextual motivation. Bolingbroke's submission with :

> Your will be done. This must my comfort be,
> That sun that warms you here, shall shine on me. . . .

may seem to veil a rivalry with the King himself. Richard dominates the stage as he gives judgement, but at the close of the scene

Bolingbroke is left alone with his friends and, as he fails to acknowledge their farewells, the course of the drama waits upon the expression of his personal and private feelings. So a newly clarified interest is balanced between Richard and Bolingbroke.

To sum up the visual effects so far, we can say that Shakespeare has introduced the action with a wide focus so that the audience is made aware of the patterns of the King's relationship to nobles and officials, and of father to son and fatherless nephew. But a more intimate focus is then induced with a short scene which adds notably, but quietly, to the exposition, and so when the next crowded, formal scene follows there are momentary intensifications of focus; but these never lead to direct narrative statement. Sometimes the audience's curiosity is aroused by some action or speech after it has been completed; or one character, by his words, provokes a closer scrutiny of another, or of relationships between several other characters. So the moments of close interest are sporadic and always lead back to a comprehensive view of the stage, or to a quick review of the preceding action. The audience's intense interest is not engaged for any single character or event, and yet, since the wider issues have been resolved in judgement and banishment, it is these insights which arouse most of the audience's expectation of further development. We can say that the stage-picture is at once comprehensive and subtle, that the focus is potentially intense over a wide design.

More informal scenes follow which complicate the audience's view, extending their interest and knowledge without co-ordinating individual impressions. While the splendours and proprieties are still alive in the memory, Richard is seen disrobed and at ease with his intimates. Now he is sarcastic about 'High Hereford' and answers the national threat of rebellion in Ireland by deciding to lease his royal estates and exact subscriptions from wealthy subjects. When news comes that Gaunt is sick, Richard wishes his uncle were dead so that he might seize his possessions, and then goes to visit him : 'Pray God we may make haste, and come too late', he says, and 'Amen' respond his companions. In all this the pious and responsible solemnities of the first regal scenes are mocked : is this erratic informality a truer picture of Richard and of his country ?

In a solemn, static scene that follows, the dying Gaunt speaks of

the 'scepter'd isle' of England with a reiterative eloquence that
lends fire to patriotic commonplaces and has made the speech
famous out of its context: this is a self-contained, largely verbal
episode. Next Richard enters, and Gaunt denounces his husbandry and openly accuses him of the murder of Gloucester.
Gaunt leaves the royal presence and, as York tries to placate the
King, his death is announced. Immediately Richard confiscates
Gaunt's possessions and York is no longer patient but denounces
Richard like Gaunt had done: his remonstrance is breathless,
not so imposing but more pitiful than Gaunt's, yet the King does
not listen; rather, with surprising decision, he makes York governor in England during his own absence in Ireland, and then again
hurries from the scene. As Gaunt and York have taken the centre
of the stage in denunciation, Shakespeare has ensured that the
King prevents a prolonged close focus by jests and rapid decisions
and movements. Verbally the situation is clearer, but the focus is
still predominantly wide; it has only become more insecure, more
uncertain and more frequently disturbed by momentary clari-
fications and intensities.

As soon as Richard has left the stage, the Earl of Northumberland and the lords, Ross and Willoughby, agree together that the
King 'is not himself' but transformed by his flatterers, and then
they hasten to join Bolingbroke newly returned at the head of an
army to redress all wrongs. Here is a simpler, stronger interest
in the narrative development, but before the audience is allowed
to follow it, there is a quiet moment in which the Queen mourns
the absence of her 'sweet Richard'—an entirely new reaction to
this baffling figure. When she hears of Bolingbroke's arrival she
despairs and York is unable to reassure her: 'Comfort's in
heaven', he warns, 'and we are on the earth'. He has little confidence in his resources or decisions: and, as he leaves with the
Queen, the audience sees Richard's lesser friends count their
chances and promptly decide to save their own skins, two fleeing
to Bristol and one to Ireland. So from this gentle and then hesi-
tating and shifting scene, the audience will turn with relief to
Bolingbroke who now appears confident in arms and attended
by Northumberland. They are joined by other nobles and all
speak courteously, as if in homage to the new central figure. Bolingbroke's speeches are both strong and relaxed, so that the stage

picture is at last ordered and assured (as it had *seemed* to be at the beginning), and the action steadily developing. York enters to denounce the rebel, but then declares himself neutral. There is a brief scene recounting the dispersal of the King's Welsh army on hearing rumours of his death, and then the action moves to Bristol where Bolingbroke, now accompanied by York as well, condemns to death Bushy and Green, Richard's cowardly friends. He takes charge of the realm as if he were the king of it, and holds the centre of the stage; again echoing the first 'set' scene.

The narrative encourages the audience to expect the uneasy focus to settle on the opposition of two main figures, two potential centres of the stage. But when Richard returns as from Ireland with Aumerle and the Bishop of Carlisle, after being absent for some four hundred and sixty lines (over one sixth of the whole play), he does not meet Bolingbroke at once. The scene of his return (III, ii) is antithetical to that of Bolingbroke's: Richard is joined by other friends, as his rival had been, but they bring bad news and not an easy courtesy; and, whereas the rebel's course was clear, the King's is makeshift. Yet from this point to his death the dramatic focus grows more and more intent upon Richard for his own sake, whenever he appears; the audience sees progressively deeper into his consciousness. Sometimes the more stable Bolingbroke is a potential rival for attention in the centre of a crowded stage, but after his opponent has surrendered he says very little: he assumes the crown, but never mentions his intention to do so; he deposes Richard, but leaves most of the business and persuasion to Northumberland and York. The audience is continually aware of Bolingbroke's presence, but he seems to stand further away from them than Richard, or than he himself had done formerly. Such is the cunning perspective of the stage picture.

The focus is intensified on Richard by huge transitions of thought and feeling, and by silences. He easily dominates the stage on his return because all the ill-tidings are known to the audience before they are told to him, and so there is no competitive narrative interest. Moreover he is eloquent and the other characters dependent upon him. But the focus is so narrowly intense because of his silences: it seems as if the extremes of his spoken despair and hope are impelled by some unexpressed fear, some knowledge or state of being which he cannot escape and cannot fully meet. He tries many ways to hope or despair, to some stable and 'true' reaction : at first plain fantasy, then affirmation of trust in God, then meditation on the oblivion of death, then renunciation of his duties. But his friends on stage cannot believe or join in any of them, and silence always follows—as if none of his words were valid the moment after they have been spoken. Richard himself is aware of this ineffectiveness and directs attention to it verbally : he thinks he will be mocked for 'senseless conjuration' and that he has been 'mistaken all this while'.

At the end of the scene he discharges his army and hurries offstage, 'From Richard's night, to Bolingbroke's fair day' and forbids anyone to speak further. He seems to know that it is from the expression of his own thoughts that he tries to escape at the end, rather than from physical or political danger. Between the rhetoric and the silences, the audience's attention is drawn towards Richard at the centre of the stage and towards the unexpressed insecurity and suffering at the centre of his being.

The scene in which Richard confronts Bolingbroke's army provides a wide stage-picture organised, for the first time, on two opposing centres. As Richard speaks and looks royally, claiming the power of 'God omnipotent' and prophesying war as the result of Bolingbroke's treason, he seems once more to justify his position on the upper level of the stage at the centre of the picture. Yet when Northumberland promises that the rebel claims only his own inheritance, Richard suddenly changes and agrees to meet his demanns : it is as if the focal point of the composition suddenly lost its substance. As his message is carried back, Richard acknowledges :

> O that I were as great
> As is my grief, or lesser than my name !
> Or that I could forget what I have been !
> Or not remember what I must be now ! (iii, iii, 136–9)

Then again his insecurity is made apparent by the extremity and variety of his reactions : he speaks openly and fluently of future defeat, a life of pious poverty and an obscure death. As Aumerle weeps, Richard retreats still further into the fantasy of 'two kins-

men' digging 'their graves with weeping eyes'. Mildly he submits
to Northumberland's request that he should meet Bolingbroke
in the base court; but before he descends from his dominating
position in the picture, his mind flashes to his former power and
glory :

> Down, down I come, like glist'ring Phaethon,
> Wanting the manage of unruly jades.

To his enemies it seems that :

> Sorrow and grief of heart
> Makes him speak fondly [foolishly], like a frantic [mad] man;
> Yet he is come.

The visual submission is criticised, as it were, by Richard's words,
which he can not wholly control. He cuts short all argument by
placing himself in the enemy's power before that is demanded
of him; and, as before, he hurries to conclude the scene. From
now on, the picture will tend to be dominated by Bolingbroke
and his agents, but the focus is still intent upon Richard whenever he speaks or moves. Borrowing phrases from the criticism of
paintings, we may say that the whole composition is static, at
rest; but it is disturbed by the figure of Richard which is mobile
and restless.

A wholly static interlude follows, of wide focus. It is set in a
garden where Richard's Queen overhears two gardeners talk of
affairs of state. They speak solemnly and pityingly of the 'wasteful
king' who has not 'trimm'd and dress'd his land' as they their
garden, and repeat the news that he is to be deposed. They are
not Shakespeare's usual comic characters impressing their own
personalities or points of view. Their quaint, slow-moving dialogue acts as a fixed point of reference like Gaunt's talk of a
'scepter'd isle', and unequivocal statement of the widest dramatic
issues from outside Richard's personal dilemma.

Then the action moves to London, with Bolingbroke in full
control. The Bishop of Carlisle boldly denounces the rebel and
prophesies 'Disorder, horror, fear, and mutiny' to future generations. He is arrested by Northumberland and at this tense moment
Richard is brought on to the stage. He has already decided to
resign the crown—Shakespeare does not use this incident to argue
about political issues—and now gives effect to his decision step

by step, as if obeying instructions or as if seeking to re-create the ceremonial solemnity of the early scenes. But he is now aware that his words and actions do not reflect his inward nature, neither his 'regal thoughts' nor his deep sorrow. And his audience, both on stage and in the auditorium, is made aware of this disparity. When he cries 'God save the King', no one dares respond 'Amen', and when he calls Bolingbroke to stand opposite him with one hand on the crown he is forced to protest that he cannot resign his cares with the resignation of his office. As he tries to speak of this, his words have a new authority : they do not express conflicting extremes and do not issue from nervous silences. The man who submits now dominates the scene : he draws all attention to himself and, within the pattern of ordained events, he controls the nature of the action and denounces his enemies. Yet this new strength derives from weakness : he speaks more firmly and steadily because he now knows he *cannot* speak of his own crimes nor alleviate his grief; he cannot tell 'what name to call himself'. It is at this point that Shakespeare introduced an incident for which his sources gave not the slightest suggestion : Richard calls for a looking glass and when he sees few signs of his suffering in it, he dashes it to pieces. The true image of Richard is not in his appearance, nor his words. Again the scene is quickly finished : he asks for leave to go and is conveyed to the Tower. Shakespeare has at once presented a wide picture and led the audience's interest intently towards a single figure standing to one side of the composition; and as the focus intensifies the drama becomes abruptly disturbed by subtextual realities and the whole wide picture is disturbed and rapidly dissolved.

There is a brief scene as the Queen greets her husband on his way to prison, not recognising the royal lion in his meek submission. There is no nervous alternation of mood now, nor anxious silence. They exchange short rhymed speeches, and then part with a kiss, in accepted silence. But the audience whose interest has been so intensified upon Richard may see the very fluency of the scene as a deliberately external manner of valediction; Richard communicates his inward grief by trying to conceal it, and in performance the dialogue can sound tender and precarious, as well as controlled. Richard yet again hurries from the

stage, lest they 'make woe wanton with this fond delay' : he is
still afraid of what he might say; for all the verbal formalism
of this scene, the centre of the picture is still mysterious, still lacking a defined and static quality.

The audience hears of further indignities that Richard is made
to suffer, but it has to wait through two bustling, half-comic
scenes before he is presented again. Then—and this is for the
first time in the play—he appears alone. In soliloquy the audience's attention is drawn wholly to him. The focus is now un-
deniably intense, and yet Shakespeare introduces a considered,
reflective, almost literary tone :

> I have been studying how I may compare
> This prison where I live unto the world. . . . (v, v, 1–2)

In due order Richard now describes his disordered thoughts—
religious, ambitious, flattering—and acknowledges that he is content in none of them. As music is played off-stage, he speaks of
'wasting' his 'time', and of his recompense in being 'wasted' by
time and being forced to 'mark the time' of Bolingbroke's progress. Grief, folly, faults, defeat and insecurity are all acknowledged; he no longer tries to escape from such thoughts but seeks
to tame them by expressing them thoughtfully. The tone is almost
unvaried and the pace almost steady : not quite, for still the balance is not easy. The change has left him helpless, expecting that :

> Nor I, nor any man that but man is,
> With nothing shall be pleas'd till he be eas'd
> With being nothing.

Yet music, played out of time, threatens this composure. Only
when he remembers that it is meant for his comfort and is a sign
of love, can he bear that too, and the scene is once more composed. Then comes a quickening of interest in an unexpected
entry : he is hailed as 'royal Prince !', and Richard answers the
visitor quickly with a sharply ironic 'Thanks, noble peer !' He
is a groom of his stable, and tells Richard of his horse, the roan
Barbary, and of this creature's pride in bearing Bolingbroke in
triumph. Richard curses the horse, but then stops to consider :
because the animal was 'created to be aw'd by man' he begs its
forgiveness, and remembers that he himself has been forced to
bear a burden and submit as if he were an animal. Immediately

a warder enters with food and orders the groom away; the focus is sharpened by the unknown, and by an attendant sense of immediate danger. Richard, however, thinks of his servant—'If thou love me, 'tis time thou wert away'—and a silence can be held in performance, despite the excitement, by an undefined and unexpressed sympathy between master and groom. The latter replies: 'What my tongue dares not, that my heart shall say'. Such a silence does not require utterance; momentarily there is intimacy and understanding, and even perhaps, a deep peace.

After this intensely focused moment, Shakespeare returned to his primary sources with the warder's harsh words asking Richard to eat. The warder refuses to taste the food to guard against poison, saying that Bolingbroke's order forbids this, and then Richard leaps at him with :

> The devil take Henry of Lancaster and thee !
> Patience is stale, and I am weary of it.

There are cries for help and Exton and his assistants rush in. Action is violent and general : Richard kills two men, and then is overpowered by numbers and struck down. Suddenly the stage is fully alive with his anger, authority and physical strength, with a struggle and then defeat—all in an instant. The deep, necessarily static focus has been broken, and then when the violence is past —violence can sustain interest in the theatre only for comparatively short times—Richard speaks his last, presumably faint, words (again wholly Shakespeare's invention) that are all the more impressive by contrast with the tumult :

> Mount, mount, my soul ! thy seat is up on high;
> Whilst my gross flesh sinks downward, here to die.

Richard had often longed for death because it would bring oblivion and perhaps pity, but as he faces assassination he finds new aspiration : royal anger and, then, hope in a world beyond death and change, spring from his deepest being.

Shakespeare's Richard talks a great deal about himself—some critics have called him a poet rather than a king—but an understanding of his part in the play cannot be found by simply analysing what he says, weighing the word against the word; his stage reality depends also on subtext, and on the changing picture as it directs the audience's attention progressively towards the thoughts behind the words and the thoughts of silence, and towards his last unthinking, physical reactions. By simple quotation it can be shown that Richard is a man who talks 'too idly', one 'who wastes time' and is then 'wasted by it'; or that he is a king who must uncrown himself and yet cannot escape the cares that 'tend the crown'. But such formulae do not embrace the whole experience the play provides in a theatre.

*   *   *

In a tragedy, after death there is always more to say. If only the eyes are closed and pious ceremonies performed in silence, the audience is shown that death affects other people besides the protagonist. A hushed drum, a bowed head, or a moment without sound or motion is enough to establish death as a fact for others' comprehension; the hero may have unpacked his heart with words but this must still be presented, his death must have this consequence. Many dramatists have made the further communication explicitly, in a chorus which tells the men and women of Thebes that no one can be called happy until he has died in peace, that there is always an end to tears, that wisdom is taught by suffering. Some authors, more busily, have recounted death's manifold implications through a group of women tidying their thoughts aloud; others have announced a long-kept secret through the mouth of some wise, experienced man—how he who has died had been true to his heritage, or had been struck down by some hidden guilt. Authors who prefer to maintain a full dramatic illusion have presented retaliation or submission, praise or blame, in continued action, or have concluded with a prayer that begs some god to appease man's misery and remorse. In Shakespeare's day the standard procedure was explicit comment, a statement of the play's meaning or significance. Elizabethan tragedy usually drew a firm line after the death of the hero, and then totalled up good deeds and bad. In this play, Shakespeare's method is to give another scene, another picture with different figures: after the death of Richard, when the focus has been more intense than ever before, Shakespeare transferred attention to Bolingbroke seated in Richard's throne; a formal 'set' scene, with a predominantly wide focus.

The transference is, however, long prepared for : the wide focus of the early scenes had not been invoked needlessly. The first stage-pictures with Richard as judge of Mowbray and Bolingbroke, were repeated half-way through when Bolingbroke stood as judge of Bushy and Green, and then of Aumerle and Surrey against the charges of Bagot, Fitzwater and others. In his second judgement Bolingbroke dealt with the same offence as had concerned Richard : the murder of Thomas, Duke of Gloucester. But there were significant differences : the contestants were more numerous and more quick-tempered; the judge said far less than his pre-decessor, his most arresting contributions being his silence, his re-peal of Mowbray and then, on hearing of this old enemy's death after fighting in the crusades, his praise and prayer for him. All these scenes are echoed in the last formal scene, and so strengthen it; once the momentary surprise has passed, it seems the inevit-able close to the play as a whole.

Again, between Richard's farewell to his Queen and his last appearance, Shakespeare elaborated on accounts in his sources by introducing two scenes showing the Duke of York's discovery that his son, Aumerle, is engaged in conspiracy against Boling-broke. The audience need not know these events in order to follow Richard's story—indeed, almost invariably the scenes are cut from modern productions—so Shakespeare must have had other reasons for inventing them. Firstly they demonstrate the effects of revolution; and, secondly, their comic details of calling for boots to a loquacious wife, provide a release from the tension of following Richard's story. And they also affect the dramatic focus. By introducing these scenes Bolingbroke is again seated as judge. At first he seems well able to manage the danger to his person, reducing the stature of both Aumerle and his mother with an ironic : 'My dangerous cousin, let your mother in' (v, iii, 81). But, as the Duchess kneels in supplication and refuses to obey Bolingbroke's thrice repeated 'Rise up, good aunt' until he has promised, and doubly promised, pardon for her son's life, the audience is shown both the new king's power and his subject's tendency to doubt the effect of his commanding words of friend-ship and forgiveness. The irony touches Bolingbroke closely, for as the suppliant rises she cries (and this is all she says) : 'A God on earth thou art'—the rebel, the silent king, has to hear him-

self called a god by those he favours. To this salutation he answers
nothing: but his tone changes and, ignoring the agonised and
flustered woman, he speaks directly of tracking down other conspirators and swears that all of them shall die. The episode ends
when the Duchess leaves with her pardoned son and places such
revolutions of fortune in another perspective: 'Come my old son;
I pray God make thee new.'

I have dwelt so long on this scene because the final scene of the
play is again, for the fourth time, Bolingbroke enthroned as king
and judge. The picture including its central figure is now quite
familiar, so that despite its wide focus the audience may give
particular attention to small points of difference, or imprecision.
York, Northumberland and Fitzwater bring news that his enemies are defeated and slain; only the Bishop of Carlisle is brought
a prisoner before him, and he—strangely perhaps—is pardoned
because Bolingbroke has seen 'sparks of honour' in this implacable
enemy. Then there follows another, more impressive entry into
the royal presence: Sir Pierce of Exton with Richard's body in a
coffin. At least four men are needed to bear this burden on to
the stage, and they must move more slowly and ceremonially than
the eager messengers who have preceded them. Bolingbroke does
not speak, but as the coffin is deliberately placed before him, Exton
announces:

> Great King, within this coffin I present
> Thy buried fear.

The answer is:

> Exton, I thank thee not; for thou hast wrought
> A deed of slander with thy fatal hand
> Upon my head and all this famous land.
> ... Though I did wish him dead,
> I hate the murderer, love him murdered.
> The guilt of conscience take thou for thy labour,
> But neither my good word nor princely favour;
> With Cain go wander thorough shades of night,
> And never show thy head by day nor light.

He turns from Exton, to address his silent, watchful noblemen:

> Lords, I protest my soul is full of woe
> That blood should sprinkle me to make me grow.

And the play ends with self-assumed penance :

> Come, mourn with me for what I do lament,
> And put on sullen black incontinent :
> I'll make a voyage to the Holy Land,
> To wash this blood off from my guilty hand.

A reader of the play might claim that Bolingbroke's last words are prompted by his practised political intelligence : to dash Exton's hopes, or to announce new business to employ the energies of fractious nobles (following such counsel as, in *Henry IV*, Shakespeare was to put in Bolingbroke's own mouth). But in performance such interpretations are not fully satisfying, for the picture, the visual impression, qualifies the words. On the crowded stage all are silent and intent upon their king, so that if he attempted dissimulation he would scarcely be content with the continued silence which is the only response to his words (compare Prince John and the Lord Chief Justice talking together after Henry V has made a similar announcement of foreign wars at the end of *2 Henry IV*). Moreover this moral note has been heard before where it could serve no political purpose : as Bolingbroke prayed for Mowbray, as he spoke of his son's irresponsibility hanging like a plague over him, and perhaps as he pardoned Aumerle 'as God shall pardon me', and as he pardoned the Bishop of Carlisle. Possibly Bolingbroke's silence when he heard his subjects accuse each other of treason and when he heard the Bishop denounce his assumption of the throne, should be viewed as earlier attempts to conceal a subtextual guilt. These moments passed quickly and without emphasis, but the repetition of the picture of a king crowned and surrounded by his nobles directs the audience attention progressively upon variations and movement : slight tensions beneath formal poses can thus become impressive.

As at the end of a sonnet, the last line can send the reader back to the first, till the experience which the sonnet gives is viewed whole and complete, contained and understood, so at the end of this tragedy, the audience's visual sense will retravel to its beginning, to a group of ambitious, striving, related and insecure human-beings. To ensure this response the awakening of a new Richard in his death-scene has been presented so briefly; Boling-

S. : R.II.—D

broke has been held uncommunicative within the wide picture of the drama while the intense focus was directed more and more upon Richard; and the early scenes were allowed no single dominant interest. Instead of concentrating the drama upon a hero's story, Shakespeare has presented a man in isolation and defeat who overcomes fear and learns to recognise guilt, responsibility and courage in himself; and has off-set this with a man who knows little of fear and recognises guilt only when he assumes the responsibility he has continually sought. The last scene presents Bolingbroke in a new way, verbally: and Richard is there in his coffin, eloquent of his own story, visually.

Both Bolingbroke's and Richard's last words are about their souls, and of Heaven or the Holy Land; and this also completes a series of scenes, still moments when an isolated figure appeals to a state of being outside the world of the stage. In the second scene, the Duchess of Gloucester is told to 'complain' to 'God, the widow's champion and defence', and this resource is again invoked by the unexpected report of the banished Mowbray fighting in the crusades, by York reminding the distressed Queen that 'Comfort's in heaven, and we are on the earth', and his warning to Bolingbroke:

> Take not, good cousin, further than you should,
> Lest you mistake. The heavens are over our heads.

The last scene, in a moment of piety, lightly draws these moments together too.

The surest and most comprehensive effects of the conclusion are carried by the stage picture: viewing the wide picture the audience may see deeply into the characters and the society portrayed, and even into a timeless perspective associated with traditional religion. This visual and formal language is not so precise as words, but it can affect the audience subtly and without its conscious knowledge; it can suggest vast implications and sensitive psychological reactions; it can awaken a response without limiting it by definition, declaration or propaganda.

SOURCE: *Shakespeare's Plays in Performance* (1966).

PART THREE

Modern Studies of *Richard II*

Richard D. Altick

SYMPHONIC IMAGERY IN
RICHARD II (1947)

Critics on occasion have remarked the peculiar unity of tone which distinguishes *Richard II* from most of Shakespeare's other plays. Walter Pater wrote that, like a musical composition, it possesses 'a certain concentration of all its parts, a simple continuity, an evenness in execution, which are rare in the great dramatist. . . . It belongs to a small group of plays, where, by happy birth and consistent evolution, dramatic form approaches to something like the unity of a lyrical ballad, a lyric, a song, a single strain of music.' And J. Dover Wilson, in his edition of the play, has observed that '*Richard II* possesses a unity of tone and feeling greater than that attained in many of his greater plays, a unity found, I think, to the same degree elsewhere only in *Twelfth Night, Antony and Cleopatra,* and *The Tempest*.'[1]

How can we account for that impression of harmony, of oneness, which we receive when we read the play or listen to its lines spoken upon the stage? The secret, it seems to me, lies in an aspect of Shakespeare's genius which has oftener been condemned than praised. Critics and casual readers alike have groaned over the fine-drawn ingenuity of the Shakespearean quibble, which, as Dr Johnson maintained, was 'the fatal Cleopatra for which he lost the world, and was content to lose it'. But it is essentially the same habit of the creative imagination—a highly sensitized associational gift—that produces iterative symbolism and imagery. Simple word-play results from the poet's awareness of the diverse meanings of words, of which, however, he makes no better use than to demonstrate his own cleverness and to tickle for a moment the wit of the audience. These exhibitions of verbal agility are simply decorations scattered upon the surface of the poetic fabric; they can be ripped out without loss. But suppose that to the poet's associational sensitivity is added a further awareness of the multitudinous emotional overtones of words. When he puts this faculty to use he is no longer merely playing a game; instead, words have become the shells in which ideas and symbols are enclosed. Suppose furthermore that instead of being the occupation of a few fleeting lines of the text, certain words of multifold meanings are played upon throughout the five acts, recurring time after time like lietmotivs in music. And suppose finally that this process of repetition is applied especially to words of sensuous significance, words that evoke vivid responses in the imagination. When these things happen to certain words—when they cease to be mere vehicles for a brief indulgence of verbal fancy and, taking on a burden of serious meaning, become thematic material—the poet has crossed the borderline that separates word-play from iterative imagery. Language has become the willing servant of structure, and what was on other occasions only a source of exuberant but undisciplined wit now is converted to the higher purpose of poetic unity.

That, briefly, is what happens in *Richard II*. The familiar word-plays of the earlier Shakespearean dramas persist: John of Gaunt puns endlessly upon his own name. But in this drama a word is not commonly taken up, rapidly revolved, so that all its various facets of meaning flash out, and then discarded. Instead, certain words are played upon throughout the drama. Far from being decorations, 'gay, fresh, variegated flowers of speech', as Pater called them, they are woven deeply into the thought-web of the play. Each word-theme symbolises one or another of the fundamental ideas of the story, and every time it reappears it perceptibly deepens and enriches those meanings and at the same time charges the atmosphere with emotional significance.

The most remarkable thing about these leitmotivs is the way in which they are constantly mingling and coalescing, two or three of them joining to form a single new figure, very much in the manner in which 'hooked images', as Professor Lowes called them, were formed in the subconscious mind of Coleridge. This repeated criss-crossing of familiar images[2] makes of the whole text one vast arabesque of language, just as a dozen lines of *Love's Labour's Lost* form a miniature arabesque when the poet's quibbling mood is upon him. And since each image motif represents

one of the dominant ideas of the play (heredity, patriotism, syco-
phancy, etc.) the coalescing of these images again and again emphasizes the complex relationship between the ideas themselves,
so that the reader is kept ever aware that all that happens in
Richard II results inevitably from the interaction of many
elements.

It is pointless to try to explain by further generalizations this
subtle and exceedingly intricate weaving together of metaphor
and symbol—this glorified word-play, if you will—which is the
key to the total poetic effect of *Richard II*. All I can do is to draw
from the fabric, one by one, the strands that compose it, and to
suggest in some manner the magical way in which they interact
and by association and actual fusion reciprocally deepen their
meaning.

Miss Spurgeon has pointed out how in *Antony and Cleopatra*
the cosmic grandeur of the theme is constantly emphasized by
the repetition of the word *world*.[3] In a similar manner the symbolism of *Richard II* is dominated by the related words *earth*,
land, and *ground*. In no other play of Shakespeare is the complex
of ideas represented by these words so tirelessly dwelt upon.[4] The
words are but three in number, and superficially they seem
roughly synonymous; but they have many intellectual ramifica-
tions, which become more and more meaningful as the play pro-
gresses and the words are used first for one thing and then for
another. As our experience of the words increases, their connotation steadily deepens. In addition to their obvious meaning in a
particular context they come to stand for something larger and
more undefinable—a mingling of everything they have represented earlier.

Above all, *earth* is the symbol of the English nation. It is used
by Shakespeare to connote those same values which we find in the
equivalent synecdoche of *soil*, as in 'native soil'. It sums up all the
feeling inherent in the sense of pride in nation—of jealousy when
the country is threatened by foreign incursion, of bitter anger
when its health has been destroyed by mismanagement or greed.
'This earth of majesty,' John of Gaunt calls England in his famous
speech, 'This blessed plot, this earth, this realm, this England'
(II, i, 41, 50).[5] And a few lines farther on : 'This land of such
dear souls, this dear dear land . . .' (II, i, 57). Having

once appeared, so early in the play, in such lustrous context, the words *earth* and *land* forever after have richer significance. Whenever they recur, they are more meaningful, more powerful. Thus Richard's elaborate speech upon his arrival in Wales—

> As a long-parted mother with her child
> Plays fondly with her tears and smiles in meeting,
> So, weeping, smiling, greet I thee, my earth,
> And do thee favours with my royal hands.
>
> .   .   .   .
>
> Mock not my senseless conjuration, lords.
> This earth shall have a feeling, and these stones
> Prove armed soldiers, ere her native king
> Shall falter under foul rebellion's arms (III, ii, 8–11, 23–6)

—undoubtedly gains in emotional splendor (as well as dramatic irony) by its reminiscences of John of Gaunt's earlier language. The two men between them make the English earth the chief verbal theme of the play.

Richard, we have just seen, speaks pridefully of '*my* earth'. To him, ownership of the land is the most tangible and positive symbol of his rightful kingship. He bids Northumberland tell Bolingbroke that 'every stride he makes upon my land/ Is dangerous treason' (III, iii, 92–3), and as he lies dying from the stroke of Exton's sword his last thought is for his land: 'Exton, thy fierce hand/ Hath with the king's blood stained the king's own land' (V, v, 110–11). It is only natural, then, that *land* should be the key word in the discussions of England's sorry condition. Symbol of Englishmen's nationalistic pride and of the wealth of kings, it becomes symbol also of Englishmen's shame and kings' disgrace:

> Why, cousin, wert thou regent of the world,
> It were a shame to let this land by lease;
> But for thy world enjoying but this land,
> Is it not more than shame to shame it so?
> Landlord of England art thou now, not king. (II, i, 109–13)

Northumberland's sad allusion to 'this declining land' (II, i, 240), York's to 'this woeful land' (II, ii, 99) and Richard's to 'this revolting land' (III, iii, 163) carry on this motif.

But *earth*, while it emblematizes the foundation of kingly pride
and power, is also a familiar symbol of the vanity of human life
and of what, in the middle ages, was a fascinating illustration of
that vanity—the fall of kings. 'Men,' Mowbray sighs, 'are but
gilded loam or painted clay' (i, i, 179); and Richard, luxuriating in self-pity, often remembers it; to earth he will return.

> Ah, Richard [says Salisbury], with the eyes of heavy mind
> I see thy glory like a shooting star
> Fall to the base earth from the firmament. (ii, iv, 18–20)

The earth, Richard knows, is accustomed to receive the knees of
courtiers : 'Fair cousin,' he tells Bolingbroke after he has given
away his kingdom for the sheer joy of listening to himself do so,
'you debase your princely knee/ To make the base earth proud
with kissing it' (iii, iii, 190–1). And the idea of the ground as
the resting place for suppliant knees, and therefore the antithesis
of kingly elevation, is repeated thrice in the two scenes dealing
with Aumerle's conspiracy.[6]

The irony of this association of *earth* with both kingly glory
and abasement is deepened by another role the word has in this
earth-preoccupied play. For after death, earth receives its own;
and in *Richard II* the common notion of the grave has new meaning, because the ubiquitous symbol of *earth* embraces it too. By
the beginning of the third act, *earth* has lost its earlier joyful connotation to Richard, and this king, whose feverish imagination
no amount of woe can cool, eagerly picks up a hint from Scroop :

> SCROOP   Those whom you curse
>   Have felt the worst of death's destroying wound
>   And lie full low, grav'd in the hollow ground.
>
>   .   .   .   .   .
>
> RICHARD   Let's talk of graves, of worms, and epitaphs;
>   Make dust our paper and with rainy eyes
>   Write sorrow on the bosom of the earth.
>   Let's choose executors and talk of wills;
>   And yet not so; for what can we bequeath
>   Save our deposed bodies to the ground?
>   Our lands, our lives, and all are Bolingbroke's,
>   And nothing can we call our own but death,

And that small model of the barren earth
Which serves as paste and cover to our bones.
For God's sake, let us sit upon the ground
And tell sad stories of the death of kings.

(III, ii, 138–40, 145–56)

And later, in another ecstasy of self-pity, he conjures up an elaborate image of making some pretty match with shedding tears:

As thus, to drop them still upon one place,
Till they have fretted us a pair of graves
Within the earth. (III, iii, 166–8)

The same association occurs in the speeches of the other characters. Surrey, casting his gage at Fitzwater's feet, envisions his father's skull lying quietly in earth (IV, i, 66–9); a moment or two later the Bishop of Carlisle brings news that the banished Mowbray, having fought for Jesu Christ in glorious Christian field, 'at Venice gave/ His body to that pleasant country's earth' (IV, i, 97–8); and in the same scene Richard, having handed over his crown to the usurper, exclaims,

Long mayst thou live in Richard's seat to sit,
And soon lie Richard in an earthy pit! (IV, i, 218–19)

A final theme in the symphonic pattern dominated by the symbol of earth is that of the untended garden. Miss Spurgeon has adequately emphasized the importance of this iterated image in the history plays, and, as she points out, it reaches its climax in *Richard II*, particularly in the allegorical scene of the Queen's garden.[7] In Shakespeare's imagination the misdeeds of Richard and his followers constituted an overwhelming indignity to the precious English earth—to a nation which, in happier days, had been a sea-wall'd garden. And thus the play is filled with references to ripeness and the seasons, to planting and cropping and plucking and reaping, to furrows and plowing, and caterpillars and withered bay trees and thorns and flowers.[8]

Among the host of garden images in the play, one especially is unforgettable because of the insistence with which Shakespeare thrice echoes it. It is the terrible metaphor of the English garden being drenched by showers of blood.

> I'll use the advantage of my power
> And lay the summer's dust with showers of blood
> Rain'd from the wounds of slaughtered Englishmen;
>   (III, iii, 42–4)

threatens Bolingbroke as he approaches Flint castle; and when
the King himself appears upon the walls, he casts the figure back
in Bolingbroke's face :

> But ere the crown he looks for live in peace,
> Ten thousand bloody crowns of mothers' sons
> Shall ill become the flower of England's face,
> Change the complexion of her maid-pale peace
> To scarlet indignation, and bedew
> Her pastures' grass with faithful English blood. (III, iii, 95–100)

The Bishop of Carlisle takes up the theme :

> And if you crown him, let me prophesy,
> The blood of English shall manure the ground,
> And future ages groan for this foul act. (IV, i, 136–8)

And the new King—amply justifying Professor Van Doren's remark that not only are most of the characters in this play poets,
but they copy one another on occasion[9]—echoes it :

> Lords, I protest, my soul is full of woe
> That blood should sprinkle me to make me grow. (V, vi, 45–6)

This extraordinary series of four images is one of the many
examples of the manner in which the principal symbols of
Richard II so often chime together, bringing the ideas they represent into momentary conjunction and thus compounding those
single emotional strains into new and revealing harmonies. In
this case the 'showers of blood' metaphor provides a recurrent
nexus between the pervasive symbol of earth and another, equally
pervasive, symbol : that of blood.

Both Professor Bradley[10] and Miss Spurgeon[11] have pointed out
the splendid horror which Shakespeare achieves in *Macbeth* by
his repeated allusions to blood. Curiously enough, the word *blood*,
together with such related words as *bloody* and *bleed*, occurs much
less frequently in *Macbeth* than it does in most of the history plays.
What gives the word the tremendous force it undoubtedly possesses in *Macbeth* is not the frequency with which it is spoken,

but rather the intrinsic magnificence of the passages in which it appears and the fact that in this play it has but one significance —the literal one. In the history plays, however, the word *blood* plays two major roles. Often it has the same meaning it has in *Macbeth*, for these too are plays in which men's minds often turn toward the sword :

> ... our kingdom's earth should not be soil'd
> With that dear blood which it hath fostered (i, iii, 125–6)

says Richard in one more instinctive (and punning!) association of blood and earth. But *blood* in the history plays also stands figuratively for inheritance, descent, familial pride; and this is the chief motivating theme of the play—the right of a monarch of unquestionably legitimate blood to his throne. The two significances constantly interplay, giving the single word a new multiple connotation wherever it appears. The finest instance of this merging of ideas is in the Duchess of Gloucester's outburst to John of Gaunt. Here we have an elaborate contrapuntal metaphor, the basis of which is a figure derived from the familiar medieval genealogical symbol of the Tree of Jesse, and which is completed by a second figure of the seven vials of blood. The imposition of the figure involving the word *blood* (in its literal and therefore most vivid use) upon another figure which for centuries embodied the concept of family descent, thus welds together with extraordinary tightness the word and its symbolic significance. The occurrence of *blood* in other senses on the borders of the metaphor (in the first and next-to-last lines of the passage) helps to focus attention upon the process occurring in the metaphor itself.

> Hath love in thy old blood no living fire?
> Edward's seven sons, whereof thyself art one,
> Were as seven vials of his sacred blood,
> Or seven fair branches springing from one root.
> Some of those seven are dried by nature's course,
> Some of those branches by the Destinies cut;
> But Thomas, my dear lord, my life, my Gloucester,
> One vial full of Edward's sacred blood,
> One flourishing branch of his most royal root,
> Is crack'd, and all the precious liquor spilt,
> Is hack'd down, and his summer leaves all faded,

> By Envy's hand and Murder's bloody axe.
> Ah, Gaunt, his blood was thine ! (I, ii, 10–22)

Because it has this multiple function, the word *blood* in this play loses much of the concentrated vividness and application it has in *Macbeth*, where it means but one unmistakable thing; but its ambiguity here gives it a new sort of power. If it is less effective as imagery, it does serve to underscore the basic idea of the play, that violation of the laws of blood descent leads but to the spilling of precious English blood. That is the meaning of the word as it pulses from beginning to end, marking the emotional rhythm of the play.

In *Richard II*, furthermore, the word has an additional, unique use, one which involves an especially striking symbol. It has often been remarked how Shakespeare, seizing upon a hint in his sources, plays upon Richard's abnormal tendency to blanch and blush. In the imagery thus called forth, *blood* has a prominent part. How, demands the haughty king of John of Gaunt, dare thou

> with thy frozen admonition
> Make pale our cheek, chasing the royal blood
> With fury from his native residence. (II, i, 117–19)

And when the King hears the news of the Welshmen's defection, Aumerle steadies his quaking body :

> Comfort, my liege; why looks your Grace so pale ?
> RICHARD   But now the blood of twenty thousand men
> Did triumph in my face, and they are fled;
> And, till so much blood thither come again,
> Have I not reason to look pale and dead? (III, ii, 75–9)

This idiosyncrasy of the King is made the more vivid because the imagery of the play constantly refers to pallor, even in contexts far removed from him. The Welsh captain reports that 'the pale-fac'd moon looks bloody on the earth' (II, iv, 10). In another speech, the words *pale* and *blood*, though not associated in a single image, occur so close to each other that it is tempting to suspect an habitual association in Shakespeare's mind :

> Pale trembling coward, there I throw my gage,
> Disclaiming here the kindred of the King,
> And lay aside my high blood's royalty. (I, i, 69–71)

And as we have already seen, the King prophesied that 'ten thousand bloody crowns of mothers' sons/ Shall . . . change the complexion of [England's] maid-pale peace' (III, iii, 96–8). Elsewhere Bolingbroke speaks of 'pale beggar-fear' (I, i, 189); the Duchess of Gloucester accuses John of Gaunt of 'pale cold cowardice' (I, ii, 34); and York describes how the returned exile and his army fright England's 'pale-fac'd villages' with war (II, iii, 94).

The idea of pallor and blushing is linked in turn with what is perhaps the most famous image-motif of the play, that of Richard (or the fact of his kingship) emblematized by the sun. More attention probably has been paid to the sun-king theme than it is worth, for although it occurs in two very familiar passages, it contributes far less to the harmonic unity of the play than do a number of other symbol strains. In any event, the conjunction of the sun image with that of blushing provides one more evidence of the closeness with which the poetic themes of the play are knit together. In the first of the sun-king speeches, Richard compares himself, at the length to which he is addicted, with 'the searching eye of heaven' (III, ii, 37). Finally, after some ten lines of analogy:

> So when this thief, this traitor, Bolingbroke,
> Who all this while hath revell'd in the night
> Whilst we were wand'ring with the antipodes,
> Shall see us rising in our throne, the east,
> His treasons will sit blushing in his face. . . . (III, ii, 47–51)

And Bolingbroke in a later scene does him the sincere flattery of imitation:

> See, see, King Richard doth himself appear,
> As doth the blushing discontented sun
> From out the fiery portal of the east. (III, iii, 62–4)

Another occurrence of the sun image provides a link with the pervasive motif of tears. Salisbury, having envisioned Richard's glory falling to the base earth from the firmament, continues:

> Thy sun sets weeping in the lowly west,
> Witnessing storms to come, woe, and unrest. (II, iv, 21–2)

In no other history play is the idea of tears and weeping so in-
sistently presented.[12] It is this element which enforces most strongly
our impression of Richard as a weakling, a monarch essentially
feminine in nature, who has no conception of stoic endurance
or resignation but a strong predilection for grief. This is why the
play seems so strangely devoid of the heroic; the King and Queen
are too much devoted to luxuriating in their misery, and the
other characters find a morbid delight in at least alluding to unmanly tears. Characteristically, Richard's first question to Aumerle, when the latter returns from bidding farewell to Bolingbroke, is, 'What store of parting tears were shed?' (I, iv, 5).
Bushy, discussing with the Queen her premonitions of disaster,
speaks at length of 'sorrow's eye, glazed with blinding tears'
(II, ii, 16). Richard greets the fair soil of England with mingled
smiles and tears; and from that point on, his talk is full of 'rainy
eyes' (III, ii, 146) and of making 'foul weather with despised
tears' (III, iii, 161). He counsels York,

> Uncle, give me your hands : nay, dry your eyes;
> Tears show their love, but want their remedies. (III, iii, 202–3)

In the garden scene the Queen, rejecting her lady's offer to sing,
sadly tells her :

> 'Tis well that thou hast cause;
> But thou shouldst please me better wouldst thou weep.
> LADY   I could weep, madam, would it do you good.
> QUEEN   And I could sing, would weeping do me good,
> And never borrow any tear of thee. (III, iv, 19–23)

And echoing that dialogue, the gardener, at the close of the scene,
looks after her and says :

> Here did she fall a tear: here in this place
> I'll set a bank of rue, sour herb of grace.
> Rue, even for ruth, here shortly shall be seen,
> In the remembrance of a weeping queen. (III, iv, 104–7)

The theme reaches a climax in the deposition scene, in which
the agonised King, handing his crown to Bolingbroke, sees himself as the lower of the two buckets in Fortune's well :

> . . . full of tears am I,
> Drinking my griefs, whilst you mount up on high. (IV, i, 188–9)

And a few lines later he merges the almost ubiquitous motif of tears with another constant theme of the play: 'With mine own tears I wash away my balm' (IV, i, 207). Of the frequent association of the anointing of kings, blood, and the act of washing, I shall speak a little later.

Professor Van Doren, in his sensitive essay on *Richard II*, eloquently stresses the importance of the word *tongue* in the play.[13] *Tongue*, he says, is the key word of the piece. I should prefer to give that distinction to *earth*; but there is no denying the effectiveness of Shakespeare's tireless repetition of the idea of speech, not only by the single word *tongue* but also by such allied words as *mouth, speech,* and *word*. A few minutes' study of Bartlett's *Concordance* will show that *Richard II* is unique in this insistence upon the concept of speech; that the word *tongue* occurs here oftener than in any other play is but one indication.

This group of associated words heavily underscores two leading ideas in the play. In the first place, it draws constant attention to the propensity for verbalizing (as Shakespeare would not have called it!) which is Richard's fatal weakness. He cannot bring himself to live in a world of hard actuality; the universe to him is real only as it is presented in packages of fine words. Aumerle tries almost roughly to recall him from his weaving of sweet, melancholy sounds to a realization of the crucial situation confronting him, but he rouses himself only momentarily and then relapses into a complacent enjoyment of the sound of his own tongue. It is of this trait that we are constantly reminded as all the characters regularly use periphrases when they must speak of what they or others have said. By making the physical act of speech, the sheer fact of language, so conspicuous, they call attention to its illusory nature—to the vast difference between what the semanticists call the intensional and extensional universes. That words are mere conventional sounds moulded by the tongue, and reality is something else again, is constantly on the minds of all the characters. The initial dispute between Mowbray and Bolingbroke is 'the bitter clamour of two eager tongues' (I, i, 49); Mowbray threatens to cram his antagonist's lie 'through the false passage of thy throat' (I, i, 125); and later, in a fine cadenza, he conceives of his eternal banishment in terms of the engaoling of his tongue, whose 'use is to me no more/ Than an unstringed viol or a harp', and concludes :

> What is thy sentence [then] but speechless death,
> Which robs my tongue from breathing native breath?
>   (I, iii, 161–2, 172–3)

Bolingbroke, for his part, marvels over the power of a single word
to change the lives of men :

> How long a time lies in one little word !
> Four lagging winters and four wanton springs
> End in a word : such is the breath of kings. (I, iii, 213–15)

Gaunt too is preoccupied with tongues and speech; and when
Aumerle returns from his farewell with Bolingbroke, from tears
the image theme swiftly turns to tongues :

> RICHARD   What said our cousin when you parted with him?
> AUMERLE   'Farewell !'
> And, for my heart disdained that my tongue
> Should so profane the word, that taught me craft
> To counterfeit oppression of such grief
> That words seem'd buried in my sorrow's grave.
> Marry, would the word 'farewell' have length'ned hours
> And added years to his short banishment,
> He should have had a volume of farewells. (I, iv, 10–18)

And we have but reached the end of Act I; the remainder of the
play is equally preoccupied with the unsubstantiality of human
language.[14]

But the unremitting stress laid upon tongues and words in this
play serves another important end : it reminds us that Richard's
fall is due not only to his preference for his own words rather than
for deeds, but also to his blind predilection for comfortable flattery
rather than sound advice. Words not only hypnotize, suspend
the sense of reality : they can sting and corrupt. And so the
tongues of *Richard II* symbolize also the honeyed but poison-
ous speech of the sycophants who surround him. 'No,' replies
York to Gaunt's suggestion that his dying words might yet undeaf
Richard's ear,

> it is stopp'd with other flattering sounds,
> As praises, of whose taste the wise are found,
> Lascivious metres, to whose venom sound
> The open ear of youth doth always listen. (II, i, 17–20)

The venom to which York refers and the snake which produces it form another theme of the imagery of this play. The snake-venom motif closely links the idea of the garden on the one hand (for what grossly untended garden would be without its snakes?) and the idea of the tongue on the other. All three meet in the latter part of Richard's speech in III, ii :

> But let thy spiders, that suck up thy venom,
> And heavy-gaited toads lie in their way,
> Doing annoyance to the treacherous feet
> Which with usurping steps do trample thee
> Yield stinging nettles to mine enemies;
> And when they from thy bosom pluck a flower,
> Guard it, I pray thee, with a lurking adder
> Whose double tongue may with a mortal touch
> Throw death upon thy sovereign's enemies. (III, ii, 14–22)

And the double association occurs again in the garden scene, when the Queen demands of the gardener,

> Thou, old Adam's likeness, set to dress this garden,
> How dares thy harsh rude tongue sound this unpleasing news?
> What Eve, what serpent, hath suggested thee
> To make a second fall of cursed man? (III, iv, 73–6)

Mowbray elsewhere speaks of 'slander's venom'd spear' (I, i, 171), and to Richard, the flatterers who have deserted him are, naturally enough, 'villains, vipers, damn'd without redemption!/ . . . Snakes, in my heart-blood warm'd, that sting my heart!' (III, ii, 129–31).

Although England's sorry state is most often figured in the references to the untended garden and the snakes that infest it, the situation is emphasized time and again by at least four other recurrent themes, some of which refer as well to the personal guilt of Richard. One such theme—anticipating a similar motif in *Hamlet*—involves repeated references to physical illness and injury. Richard in seeking to smooth over the quarrel between Mowbray and Bolingbroke says:

> Let's purge this choler without letting blood.
> This we prescribe, though no physician;
> **Deep malice makes too deep incision.** (i, i, 153–5)

There are repeated allusions to the swelling caused by infection. Richard in the same scene speaks of 'the swelling difference of your settled hate' (i, i, 201), and much later, after he has been deposed, he predicts to Northumberland that

> The time shall not be many hours of age
> More than it is, ere foul sin gathering head
> Shall break into corruption. (v, i, 57–9)

Thus too there are vivid mentions of the remedy for such festering:

> Fell Sorrow's tooth doth never rankle more
> Than when he bites, but lanceth not the sore. (i, iii, 302–3)

> This fest'red joint cut off, the rest rest sound. (v, iii, 85)

Plague, pestilence, and *infection* are words frequently in the mouths of the characters of this play. Aumerle, during the furious gage-casting of iv, i, cries, 'May my hands rot off' if he does not seize Percy's gage (iv, i, 49); and elsewhere York, speaking to the unhappy Queen, says of the King,

> Now comes the sick hour that his surfeit made;
> Now shall he try his friends that flatter'd him. (ii, ii, 84–5)

Indeed, the imagery which deals with bodily injury directly associates the wretchedness of the monarch and his country with the tongues of the sycophants. A verbal juxtaposition of *tongue* and *wound* occurs early in the plays: 'Ere my tongue / Shall wound my honour with such feeble wrong' (i, i, 190–1). Gaunt carries the association one step farther when he explicitly connects Richard's and England's illness with the presence of gross flatterers in the King's retinue:

> Thy death-bed is no lesser than thy land
> Wherein thou liest in reputation sick;
> And thou, too careless patient as thou art,
> Commit'st thy anointed body to the cure
> Of those physicians that first wounded thee.
> A thousand flatterers sit within thy crown,
> Whose compass is no bigger than thy head. (ii, i, 95–101)

And Richard himself completes the circuit between the tongue-wound association and his personal grief : 'He does me double wrong/ That wounds me with the flatteries of his tongue' (III, ii, 215–16).

Again, the evil that besets England is frequently symbolized as a dark blot upon fair parchment—an image which occurs oftener in this play than in any other. The suggestion for the image undoubtedly came from contemplation of the deeds and leases by which the King had farmed out the royal demesnes; as John of Gaunt said, England 'is now bound in with shame,/ With inky blots and rotten parchment bonds' (II, i, 63–4). The image recurs several times. 'No, Bolingbroke,' says Mowbray in I, iii, 'if ever I were traitor,/ My name be blotted from the book of life' (I, iii, 201–2). Richard sighs through blanched lips, 'Time hath set a blot upon my pride' (III, ii, 81) and later speaks of the record of Northumberland's offenses as including

> one heinous article,
> Containing the deposing of a king
> And cracking the strong warrant of an oath,
> Mark'd with a blot, damn'd in the book of heaven. (IV, i, 233–6)

Carlisle and Aumerle in a duet harmonize the image with the two other motifs of gardening and generation :

> CARLISLE   The woe's to come; the children yet unborn
>   Shall feel this day as sharp to them as thorn.
> AUMERLE   You holy clergymen, is there no plot
>   To rid the realm of this pernicious blot? (IV, i, 322–5)

Aumerle's conspiracy which stems from this conversation is itself spoken of by Bolingbroke in Aumerle's own terms: 'Thy abundant goodness shall excuse/ This deadly blot in thy digressing son' (V, iii, 65–6). The vividness of the image is increased by the presence elsewhere of allusions to books and writing : 'He should have had a volume of farewells' (I, iv, 18); 'The purple testament of bleeding war' (III, iii, 94);

> Let's talk of graves, of worms, and epitaphs;
> Make dust our paper and with rainy eyes
> Write sorrow on the bosom of the earth (III, ii, 145–7)

(an interesting example of double association of imagery—tears, earth–grave, and writing); and in the deposition scene, when Richard calls for a mirror :

> I'll read enough,
> When I do see the very book indeed
> Where all my sins are writ, and that's myself. (iv, i, 273–5)

The blot image has a very direct relationship with another class of figures by which Shakespeare symbolizes guilt or evil : that of a stain which must be washed away. This image is most commonly associated with *Macbeth*, because of the extraordinary vividness with which it is used there. But the theme is much more insistent in *Richard II*. Twice it is associated, as in *Macbeth*, with blood :

> Yet, to wash your blood
> From off my hands, here in the view of men
> I will unfold some causes of your deaths. (iii, i, 5–7)

> I'll make a voyage to the Holy Land,
> To wash this blood off from my guilty hand. (v, vi, 49–50)

Elsewhere the association is with the story of the crucifixion, in a repetition of which Richard fancies he is the sufferer :

> Nay, all of you that stand and look upon me
> Whilst that my wretchedness doth bait myself,
> Though some of you with Pilate wash your hands
> Showing an outward pity; yet you Pilates
> Have here deliver'd me to my sour cross,
> Have ever made me sour my patient cheek. (ii, i, 165–6, 169)

But in this play the absolution of guilt requires not merely the symbolic cleansing of bloody hands; it entails the washing-off of the sacred ointment of royalty—the ultimate expiation of kingly sin. The full measure of Richard's fall is epitomized in two further occurrences of the metaphor, the first spoken when he is in the full flush of arrogant confidence, the second when nemesis has overtaken him :

> Not all the water in the rough rude sea
> Can wash the balm off from an anointed king. (iii, ii, 54–5)

> With mine own tears I wash away my balm,
> With mine own hands I give away my crown. (iv, i, 207–8)

Whatever the exact context of the image of washing, one suggestion certainly is present whenever it appears: a suggestion of momentous change—the deposition of a monarch, the cleansing of a guilt-laden soul.

But the most unusual of all the symbols of unpleasantness which occur in *Richard II* is the use of the adjective *sour*, together with the repeated contrast of sweetness and sourness. A reader of the play understandably passes over the frequent use of *sweet* as a conventional epithet used both of persons and of things. But the word, however commonplace the specific phrases in which it occurs, has a role in the poetic design which decidedly is not commonplace, for it acts as a foil for the very unaccustomed use of its antonym. There is nothing less remarkable in Shakespeare than such phrases as 'sweet Richard', 'your sweet majesty', 'sweet York, sweet husband', even such passages as this:

> And yet your fair discourse hath been as sugar,
> Making the hard way sweet and delectable. (II, iii, 6–7)

But what is remarkable is the manner in which, in this play alone, mention of *sweet* so often invites mention of *sour*: 'Things sweet to taste prove in digestion sour' (I, iii, 236); 'Speak sweetly, man, although thy looks be sour' (III, ii, 193); 'how sour sweet music is!' (V, v, 42);

> Sweet love, I see, changing his property,
> Turns to the sourest and most deadly hate. (III, ii, 135–6)

In addition to this repeated collocation of *sweet* and *sour*, the text of *Richard II* is notable for a persistent use, unmatched in any other play, of *sour* alone, as an adjective or verb:

> Not Gloucester's death, nor Hereford's banishment
> Not Gaunt's rebukes, nor England's private wrongs,
>
> •   •   •   •
>
> Have ever made me sour my patient cheek. (II, i, 165–6, 169)

'I'll set a bank of rue, sour herb of grace' (III, iv, 105: this in significant collocation with the motif of tears, as the next is joined with the motif of washing)—'yet you Pilates/ Have here deliver'd me to my sour cross' (IV, i, 240–1);

> The grand conspirator, Abbot of Westminster,
> With clog of conscience and sour melancholy
> Hath yielded up his body to the grave. (v, vi, 19–21)

The occurrence of *sour* thus lends unmistakable irony to every occurrence of *sweet*, however unimportant the latter may be in itself. Even at a distance of a few lines, mention of one quality seems to invite mention of the other, as if Shakespeare could never forget that the sour is as frequent in life as the sweet :

> DUCHESS   The word is short, but not so short as sweet;
> No word like 'pardon' for kings' mouths so meet.
> YORK   Speak it in French, King; say *'Pardonne moi.'*
> DUCHESS   Dost thou teach pardon pardon to destroy?
> Ah, my sour husband, my hard-hearted lord,
> That set'st the word itself against the word ! (v, iii, 117–22)

This contrapuntal use of *sweet* and *sour* is one of the most revealing instances of the artistry by which the poetry of *Richard II* is unified.[15]

Two more image themes, one of major importance, the other less conspicuous, remain to be mentioned. For one of them, we must return to the Tree of Jesse passage (I, ii, 10–22) quoted above. This passage is the fountainhead of one of the chief themes of the play—the idea of legitimate succession, of hereditary kingship. We have already noticed how, largely as a result of this early elaborate metaphor, the close identification of the word *blood* with the idea of family descent deepens the symbolic significance of that word as it recurs through the play. In addition, as Miss Spurgeon has pointed out, in *Richard II* there are many other cognate images derived from the ideas of birth and generation, and of inheritance from father to son.[16] The Tree of Jesse metaphor (whose importance Miss Spurgeon failed to note) is followed in the next scene by one involving the symbol of earth and thus suggesting the vital relationship between generation and patriotism :

> Then, England's ground, farewell; sweet soil, adieu;
> My mother, and my nurse, that bears me yet ! (I, iii, 306–7)

In John of Gaunt's dying speech, earth and generation again appear, significantly, in conjunction :

> This blessed plot, this earth, this realm, this England,
> This nurse, this teeming womb of royal kings. (II, i, 50–1)

In her scene with Bagot and Bushy, the Queen dwells constantly on the idea of birth :

> Some unborn sorrow, ripe in fortune's womb,
> Is coming towards me.
>
> .   .   .   .
>   Conceit is still deriv'd
> From some forefather grief; mine is not so,
> For nothing hath begot my something grief,
>
> .   .   .   .
> So, Green, thou art the midwife to my woe,
> And Bolingbroke my sorrow's dismal heir.
> Now hath my soul brought forth her prodigy,
> And I, a gasping new-deliver'd mother,
> Have woe to woe, sorrow to sorrow join'd.
>   (II, ii, 10–11, 34–6, 62–6)

Richard's last soliloquy begins with the same sort of elaborated conceit :

> My brain I'll prove the female to my soul,
> My soul the father; and these two beget
> A generation of still-breeding thoughts,
> And these same thoughts people this little world,
> In humours like the people of this world.
> For no thought is contented. (v, v, 6–11)

And throughout the play, as Miss Spurgeon notes, 'the idea of inheritance from father to son . . . increases the feeling of the inevitable and the foreordained, as also of the unlimited consequences of action'.

The word *crown* as the symbol of kingship is of course common throughout the history plays. In *Richard II*, however, the vividness of the image and the relevance of its symbolism to the grand theme of the play are heightened by several instances in which its metaphorical function goes beyond that of a simple, conventional metonymy :

> A thousand flatterers sit within thy crown,
> Whose compass is no bigger than thy head; (II, i, 100–1)

> for within the hollow crown
> That rounds the mortal temples of a king
> Keeps Death his court, (III, ii, 160–2)

But ere the crown he looks for live in peace,
Ten thousand bloody crowns of mothers' sons
Shall ill become the flower of England's face, (III, iii, 95–7)

> Now is this golden crown like a deep well
> That owes two buckets, filling one another,
> The emptier ever dancing in the air,
> The other down, unseen, and full of water. (IV, i, 184–7)

In addition, the actual image of the crown is made more splendid by the occurrence, in the play's poetic fabric, of several images referring to jewels:

> A jewel in a ten-times-barr'd-up chest
> Is a bold spirit in a loyal breast. (I, i, 180–1)

GAUNT   The sullen passage of thy weary steps
Esteem as foil wherein thou art to set
The precious jewel of thy home return.
BOLINGBROKE   Nay, rather, every tedious stride I make
Will but remember me what a deal of world
I wander from the jewels that I love. (I, iii, 265–70)

And again: 'I'll give my jewels for a set of beads' (III, iii, 147), 'This precious stone set in the silver sea' (II, i, 46), and 'Love to Richard/ Is a strange brooch in this all-hating world' (V, v, 65–6).

Keeping in mind the leading metaphors and verbal motifs which I have reviewed—*earth–ground–land*, *blood*, pallor, garden, sun, tears, *tongue–speech–word*, *snake–venom*, physical injury and illness, *blot*, washing, *sweet–sour*, generation, and jewel–crown—it is profitable to re-read the whole play, noting especially how widely the various themes are distributed, and how frequently their strands cross to form new images. There is no extended passage of the text which is not tied in with the rest of the play by the occurrence of one or more of the familiar symbols. However, the images are not scattered with uniform evenness. As in *The Merchant of Venice*, metaphorical language tends to be concentrated at the emotional climaxes of *Richard II*. At certain crucial points in the action, a large number of the unifying image-threads appear almost simultaneously, so that our minds are virtually flooded with many diverse yet closely related ideas. The first part of II, i (the prophecy of Gaunt) offers a good instance of this rapid cumulation of symbols and the resultant heightening of emotional effect. The whole passage should be read as Shakespeare wrote it; here I list simply the phrases that reveal the various image themes, omitting a number which glance obliquely at the themes but are not directly connected with them :

line	
5	the tongues of dying men
7	words
8	words
12	the setting sun
13	As the last taste of sweets, is sweetest last
14	Writ in remembrance
17	flattering sounds
19	Lascivious metres, to whose venom sound
23	limps
41	The earth of majesty
44	infection
45	breed
46	This precious stone
49	less happier lands
50	This earth
51	This nurse, this teeming womb of royal kings
52	breed . . . birth
57	land . . . land
64	With inky blots and rotten parchment bonds
83	hollow womb
95	land
96	sick [followed by extended metaphor]
100	thy crown
103	thy land
104–5	thy grandsire . . . his son's son . . . his sons
110–13	this land . . . this land . . . landlord
116	ague
118	pale . . . blood
122	This tongue
126	blood
131	blood
134	To crop at once a too long withered flower
136	words

Thus in the first 157 lines of the scene we meet no less than twelve of the motifs of the play.

In another sort of harmonization, Shakespeare strikes a long chord containing a number of the image strains and then in the following minutes of the play echoes them separately. The 'Dear earth, I do salute thee with my hand' speech at the beginning of III, ii interweaves at least six themes which shortly are unravelled into individual strands. The idea of the garden which is the framework for the whole speech (6–26) recurs in the line 'To ear the land that hath some hope to grow' (212). The repeated references to weeping in the initial speech ('I weep for joy' . . . 'with her tears' . . . 'weeping') are echoed in 'as if the world were all dissolv'd to tears' (108) and 'rainy eyes' (146). Richard's 'Nor with thy sweets comfort his ravenous sense' (13) is recalled in Scroop's 'Sweet love . . . changing his property,/ Turns to the sourest and most deadly hate' (135–6) and in Richard's 'speak sweetly, man, although thy looks be sour' (193) and 'that sweet way I was in to despair' (205). The lurking adder and the venom which the spiders suck up (20, 14) find their sequel in Richard's later 'vipers . . . snakes . . . that sting my heart' (129–31). The double tongue (21) is succeeded by 'discomfort guides my tongue' (65), 'my care-tun'd tongue' (92), the tongue that 'hath but a heavier tale to say' (197), and the one whose flatteries wound the King at the end of the scene (216). The initial reference to wounding ('though rebels wound thee with their horses' hoofs,' 7) is succeeded by 'death's destroying wound' (139); and the same general motif of bodily hurt is carried out by 'this ague fit of fear is over-blown' (190), which links the disease-theme to that of the garden. Finally, the frequent use of *earth* in Richard's first speech (6, 10, 12, 24) prepares the ear for the five-times-repeated occurrence of the idea (earth . . . ground . . . lands . . . earth . . . ground) in the 'Let's talk of graves, of worms, and epitaphs' speech. This progressive analysis of the components of the original chord of images is accompanied by a succession of other images not included in the chord: an extended sun metaphor (36–50), a reference to washing (54–5), the most famous instance of the pallor–blood motif (76–81), two references to the crown (59, 115), and two allusions to writing (81, 146–7). And thus the mind is crowded with a richly overlapping series of images.

Another example of the close arraying of image patterns (without the initial chord) occurs in III, iii, 85–100 :

Yet know, my master, God omnipotent,	
Is mustering in his clouds on our behalf	
Armies of pestilence ; and they shall strike	(illness)
Your children yet unborn and unbegot,	(generation)
That lift your vassal hands against my head	
And threat the glory of my precious crown.	(crown)
Tell Bolingbroke—for yon methinks he stands—	
That every stride he makes upon my land	(earth)
Is dangerous treason. He is come to open	
The purple testament of bleeding war ;	(books, blood)
But ere the crown he looks for live in peace,	(crown)
Ten thousand bloody crowns of mothers' sons	(blood, crown, generation)
Shall ill become the flower of England's face,	(garden)
Change the complexion of her maid-pale peace	(pallor)
To scarlet indignation, and bedew	
Her pastures' grass with faithful English blood.	(blood)

Curiously, the deposition scene, though it is rich enough in individual appearances of the familiar themes, does not mesh them so closely as one might expect.

A final aspect of the use of iterative imagery in *Richard II* is the manner in which a particularly important passage is prepared for by the interweaving into the poetry, long in advance, of inconspicuous but repeated hints of the imagery which is to dominate that passage. The method is exactly analogous to that by which in a symphony a melody appears, at first tentatively, indeed almost unnoticed, first in one choir of the orchestra, then another, until ultimately it comes to its reward as the theme of a climactic section. In such a manner is the audience prepared, although unconsciously, for Richard's last grandiose speech. One takes little note of the first timid appearance of a reference to beggary or bankruptcy in Bolingbroke's 'Or with pale beggar-

fear impeach my height' (I, i, 189). But in the second act the
motif recurs :

> Be York the next that must be bankrupt so !
> Though death be poor, it ends a mortal woe, (II, i, 151–2)

and a hundred lines later the idea is repeated : 'The king's grown
bankrupt, like a broken man' (II, i, 257). The haunting dread
of destitution, then, however obliquely alluded to, is a recurrent
theme, and adds its small but perceptible share to the whole atmosphere of impending disaster. It forms the burden of two plaints
by Richard midway in the play :

> Let's choose executors and talk of wills;
> And yet not so; for what can we bequeath
> Save our deposed bodies to the ground?
> Our lands, our lives and all are Bolingbroke's. (III, ii, 148–51)

>> I'll give my jewels for a set of beads,
>> My gorgeous palace for a hermitage,
>> My gay apparel for an almsman's gown,
>> My figur'd goblets for a dish of wood,
>> My sceptre for a palmer's walking-staff,
>> My subjects for a pair of carved saints,
>> And my large kingdom for a little grave. (III, iii, 147–53)

But the time is not ripe for the climactic utterance of this motif.
It disappears, to return for a moment in a verbal hint in the deposition scene :

>> Let it command a mirror hither straight,
>> That it may show me what a face I have
>> Since it is bankrupt of his majesty. (IV, i, 265–7)

>> Being so great, I have no need to beg. (IV, i, 309)

The Duchess of York momentarily takes up the motif : 'A beggar
begs that never begg'd before' (V, iii, 78), and Bolingbroke
replies :

> Our scene is alt'red from a serious thing,
> And now chang'd to 'The Beggar and the King'. (V, iii, 79–80)

And now finally comes the climax toward which these fleeting
references have been pointing : a climax which illuminates the
purpose and direction of the earlier talk about beggary and bankruptcy :

> Thoughts tending to content flatter themselves
> That they are not the first of fortune's slaves,
> Nor shall not be the last; like silly beggars
> Who, sitting in the stocks, refuge their shame,
> That many have and others must sit there;
> And in this thought they find a kind of ease,
> Bearing their own misfortunes on the back
> Of such as have before endur'd the like.
> Thus play I in one person many people,
> And none contented. Sometimes am I king;
> Then treasons make me wish myself a beggar;
> And so I am. Then crushing penury
> Persuades me I was better when a king. (v, v, 23–35)

A similar process can be traced in the repetition of the word *face*, which, besides being obviously connected with the idea of Richard's personal comeliness, underscores the hovering sense the play contains of the illusory quality of life, of the deceptions that men accept as if they were reality. The word occurs casually, unremarkably, often without metaphorical intent; but its frequent appearance not only reinforces, however subtly, a dominant idea of the play, but also points toward a notable climax. 'Mowbray's face' (I, i, 195) . . . 'Nor never look upon each other's face' (I, iii, 185) . . . 'the northeast wind/ Which then blew bitterly against our faces' (I, iv, 6–7) . . . 'His face thou hast, for even so look'd he' (II, i, 176) . . . 'Frighting her pale-fac'd villages with war' (II, iii, 94) . . . 'The pale-fac'd moon looks bloody on the earth' (II, iv, 10) . . . 'His treasons will sit blushing in his face' (III, ii, 51) . . . 'But now the blood of twenty thousand men/ Did triumph in my face' (III, ii, 76–7) . . .

> Ten thousand bloody crowns of mothers' sons
> Shall ill become the flower of England's face. (III, iii, 96–7)

Meanwhile Bushy has introduced the corollary idea of shadow:

> Each substance of a grief hath twenty shadows,
> Which shows like grief itself, but is not so (II, ii, 14–15)

> Which, look'd on as it is, is nought but shadows
> Of what it is not. (II, ii, 23–4)

The related themes merge as, in retrospect, it is plain they were destined to do, in the deposition scene:

                     Was this face the face
        That every day under his household roof
        Did keep ten thousand men? Was this the face
        That, like the sun, did make beholders wink?
        Is this the face which fac'd so many follies,
        That was at last out-fac'd by Bolingbroke?
        A brittle glory shineth in this face;
        As brittle as the glory is the face,
        For there it is, crack'd in an hundred shivers.
        Mark, silent king, the moral of this sport,
        How soon my sorrow hath destroy'd my face.
    BOLINGBROKE   The shadow of your sorrow hath destroy'd
        The shadow of your face.
    RICHARD   Say that again.
        The shadow of my sorrow! Ha! let's see. (IV, i, 281–94)

And thus from beginning to end *Richard II* is, in a double
sense of which Shakespeare would have approved, a play on
words. As countless writers have affirmed, it is entirely fitting
that this should be so. King Richard, a poet *manqué*, loved words
more dearly than he did his kingdom, and his tragedy is made
the more moving by the style, half rhetorical, half lyrical, in which
it is told. Splendid words, colorful metaphors, pregnant poetic
symbols in this drama possess their own peculiar irony.

   But the language of *Richard II*, regarded from the viewpoint
I have adopted in this paper, has another significance, entirely
apart from its appropriateness to theme. It suggests the existence
of a vital relationship between two leading characteristics of
Shakespeare's poetic style: the uncontrolled indulgence of verbal
wit in the earlier plays and the use of great image-themes in the
plays of his maturity. As I suggested in the beginning, word-play
and iterative imagery are but two different manifestations of a
single faculty in the creative imagination—an exceedingly well
developed sense of association. In *Richard II* we see the crucial
intermediate stage in the development, or perhaps more accur-
ately the utilization, of Shakespeare's singular associative gift. In
such passages as John of Gaunt's speech upon his name, we are
reminded of the plays which preceded this from Shakespeare's
pen. But, except on certain occasions when they contribute to
the characterization of the poet-king, the brief coruscations of

verbal wit which marked the earlier plays are less evident than formerly. On the other hand, when we stand back and view the play as a whole, its separate movements bound so closely together by image themes, we are enabled to anticipate the future development of Shakespeare's art. The technique that is emerging in *Richard II* is the technique that eventually will have its part in producing the poetry of *Lear* and *Macbeth* and *Othello*. Here we have the method : the tricks of repetition, of cumulative emotional effect, of interweaving and reciprocal coloration. What is yet to come is the full mastery of the artistic possibilities of such a technique. True, thanks to its tightly interwoven imagery *Richard II* has a poetic unity that is unsurpassed in any of the great tragedies; so far as structure is concerned, Shakespeare has levied from iterative language about all the aid that it will give. The great improvement will come in another region. Taken individually, in *Richard II* Shakespeare's images lack the qualities which they will possess in the later plays. They are, many of them, too conventional for our tastes; they are marred by diffuseness; they bear too many lingering traces of Shakespeare's affection for words for words' sake. The ultimate condensation, the compression of a universe of meaning into a single bold metaphor, remains to be achieved. But in the best imagery of *Richard II*, especially in those passages which combine several themes into a richly complex pattern of meaning, we receive abundant assurance that Shakespeare will be equal to his task. The process of welding language and thought into a single entity is well begun.

SOURCE : from *PMLA, 62* (1947).

NOTES

1. *Richard II*, ed. J. Dover Wilson (Cambridge, 1939) pp. xiv–xv.

2. Throughout this paper I use the words *image* and *imagery* in their most inclusive sense of metaphorical as well as 'picture-making' but non-figurative language.

3. Caroline F. E. Spurgeon, *Shakespeare's Imagery* (Cambridge, 1936) pp. 352–3. I should add a word concerning a relatively little known book which anticipated Miss Spurgeon's general method of

image-study as well as two or three of my own observations concerning *Richard II*. This is *Shakespeare's Way: a Psychological Study*, by the Rt Rev. Msgr F. C. Kolbe (London, 1930).

4. In *Richard II* the three words occur a total of 71 times; in *King John*, the nearest rival, 46.—I should note at this point that my identification of all the word- and image-themes to be discussed in this essay is based upon statistical study. A given word or group of related words is called a 'theme' (a) if Bartlett's *Concordance* shows a definite numerical preponderance for *Richard II* or (b) if the word or group of words is so closely related to one of the fundamental ideas of the play that it is of greater importance than the comparative numerical frequency would imply. I have not included any arithmetic in this paper because all such tabulations obviously must be subjective to some degree. No two persons, doing the same counting for the same purpose, would arrive at precisely the same numerical results. But I am confident that independent tabulation would enable anyone to arrive at my general conclusions. Statistics here, as in all such critical exercises, are merely grounds upon which to base a judgment that must eventually be a subjective one.

5. I am using the text of William A. Neilson and Charles J. Hill (Boston, 1942).

6. The much admired little passage about the roan Barbary takes on added poignancy when the other overtones of *ground* are remembered :

RICHARD   Rode he on Barbary? Tell me, gentle friend,
    How went he under him?

GROOM   So proudly as if he disdain'd the ground. (v, v, 81–3)

7. *Shakespeare's Imagery*, pp. 216–24.

8. We must not, of course, take *garden* too literally. Shakespeare obviously intended the term in its wider metaphorical sense of fields and orchards.

9. Mark Van Doren, *Shakespeare* (New York, 1939), p. 88.

10. A. C. Bradley, *Shakespearean Tragedy*, 2nd ed. (London, 1905), pp. 335–56.

11. *Shakespeare's Imagery*, p. 334.

12. There are many more references to tears and weeping in *Titus Andronicus*, but the obvious inferiority of the poetry and the crudity of characterization make their presence far less remarkable.

13. *Shakespeare*, pp. 85–7.

14. Another way in which Shakespeare adds to the constant tragic sense of unsubstantiality in this play—the confusion of appearance and reality—is the repeated use of the adjective *hollow*, especially

in connection with death : 'our hollow parting' (I, iv, 9), the 'hollow womb' of the grave (II, i, 83), 'the hollow eyes of death' (II, i, 270), a grave set in 'the hollow ground' (III, ii, 140), 'the hollow crown in which Death keeps his court (III, ii, 160).

15. The *sweet–sour* contrast occurs five times in *Richard II*; no more than twice in any other play.—Compare a similar juxtaposition in three of the sonnets :

> Such civil war is in my love and hate
>   That I an accessary needs must be
>   To that sweet thief which sourly robs from me.   (No. 35)

> O absence, what a torment wouldst thou prove
>   Were it not thy sour leisure gave sweet leave
>   To entertain the time with thoughts of love.   (No. 39)

> For sweetest things turn sourest by their deeds.   (No. 94)

It is interesting to note that in the same two groups of sonnets in which the *sweet-sour* collocation occurs can be found another word whose use is noteworthy in *Richard II* :

> And dost him grace when clouds do blot the heaven (No. 28)

> So shall those blots that do with me remain,
> Without thy help by me be borne alone.   (No. 36)

> But what's so blessed-fair that fears no blot?   (No. 92)

> Where beauty's veil doth cover every blot   (No. 95)

If we accept the hypothesis that at a given period in his life Shakespeare habitually thought of certain abstract ideas in terms of particular metaphors, there is a good case for dating these sonnets at the time of *Richard II*. Conventional though the sweet–sour and blot ideas may be, it is plain that Shakespeare had them constantly in mind when writing *Richard II*; they are a hallmark of the style of the play. Their occurrence in these sonnets is possibly significant.

16. *Shakespeare's Imagery*, pp. 238–41.

E. M. W. Tillyard

RICHARD II IN THE SECOND
TETRALOGY (1948)

Richard II is imperfectly executed, and yet, that imperfection granted, perfectly planned as part of a great structure. It is sharply contrasted, in its extreme formality of shape and style, with the subtler and more fluid nature of *Henry IV*; but it is a necessary and deliberate contrast; resembling a stiff recitative composed to introduce a varied and flexible *aria*. Coming after *King John* the play would appear the strangest relapse into the official self which Shakespeare had been shedding; taken with *Henry IV* it shows that Shakespeare, while retaining and using this official self, could develop with brilliant success the new qualities of character and style manifested in the Bastard. *Richard II* therefore betokens no relapse but is an organic part of one of Shakespeare's major achievements.

But the imperfections are undoubted and must be faced. As a separate play *Richard II* lacks the sustained vitality of *Richard III*, being less interesting and less exacting in structure and containing a good deal of verse which by the best Shakespearean standards can only be called indifferent. Not that there is anything wrong with the structure, which is that of *2 Henry VI*, the rise of one great man at the expense of another; but it is simple, as befits an exordium and does not serve through the excitement of its complications to make the utmost demand on the powers of the author. For illustrating the indifferent verse I need not go beyond the frequent stretches of couplet-writing and the occasional quatrains that make such a contrast to the verse of *Henry IV*. It is not that these have not got their function, which will be dealt with later, but that as poetry they are indifferent stuff. They are as necessary as the stiff lines in *3 Henry VI* spoken by the Father who has killed his Son, and

the Son who has killed his Father; but they are little better
poetically. For present purposes it does not matter in the least
whether they are relics of an old play, by Shakespeare or by
someone else, or whether Shakespeare wrote them with the rest.
They occur throughout the play and with the exception of perhaps two couplets are not conspicuously worse in the fifth act
than anywhere else. There is no need for a theory that in this
act, to save time, Shakespeare hurriedly began copying chunks
from an old play. Until there is decisive proof of this, it is simplest
to think that Shakespeare wrote his couplets along with the rest,
intending a deliberate contrast. He had done the same thing with
the Talbots' death in *1 Henry VI*, while, to account for the
indifferent quality, one may remember that he was never very
good at the couplet. The best couplets in *A Midsummer Night's
Dream* are weak compared with the best blank verse in that
play, while few of the final couplets of the sonnets are more than
a competent close to far higher verse.

I turn now to a larger quality of the play, of which the
couplets are one of several indications.

Of all Shakespeare's plays *Richard II* is the most formal and
ceremonial. It is not only that Richard himself is a true king in
appearance, in his command of the trappings of royalty, while
being deficient in the solid virtues of the ruler; that is a commonplace : the ceremonial character of the play extends much
wider than Richard's own nature or the exquisite patterns of
his poetic speech.

First, the very actions tend to be symbolic rather than real.
There is all the pomp of a tournament without the physical
meeting of the two armed knights. There is a great army of
Welshmen assembled to support Richard, but they never fight.
Bolingbroke before Flint Castle speaks of the terrible clash there
should be when he and Richard meet :

> Methinks King Richard and myself should meet
> With no less terror than the elements
> Of fire and water, when their thundering shock
> At meeting tears the cloudy cheeks of heaven.

But instead of a clash there is a highly ceremonious encounter
leading to the effortless submission of Richard. There are

violent challenges before Henry in Westminster Hall, but the issue is postponed. The climax of the play is the ceremony of Richard's deposition. And finally Richard, imprisoned at Pomfret, erects his own lonely state and his own griefs into a gigantic ceremony. He arranges his own thoughts into classes corresponding with men's estates in real life; king and beggar, divine, soldier, and middle man. His own sighs keep a ceremonial order like a clock :

> Now, sir, the sound that tells what hour it is
> Are clamorous groans, which strike upon my heart,
> Which is the bell : so sighs and tears and groans
> Show minutes, times, and hours.

Second, in places where emotion rises, where there is strong mental action, Shakespeare evades direct or naturalistic presentation and resorts to convention and conceit. He had done the same when Arthur pleaded with Hubert for his eyes in *King John*, but that was exceptional to a play which contained the agonies of Constance and the Bastard's perplexities over Arthur's body. Emotionally Richard's parting from his queen could have been a great thing in the play : actually it is an exchange of frigidly ingenious couplets.

> RICHARD   Go, count thy way with sighs; I mine with groans.
> QUEEN   So longest way shall have the longest moans.
> RICHARD   Twice for one step I'll groan, the way being short,
> And piece the way out with a heavy heart.

This is indeed the language of ceremony not of passion. Exactly the same happens when the Duchess of York pleads with Henry against her husband for her son Aumerle's life. Before the climax, when York gives the news of his son's treachery, there had been a show of feeling; but with the entry of the Duchess, when emotion should culminate, all is changed to prettiness and formal antiphony. This is how the Duchess compares her own quality of pleading with her husband's :

> Pleads he in earnest? look upon his face;
> His eyes do drop no tears, his prayers are jest;
> His words come from his mouth, ours from our breast :

> He prays but faintly and would be denied;
> We pray with heart and soul and all beside :
> His weary joints would gladly rise, I know;
> Our knees shall kneel till to the ground they grow :
> His prayers are full of false hypocrisy;
> Ours of true zeal and deep integrity.

And to 'frame' the scene, to make it unmistakably a piece of deliberate ceremonial, Bolingbroke falls into the normal language of drama when having forgiven Aumerle he vows to punish the other conspirators :

> But for our trusty brother-in-law and the abbot,
> And all the rest of that consorted crew,
> Destruction straight shall dog them at the heels.

The case of Gaunt is different but more complicated. When he has the state of England in mind and reproves Richard, though he can be rhetorical and play on words, he speaks the language of passion :

> Now He that made me knows I see thee ill.
> Thy death-bed is no lesser than thy land
> Wherein thou liest in reputation sick.
> And thou, too careless patient as thou art,
> Commit'st thy anointed body to the cure
> Of those physicians that first wounded thee.
> A thousand flatterers sit within thy crown,
> Whose compass is no bigger than thy head.

But in the scene of private feeling, when he parts from his banished son, both speakers, ceasing to be specifically themselves, exchange the most exquisitely formal commonplaces traditionally deemed appropriate to such a situation.

> Go, say I sent thee for to purchase honour
> And not the king exil'd thee; or suppose
> Devouring pestilence hangs in our air
> And thou art flying to a fresher clime.
> Look, what thy soul holds dear, imagine it
> To lie that way thou go'st, not whence thou com'st.

> Suppose the singing birds musicians,
> The grass whereon thou tread'st the presence strew'd,
> The flowers fair ladies, and thy steps no more
> Than a delightful measure or a dance;
> For gnarling sorrow hath less power to bite
> The man that mocks at it and sets it light.

Superficially this may be maturer verse than the couplets quoted, but it is just as formal, just as mindful of propriety and as unmindful of nature as Richard and his queen taking leave. Richard's sudden start into action when attacked by his murderers is exceptional, serving to set off by contrast the lack of action that has prevailed and to link the play with the next of the series. His groom, who appears in the same scene, is a realistic character alien to the rest of the play and serves the same function as Richard in action.

Thirdly, there is an elaboration and a formality in the cosmic references, scarcely to be matched in Shakespeare. These are usually brief and incidental, showing indeed how intimate a part they were of the things accepted and familiar in Shakespeare's mind. But in *Richard II* they are positively paraded. The great speech of Richard in Pomfret Castle is a tissue of them : first the peopling of his prison room with his thoughts, making its microcosm correspond with the orders of the body politic; then the doctrine of the universe as a musical harmony; then the fantasy of his own griefs arranged in a pattern like the working of a clock, symbol of regularity opposed to discord; and finally madness as the counterpart in man's mental kingdom of discord or chaos. Throughout the play the great commonplace of the king on earth duplicating the sun in heaven is exploited with a persistence unmatched anywhere else in Shakespeare. Finally (for I omit minor references to cosmic lore) there is the scene (iii, 4) of the gardeners, with the elaborate comparison of the state to the botanical microcosm of the garden. But this is a scene so typical of the whole trend of the play that I will speak of it generally and not merely as another illustration of the traditional correspondences.

The scene begins with a few exquisitely musical lines of dialogue between the Queen and two ladies. She refines her grief in a vein of high ceremony and sophistication. She begins by asking what sport they can devise in this garden to drive away care. But to every sport proposed there is a witty objection.

LADY Madam, we'll tell tales.
QUEEN Of sorrow or of joy?
LADY   Of either, madam.
QUEEN Of neither, girl :
    For if of joy, being altogether wanting,
    It doth remember me the more of sorrow;
    Or if of grief, being altogether had,
    It adds more sorrow to my want of joy.
    For what I have I need not to repeat,
    And what I want it boots not to complain.

Shakespeare uses language here like a very accomplished musician doing exercises over the whole compass of the violin. Then there enter a gardener and two servants : clearly to balance the Queen and her ladies and through that balance to suggest that the gardener within the walls of his little plot of land is a king. Nothing could illustrate better the different expectations of a modern and of an Elizabethan audience than the way they would take the gardener's opening words :

    Go, bind thou up yon dangling apricocks,
    Which, like unruly children, make their sire
    Stoop with oppression of their prodigal weight.

The first thought of a modern audience is : what a ridiculous way for a gardener to talk. The first thought of an Elizabethan would have been : what is the symbolic meaning of those words, spoken by this king of the garden, and how does it bear on the play? And it would very quickly conclude that the apricots had grown inflated and overweening in the sun of the royal favour; that oppression was used with a political as well as a physical meaning; and that the apricots threatened, unless restrained, to upset the proper relation between parent and offspring, to offend against the great principle of order. And the rest of the gardener's speech would bear out this interpretation.

    Go thou, and like an executioner
    Cut off the heads of too fast growing sprays,

> That look too lofty in our commonwealth.
> All must be even in our government.
> You thus employ'd, I will go root away
> The noisome weeds, which without profit suck
> The soil's fertility from wholesome flowers.

In fact the scene turns out to be an elaborate political allegory, with the Earl of Wiltshire, Bushy, and Green standing for the noxious weeds which Richard, the bad gardener, allowed to flourish and which Henry, the new gardener, has rooted up. It ends with the Queen coming forward and joining in the talk. She confirms the gardener's regal and moral function by calling him 'old Adam's likeness', but curses him for his ill news about Richard and Bolingbroke. The intensively symbolic character of the scene is confirmed when the gardener at the end proposes to plant a bank with rue where the Queen let fall her tears, as a memorial:

> Rue, even for ruth, here shortly shall be seen
> In the remembrance of a weeping queen.

In passing, for it is not my immediate concern, let me add that the gardener gives both the pattern and the moral of the play. The pattern is the weighing of the fortunes of Richard and Bolingbroke:

> Their fortunes both are weigh'd.
> In your lord's scale is nothing but himself
> And some few vanities that make him light;
> But in the balance of great Bolingbroke
> Besides himself are all the English peers,
> And with that odds he weighs King Richard down.

For the moral, though he deplores Richard's inefficiency, the gardener calls the news of his fall 'black tidings' and he sympathises with the Queen's sorrow. And he is himself, in his microcosmic garden, what neither Richard nor Bolingbroke separately is, the authentic gardener-king, no usurper, and the just represser of vices, the man who makes 'all even in our government'.

The one close Shakespearean analogy with this gardener is Iden, the unambitious squire in his Kentish garden, who stands for 'degree' in 2 *Henry VI*. But he comes in as an obvious foil to the realistic disorder just exhibited in Cade's rebellion. Why was it that in *Richard II*, when he was so much more mature, when his brilliant realism in *King John* showed him capable of making his gardeners as human and as amusing as the grave-diggers in *Hamlet*, Shakespeare chose to present them with a degree of formality unequalled in any play he wrote? It is, in a different form, the same question as that which was implied by my discussion of the other formal or ceremonial features of the play: namely, why did Shakespeare in *Richard II* make the ceremonial or ritual form of writing, found in differing quantities in the *Henry VI* plays and in *Richard III*, not merely one of the principal means of expression but the very essence of the play?

These are the first questions we must answer if we are to understand the true nature of *Richard II*. And here let me repeat that though Richard himself is a very important part of the play's ceremonial content, that content is larger and more important than Richard. With that caution, I will try to explain how the ritual or ceremonial element in *Richard II* differs from that in the earlier History Plays, and through such an explanation to conjecture a new interpretation of the play. There is no finer instance of ceremonial writing than the scene of the ghosts at the end of *Richard III*. But it is subservient to a piece of action, to the Battle of Bosworth with the overthrow of a tyrant and the triumph of a righteous prince. Its duty is to make that action a matter of high, mysterious, religious import. We are not invited to dwell on the ritual happenings as on a resting-place, to deduce from them the ideas into which the mind settles when the action of the play is over. But in *Richard II*, with all the emphasis and the point taken out of the action, we are invited, again and again, to dwell on the sheer ceremony of the various situations. The main point of the tournament between Boling-broke and Mowbray is the way it is conducted; the point of Gaunt's parting with Bolingbroke is the sheer propriety of the sentiments they utter; the portents, put so fittingly into the mouth of a Welshman, are more exciting because they are appropriate than because they precipitate an event; Richard is ever more concerned with how he behaves, with the fitness of his conduct to the occasion, than with what he actually does; the gardener may foretell the deposition of Richard yet he is far more interesting as representing a static principle of order; when Richard is deposed, it is the precise manner that comes before all—

> With mine own tears I wash away my balm,
> With mine own hands I give away my crown,
> With mine own tongue deny my sacred state,
> With mine own breath release all duty's rites.

We are in fact in a world where means matter more than ends, where it is more important to keep strictly the rules of an elaborate game than either to win or to lose it.

Now though compared with ourselves the Elizabethans put a high value on means as against ends they did not go to the extreme. It was in the Middle Ages that means were so elaborated, that the rules of the game of life were so lavishly and so minutely set forth. *Richard II* is Shakespeare's picture of that life.

Of course it would be absurd to suggest that Shakespeare pictured the age of Richard II after the fashion of a modern historian. But there are signs elsewhere in Shakespeare of at least a feeling after historical verity; and there are special reasons why the age of Richard II should have struck the imaginations of the Elizabethans.

. . . I noted at the end of *2 Henry VI* Clifford and York, though enemies, do utter some of the chivalric sentiments proper to medieval warfare. Such sentiments do not recur in *3 Henry VI*, where we have instead the full barbarities of Wakefield and Towton. Shakespeare is probably recording the historical fact that the decencies of the knightly code went down under the stress of civil carnage. But the really convincing analogy with *Richard II* is the play of *Julius Caesar*. There, however slender Shakespeare's equipment as historian and however much of his own time he slips in, he does succeed in giving his picture of antique Rome, of the dignity of its government and of the stoic creed of its great men. T. S. Eliot has rightly noted how much essential history Shakespeare extracted from Plutarch. And if from Plutarch, why not from Froissart likewise?

Till recently Shakespeare's debt to Berners's translation of

Froissart's Chronicle has been almost passed over, but now it is rightly agreed that it was considerable. To recognise the debt helps one to understand the play. For instance, one of the minor puzzles of the play is plain if we grant Shakespeare's acquaintance with Froissart. When York, horrified at Richard's confiscating Gaunt's property the moment he died, goes on to enumerate all Richard's crimes, he mentions 'the prevention of poor Bolingbroke about his marriage'. There is nothing more about this in the play, but there is a great deal about it in Froissart—Richard had brought charges against the exile Bolingbroke which induced the French king to break off Bolingbroke's engagement with the daughter of the Duke of Berry, the King's cousin. If Shakespeare had been full of Froissart when writing *Richard II* he could easily have slipped in this isolated reference. But quite apart from any tangible signs of imitation it is scarcely conceivable that Shakespeare should not have read so famous a book as Berners's Froissart, or that having read it he should not have been impressed by the bright pictures of chivalric life in those pages. Now among Shakespeare's History Plays *Richard II* is the only one that falls within the period of time covered by Froissart. All the more reason why on this unique occasion he should heed this great original. Now though Froissart is greatly interested in motives, he also writes with an eye unmatched among chroniclers for its eager observation of external things and with a mind similarly unmatched for the high value it placed on the proper disposition of those things. In fact he showed a lively belief in ceremony and in the proprieties of heraldry akin to Elizabethan belief yet altogether more firmly attached to the general scheme of ideas that prevailed at the time. Shakespeare's brilliant wit must have grasped this; and *Richard II* may be his intuitive rendering of Froissart's medievalism.

But there were other reasons why the reign of Richard II should be notable. A. B. Steel, his most recent historian, begins his study by noting that Richard was the last king of the old medieval order :

the last king ruling by hereditary right, direct and undisputed, from the Conqueror. The kings of the next hundred and ten years . . . were essentially kings *de facto* not *de jure*, successful usurpers recognised after the event, upon conditions, by their fellow-magnates or by parliament.

Shakespeare, deeply interested in titles as he had showed himself to be in his early History Plays, must have known this very well; and Gaunt's famous speech on England cannot be fully understood without this knowledge. He calls England

> This nurse, this teeming womb of royal kings,
> Fear'd by their breed and famous by their birth,
> Renowned for their deeds as far from home,
> For Christian service and true chivalry,
> As is the sepulchre in stubborn Jewry
> Of the world's ransom, blessed Mary's son.

Richard was no crusader, but he was authentic heir of the crusading Plantagenets. Henry was different, a usurper; and it is with reference to this passage that we must read the lines in *Richard II* and *Henry IV* which recount his desire and his failure to go to Palestine. That honour was reserved for the authentic Plantagenet kings. Richard then had the full sanctity of medieval kingship and the strong pathos of being the last king to possess it. Shakespeare probably realised that however powerful the Tudors were and however undisputed their hold over their country's church, they had not the same sanctity as the medieval kings. He was therefore ready to draw from certain French treatises, anti-Lancastrian in tone, that made Richard a martyr and compared him to Christ and his accusers to so many Pilates giving him over to the wishes of the London mob. Shakespeare's Richard says at his deposition :

> Though some of you with Pilate wash your hands,
> Showing an outward pity; yet you Pilates
> Have here deliver'd me to my sour cross,
> And water cannot wash away your sin.

Holy and virtuous as the Earl of Richmond is in *Richard III*, he does not pretend to the same kingly sanctity as Richard II. Such sanctity belongs to a more antique, more exotically ritual world; and Shakespeare composed his play accordingly.

Not only did Richard in himself hold a position unique among English kings, he maintained a court of excessive splendour. Froissart writes as follows in the last pages of his chronicle :

> This King Richard reigned king of England twenty-two year in great prosperity, holding great estate and signory. There was never before any king of England that spent so much in his house as he did by a hundred thousand florins every year. For I, Sir John Froissart, canon and treasurer of Chinay, knew it well, for I was in his court more than a quarter of a year together and he made me good cheer. . . . And when I departed from him it was at Windsor; and at my departing the King sent me by a knight of his, Sir John Golofer, a goblet of silver and gilt weighing two mark of silver and within it a hundred nobles, by the which I am as yet the better and shall be as long as I live; wherefore I am bound to pray to God for his soul and with much sorrow I write of his death.

But Shakespeare need not have gone to Froissart for such information. In an age that was both passionately admiring of royal magnificence and far more retentive of tradition than our own the glories of Richard's court must have persisted as a legend. Anyhow that Shakespeare was aware of them is plain from Richard's address to his own likeness in the mirror :

> Was this face the face
> That every day under his household roof
> Did keep ten thousand men?

The legend must have persisted of this court's continental elegance, of the curiosities of its dress, of such a thing as Anne of Bohemia introducing the custom of riding side-saddle, of Richard's invention of the handkerchief for nasal use. Then there were the poets. Shakespeare must have associated the beginnings of English poetry with Chaucer and Gower; and they wrote mainly in Richard's reign. There must have been much medieval art, far more than now survives, visible in the great houses of Elizabeth's day, illuminated books and tapestry; and it would be generally associated with the most brilliant reign of the Middle Ages. Finally in Richard's reign there was the glamour of a still intact nobility : a very powerful glamour in an age still devoted to heraldry and yet possessing an aristocracy who, compared with the great men of Richard's day, were upstarts.

All these facts would have a strong, if unconscious, effect on Shakespeare's mind and induce him to present the age of Richard in a brilliant yet remote and unrealistic manner. He was already master of a certain antique lore and of a certain kind of ceremonial writing : it was natural that he should use them, but with a different turn, to do this particular work. Thus he makes more solemn and elaborates the inherited notions of cosmic correspondences and chivalric procedure and he makes his ritual style a central and not peripheral concern. Hence the portentous solemnity of the moralising gardeners, the powerful emphasis on the isolated symbol of the rue-tree, the elaborate circumstances of the tournament between Bolingbroke and Mowbray, and the unique artifice of Richard's great speeches : speeches which are the true centre of the play but central with a far wider reference than to the mere character of Richard.

In speaking of medieval illuminated books and tapestry I do not wish to imply anything too literal : that Shakespeare had actual examples of such things in mind when he wrote *Richard II*. But it is true that many passages in this play call them up and that unconscious memory of them *might* have given Shakespeare help. Take a passage from one of Richard's best known speeches.

> For God's sake, let us sit upon the ground
> And tell sad stories of the death of kings :
> How some have been depos'd, some slain in war,
> Some haunted by the ghosts they have depos'd,
> Some poison'd by their wives, some sleeping kill'd ;
> All murder'd : for within the hollow crown
> That rounds the mortal temples of a king
> Keeps Death his court, and there the antic sits,
> Scoffing his state and grinning at his pomp,
> Allowing him a breath, a little scene,
> To monarchise, be fear'd, and kill with looks,
> Infusing him with self and vain conceit,
> As if this flesh which walls about our life
> Were brass impregnable, and, humour'd thus,

> Comes at the last and with a little pin
> Bores through his castle wall, and farewell king!

Critics have seen a reference here to the *Mirror for Magistrates*, but Chaucer's *Monk's Tale* would suit much better. Death, keeping his court, is a pure medieval motive. Still, these motives were inherited and need imply nothing unusual. But Death the skeleton watching and mocking the king in his trappings is a clear and concrete image that reminds one of the visual arts: and above all the exquisiteness, the very remoteness from what could have happened in an actual physical attempt, of someone boring through the castle wall with a little pin precisely recaptures the technique of medieval illumination. Before the tournament Bolingbroke prays God:

> And with thy blessings steel my lance's point
> That it may enter Mowbray's waxen coat.

That again is just like medieval illumination. When a wound is given in medieval art there is no fusion of thing striking with thing stricken; the blow simply rests in a pre-existing hole, while any blood that spouts out had pre-existed just as surely. This is the kind of picture called up by Mowbray's 'waxen coat'. Or take this comparison. If anywhere in *Henry IV* we might expect medievalism it is in the description of the Prince performing the most spectacular of chivalric actions: yaulting onto his horse in full armour.

> I saw young Harry, with his beaver on,
> His cuisses on his thighs, gallantly arm'd,
> Rise from the ground like feather'd Mercury,
> And vaulted with such ease into his seat,
> As if an angel dropp'd down from the clouds,
> To turn and wind a fiery Pegasus
> And witch the world with noble horsemanship.

There is nothing medieval here. It is a description recalling the art of the high Renaissance with fused colours and subtle transitions. Set beside it Gaunt's advice to Bolingbroke about to go into exile:

> Suppose the singing birds musicians,
> The grass whereon thou tread'st the presence strew'd,
> The flowers fair ladies, and thy steps no more
> Than a delightful measure or a dance.

Here each item is distinct, and the lines evoke the mincing figures of a medieval tapestry in a setting of birds and flowers.

The case for the essential medievalism of *Richard II* is even stronger when it is seen that the conspirators, working as such, do not share the ceremonial style used to represent Richard and his court. Once again the usual explanation of such a contrast is too narrow. It has been the habit to contrast the 'poetry' of Richard with the practical common sense of Bolingbroke. But the 'poetry' of Richard is all part of a world of gorgeous tournaments, conventionally mournful queens, and impossibly sententious gardeners, while Bolingbroke's common sense extends to his backers, in particular to that most important character, Northumberland. We have in fact the contrast not only of two characters but of two ways of life.

One example of the two different ways of life has occurred already : in the contrast noted between the mannered pleading of the Duchess of York for Aumerle's life and Henry's vigorous resolve immediately after to punish the conspirators. The Duchess and her family belong to the old order where the means, the style, the embroidery matter more than what they further or express. Henry belongs to a new order, where action is quick and leads somewhere. But other examples are needed to back up what to many readers will doubtless seem a dangerous and forced theory of the play's significance. First, a new kind of vigour, the vigour of strong and swift action, enters the verse of the play at II, i, 224, when, after Richard has seized Gaunt's property and announced his coming journey to Ireland, Northumberland, Ross, and Willoughby remain behind and hatch their conspiracy. Northumberland's last speech especially has a different vigour from any vigorous writing that has gone before : from the vigour of the jousters' mutual defiance or York's moral indignation at the King's excesses. After enumerating Bolingbroke's supporters in Brittany, he goes on :

> All these well furnish'd by the Duke of Brittain
> With eight tall ships, three thousand men of war,
> Are making hither with all due expedience
> And shortly mean to touch our northern shore :
> Perhaps they had ere this, but that they stay
> The first departing of the king for Ireland.
> If then we shall shake off our slavish yoke,
> Imp out our drooping country's broken wing,
> Redeem from broken pawn the blemish'd crown,
> Wipe off the dust that hides our sceptre's gift
> And make high majesty look like itself,
> Away with me in post to Ravenspurgh.

The four lines describing by different metaphors how the land is to be restored are not in a ritual manner but in Shakespeare's normal idiom of Elizabethan exuberance. It is not for nothing that the next scene shows the Queen exchanging elegant conceits about her sorrow for Richard's absence with Bushy and Green. But the largest contrast comes at the beginning of the third act. It begins with a very fine speech of Bolingbroke recounting to Bushy and Green all their crimes, before they are executed. It has the full accent of the world of action, where people want to get things and are roused to passion in their attempts :

> Bring forth these men.
> Bushy and Green, I will not vex your souls
> (Since presently your souls must part your bodies)
> With too much urging your pernicious lives,
> For 'twere no charity.

That is the beginning, and the speech goes on to things themselves not to the way they are done or are embroidered. And when at the end Bolingbroke recounts his own injuries it is with plain and understandable passion :

> Myself a prince by fortune of my birth,
> Near to the king in blood, and near in love
> Till you did make him misinterpret me,
> Have stoop'd my neck under your injuries .
> And sigh'd my English breath in foreign clouds,
> Eating the bitter bread of banishment.

The scene is followed by Richard's landing in Wales, his pitiful inability to act, and his wonderful self-dramatisation. As a display of externals, as an exaltation of means over ends (here carried to a frivolous excess), it is wonderful; yet it contains no lines that for the weight of unaffected passion come near Bolingbroke's single line,

> Eating the bitter bread of banishment.

The world for which Bolingbroke stands, though it is a usurping world, displays a greater sincerity of personal emotion.

Thus *Richard II*, although reputed so simple and homogeneous a play, is built on a contrast. The world of medieval refinement is indeed the main object of presentation but it is threatened and in the end superseded by the more familiar world of the present.

In carrying out his object Shakespeare shows the greatest skill in keeping the emphasis sufficiently on Richard, while hinting that in Bolingbroke's world there is the probability of development. In other words he makes the world of Bolingbroke not so much defective as embryonic. It is not allowed to compete with Richard's but it is ready to grow to its proper fulness in the next plays. This is especially true of the conspirators' characters. Hotspur, for instance, is faintly drawn yet in one place he speaks with a hearty abruptness that shows his creator had conceived the whole character already. It is when Hotspur first meets Bolingbroke, near Berkeley Castle. Northumberland asks him if he has forgotten the Duke of Hereford, and Hotspur replies :

> No, my good lord, for that is not forgot
> Which ne'er I did remember : to my knowledge
> I never in my life did look on him.

At the beginning of the same scene Northumberland's elaborate compliments to Bolingbroke show his politic nature : it is the same man who at the beginning of *2 Henry IV* lies 'crafty-sick'. Bolingbroke too is consistent with his later self, though we are shown only certain elements in his character. What marks out the later Bolingbroke and makes him a rather pathetic figure is his bewilderment. For all his political acumen he does not know himself completely on his way about the world. And the reason is that he has relied in large part on fortune. Dover Wilson remarked truly of him in *Richard II* that though he acts forcibly he appears to be borne upward by a power beyond his volition. He is made the first mover of trouble in the matter of the tournament and he wants to do something about Woodstock's murder. But he has no steady policy and having once set events in motion is the servant of fortune. As such, he is not in control of events, though by his adroitness he may deal with the unpredictable as it occurs. Now a man who, lacking a steady policy, begins a course of action will be led into those 'by-paths and indirect crook'd ways' of which Henry speaks to his son in *2 Henry IV*. Shakespeare says nothing of them in *Richard II*, but they are yet the inevitable result of Henry's character as shown in that play. It is worth anticipating and saying that Prince Hal differs from his father in having perfect knowledge both of himself and of the world around him. Of all types of men he is the least subject to the sway of fortune.

Another quality shown only in embryo is humour. It is nearly absent but there is just a touch: sufficient to assure us that Shakespeare has it there all the time in readiness. It occurs in the scene where Aumerle describes to Richard his parting from Bolingbroke.

> RICHARD   And say, what store of parting tears were shed?
> AUMERLE   Faith, none for me : except the north-east wind
>   Which then blew bitterly against our faces,
>   Awak'd the sleeping rheum, and so by chance
>   Did grace our hollow parting with a tear.

Richard II thus at once possesses a dominant theme and contains within itself the elements of those different things that are to be the theme of its successors.

It must not be thought because Shakespeare treated history, as described above, in a way new to him, that he has lost interest in his old themes. On the contrary he is interested as much as ever in the theme of civil war, in the kingly type, and in the general fortunes of England. And I will say a little on each of these before trying to sum up the play's meaning in the tetralogy to which it belongs.

Richard II does its work in proclaiming the great theme of the whole cycle of Shakespeare's History Plays: the beginning in prosperity, the distortion of prosperity by a crime, civil war, and ultimate renewal of prosperity. The last stage falls outside the play's scope, but the second scene with the Duchess of Gloucester's enumeration of Edward III's seven sons, her account of Gloucester's death, and her call for vengeance is a worthy exordium of the whole cycle. The speeches of the Bihop of Carlisle and of Richard to Northumberland . . . are worthy statements of the disorder that follows the deposition of the rightful king. In doctrine the play is entirely orthodox. Shakespeare knows that Richard's crimes never amounted to tyranny and hence that outright rebellion against him was a crime. He leaves uncertain the question of who murdered Woodstock and never says that Richard was personally responsible. The King's uncles hold perfectly correct opinions. Gaunt refuses the Duchess of Gloucester's request for vengeance, the matter being for God's decision alone. Even on his deathbed, when lamenting the state of the realm and calling Richard the landlord and not the king of England, he never preaches rebellion. And he mentions deposition only in the sense that Richard by his own conduct is deposing himself. York utters the most correct sentiments. Like the Bastard he is for supporting the existing government. And though he changes allegiance he is never for rebellion. As stated above, the gardener was against the deposition of Richard.

As well as being a study of medievalism, Richard takes his place among Shakespeare's many studies of the kingly nature. He is a king by unquestioned title and by his external graces alone. But others have written so well on Richard's character that I need say no more.

Lastly, for political motives, there is the old Morality theme of Respublica. One of Shakespeare's debts in *Richard II* is to *Woodstock*; and this play is constructed very plainly on the Morality pattern, with the King's three uncles led by Woodstock inducing him to virtue, and Tressilian Bushy and Green to vice. There are traces of this motive in Shakespeare's play, but with Woodstock dead before the action begins and Gaunt dying early in it the balance of good and evil influences is destroyed. Bushy Green and Bagot, however, remain very plainly Morality figures and were probably marked in some way by their dress as abstract vices. If Shakespeare really confused Bagot with the Earl of Wiltshire (according to a conjecture of Dover Wilson) he need not be following an old play heedlessly : he would in any case look on them all as a gang of bad characters, far more important as a gang than as individuals, hence not worth being careful over separately. Once again, as in the earlier tetralogy, England herself, and not the protagonist, is the main concern. Gaunt speaks her praises, the gardener in describing his own symbolic garden has her in mind. As part of the great cycle of English history covered by Hall's chronicle the events of the reign of Richard II take their proper place. But here something fresh has happened. The early tetralogy had as its concern the fortunes of England in that exciting and instructive stretch of her history. *Richard II* has this concern too, but it also deals with England herself, the nature and not merely the fortunes of England. In *Richard II* it is the old brilliant medieval England of the last Plantagenet in the authentic succession; in *Henry IV* it will be the England not of the Middle Ages but of Shakespeare himself. We can now see how the epic comes in and how *Richard II* contributes to an epic effect. Those works which we honour by the epic title always, among other things, express the feelings or the habits of a large group of men, often of a nation. However centrally human, however powerful, a work may be, we shall not give it the epic title for these qualities alone. It is not the parting of Hector and Andromache or the ransoming of Hector's body that make the *Iliad* an epic; it is that the *Iliad* expresses a whole way of life. Shakespeare, it seems, as well as exploiting the most central human affairs, as he was to do in his tragedies, was also impelled to fulfil through the drama that peculiarly epic function which is usually fulfilled through the narrative. Inspired partly perhaps by the example of Daniel and certainly by his own genius, he combined with the grim didactic exposition of the fortunes of England during her terrible ordeal of civil war his epic version of what England was.

This new turn given to the History Play is a great stroke of Shakespeare's genius. Through it he goes beyond anything in Hall or Daniel or even Spenser. Hall and Daniel see English history in a solemn and moral light and they are impressive writers. Spenser is a great philosophical poet and epitomises the ethos of the Elizabethan age. But none of these can truly picture England. Of the epic writers Sidney in *Arcadia* comes nearest to doing this. It is indeed only in patches that authentic England appears through mythical Arcadia, but that it can this description of Kalander's house in the second chapter of the book is sufficient proof :

> The house itself was built of fair and strong stone, not affecting so much any extraordinary kind of fineness as an honourable representing of a firm stateliness : the lights doors and stairs rather directed to the use of the guest than to the eye of the artificer, and yet, as the one chiefly heeded, so the other not neglected; each place handsome without curiosity and homely without loathsomeness; not so dainty as not to be trod on nor yet slubbered up with good fellowship; all more lasting than beautiful but that the consideration of the exceeding lastingness made the eye believe it was exceedingly beautiful.

This expresses the authentic genius of English domestic architecture.

Of this great new epic attempt *Richard II* is only the prelude. What of England it pictures is not only antique but partial : the confined world of a medieval courtly class. In his next plays Shakespeare was to picture (with much else) the whole land, as he knew it, in his own day, with its multifarious layers of society and manners of living.

Source : *Shakespeare's History Plays* (1948).

M. C. Bradbrook

TRAGICAL-HISTORICAL: *RICHARD II* (1951)

In *Richard III* very little is said of England or the troubles of the realm: the citizens' scene (II, iii) is feeble, and there are no representatives of the common people. In *Richard II* the background is not heaven and hell, but the sceptred isle, and instead of Senecan imagery of night and death, the dominant image is that of England, 'the garden of the world'[1] laid waste, her fields manured with blood and her 'fair rose', Richard, withered. The image of the trampled garden runs through the play and it is embodied in the Mirror Scene of the gardeners, when the first news of Richard's capture reaches his foreboding Queen. This scene, the stumbling-block to all naturalist readers, sets out the main theme of the play. The gardeners who expound the art of government in terms of their own labours are none the less something of an archaism in this play. For the device of the mirror scene which enabled Shakespeare to focus his poetry in *Henry VI* is now outgrown, so rapid was his development at this time. The groom who appears in the final scene is a fully dramatized character who 'quarrels' with these choric gardeners: yet in spite of such minor inconsistencies, *Richard II* presents a wonderful balance between the theme and the character, between the image which is poetically embodied and the image which is dramatically embodied. The prophecy of the Bishop of Carlisle (which Shakespeare did not find in his sources, and which appeared only in the later editions of the play) constitutes the fullest statement of the moral history, the destruction of order and degree by the usurpation of Bolingbroke.

> The bloud of English shall manure the ground,
> And future ages groane for his foul act.
> Peace shall go sleepe with turks and Infidels,
> And in this seat of peace, tumultuous warres

Shall kin with kin, and kinde with kind confound :
Disorder, horror, feare, and mutiny
Shall heere inhabit, and the land be calld
The field of Golgotha and dead mens skuls.   (iv, i, 137–44)

In place of flat verbal patterns Shakespeare develops in this play
recurrent or, as it has been called, 'symphonic' imagery[2] : and
this change of style is the outward and visible sign of a changed
conception of structure. The tableaux, set debates, laments in
chorus, give way to more complex groupings of characters, each
character contrasted not only in function but in temper and
idiom; each character a sympathetically conceived being, not
conceived indeed in isolation from the others or from the general
theme, but still conceived from within. It is the multiplicity of
points of view which gives its tragic character to this play : even
as on the early stage a multiple setting allowed the dramatist to
set several scenes on the stage side by side, so this multiple
characterization allows the dramatist several centres of sympathy.
Richard, Gaunt, York, Bolingbroke are all animated in this way.
To a modern reader this may not sound a very remarkable
achievement : yet it was something none of Shakespeare's predecessors had done since Chaucer wrote *Troilus* and *The
Canterbury Tales.* In *Richard III* he presented one man contending against 'the main sway of things' : here he presents a
whole world.

Richard himself, defined both through speech and action, has
something in common with Henry VI, the weak king crushed by
his violent subjects, as far as his history goes; but there is little in
common between their persons. The dichotomy between Man
and Office 'the deputy anointed by the Lord' and the man who

lives with bread like you, feels want,
Tastes grief, needs friends. . . . (iii, ii, 175–6)

is one which Shakespeare was to treat again and again under
many aspects : in Bolingbroke's uneasy nightwatching, and his
son's meditation on Ceremony : in Hamlet, King Lear, the Duke
of Vienna and the Duke of Milan. Here it serves as basis for the
reconciliation of opposites within a single role : Richard loves his
land, with an almost passionate devotion to its very soil, but

hopelessly misuses his office; he is sensitive and brutal, variable and obstinate, witty but not wise. The variety of his speech reflects the variety of his moods—his fanciful poetry to Aumerle or the Queen, his nervous irony to Bolingbroke and Northumberland, his cruel petulance to old Gaunt and his pitiable family likeness to old York make him consistently inconsistent, as Aristotle would say : give that peculiar depth and many-sidedness to his character which is the mark of Shakespeare's dramatic and poetic power, and by which he creates the illusion of life itself, multiform yet one.

The trampled garden of King Richard's land, in which he is the withering rose or the setting sun, is an image peculiarly fitted to govern the play of which such a man is hero. Here Shakespeare first evolved that method of embodying the main theme in a dominant image which he was to use in the greater tragedies, particularly *Hamlet* and *Macbeth* with their darkness, disease and blood. There is a fine balance between the natural and sensuous evocation of this image, as in the scene of farewell between Richard and his Queen, and the more emblematic or heraldic use of it.

Heraldry is behind the lines,

> Downe, downe I come, like glistring Phaethon;
> Wanting the manage of unrulie Iades (III, iii, 178–9)

which derive from Richard's personal badge of the sun in glory. The image is used in this sense elsewhere (III, iii, 62–7 : IV, i, 221, 260–2), and it is as fully heraldic as Richard III's badge of the boar.[3]

Here it is blended with a notion also of the turning wheel of Fortune, on which Richard is now descending, and with the image of the horse, which had been since Plato the symbol of instincts managed—or not managed—by reason the charioteer. The prominence of horsemanship in courtly education gave it particular power at this time and it is no dead simile for Richard. The account of his ride into London and the final scene in which the groom tells Richard of his ungrateful 'roan Barbary' develop the image as symbol of harmonious relations between king and subject, body and soul.[4]

This wealth and fecundity of meaning within a single image

is matched by the wealth of significance in the great dramatic tableaux. Richard's incompetence in the lists at Coventry, where all the pomp and order of the fight is broken up by his gesture, reflects directly upon his government: the confusion symbolizes the greater confusion to come. In the deposition scene, the old formal properties—the stage crown and the Mirror itself—are used in a symbolic manner warranted by tradition,[5] yet the formality of the scene is a completely adequate presentation of the personal conflict between the despairing Richard and the 'silent king' who confronts him. Bolingbroke's character, indeed, as has been noted often enough, is largely built up from what he does *not* say, and this dramatic use of a silent figure implies a grasp of full theatrical perspective. His early rejection of the conventional consolations offered for his banishment by Gaunt marks Bolingbroke as one who despises mere words : his silence in the abdication scene is as bitter a reflection upon Richard's weakness as Northumberland's taunts : and in the scene where York and his Duchess plead before the King, after Aumerle's conspiracy has come to light—a scene where Bolingbroke's mastery of the situation contrasts sharply with Richard's behaviour at Coventry—a single word suffices to give his judgment on the whole affair. It puts all his clamorous relatives in their place, and, with the neat clinching of a rhyme, adds the spice of wit to his irony. York and his son have been high in speech, the Duchess is crying without the door, when Bolingbroke turns to the culprit with :

> My *dangerous* cousin, let your mother in :
> I know she is come to pray for your foule sinne.

The scene then changes to something pretty near farce.

The use of contrasting groups in this play is dependent on the complex family likenesses and differences between Richard, Aumerle, Bolingbroke, Gaunt and York : at Coventry, Gaunt and Bolingbroke are grouped in opposition to Richard : later Gaunt and Richard, age and youth, confront each other. The variations of interplay are far more subtle than those of *Richard III*, and recall rather the plays immediately preceding or following—*Romeo and Juliet* and *A Midsummer Night's Dream*—where Shakespeare is clearly experimenting in contrasted groups or contrasted figures.

A further measure of the complexity of conception which distinguishes *Richard II* is found in the complexity of the source material upon which it is based.[6] Hall, Froissart, two French pamphlets and Daniel's *Civil Wars* seem to imply such unusually academic interests that Dover Wilson attributed all the spade-work to the unknown author of a hypothetical source-play. It might be hazarded that Shakespeare wrote this play at a moment when he had attracted the notice and perhaps the friendship of a noble patron, and that therefore he composed for the judicious and learned part of his audience and that it is the historical partner of *Love's Labour's Lost.*

The first recorded reference to *Richard II* is a letter dated 7 December 1595, written by Sir Edward Hoby, the son of Sir Thomas Hoby, translator of *Il Cortegiano*, to invite Sir Robert Cecil to a private performance of the play at his house in Cannon Row, after supper (E. K. Chambers, *William Shakespeare*, II, p. 320–1). Though it is not absolutely certain that this is Shakespeare's play, both Chambers and Dover Wilson regard it as highly probable.

It is known that this play was later of particular interest to Essex's friends, who included Southampton and Sir Charles Percy: and it is not impossible that it might have been composed with an intention specially directed towards them. Its sense of the beauty of courtesy and the graces of life might arise from Shakespeare's first encounter with the life lived according to Castiglione.

Certainly the meaning of history had changed for Shake-speare: perhaps the poetry of Daniel and of Drayton, which softened these harsh stories into decorative lyrics of love,[7] had something to do with the change. But like a later poet he had

> learnt to get the better of words
> For the thing he no longer had to say or the way in which
> He no longer had to say it. (*East Coker*, v)

For the subsequent history plays differed as widely from *Richard II*, as *Richard II* had done from its predecessors. England is no longer embodied in tragic images but in comic characters.

SOURCE: *Shakespeare and Elizabethan Poetry* (1951).

NOTES

1. The phrase is Andrew Marvell's (*Nunappleton House*, xli); *Richard II*, III, ii, 4–26; III, iii, 160–9; v, i, 76–80; v, ii, 46–7; v, vi, 45–6 and *I Henry IV*, I, i, 5–9.

2. See R. D. Altick, above.

3. Cf. III, iii, 62–7; IV, i, 221, 260–2 and for the Boar in *Richard III*, I, ii, 103; I, iii, 228; III, ii, 10–11, 28–30, 72–3; IV, v, 2–3; v, ii, 7–11.

4. See, e.g., Philip Sidney's description of horsemanship at the beginning of the *Defence of Poetry*, his Sonnet xlix; Chapman's Byron 'on his brave Pastrana' (*Byrons Conspiracy*, II, ii, 66–81), which Miss R. Freeman compares with an emblem (*English Emblem Books*, London, 1948, p. 6); Antonio's horsemanship as described in *The Duchess of Malfi* (I, i, 141–6) and compare the revolt of Adonis's horse in Shakespeare's *Venus and Adonis*.

5. The use of the stage crown symbolically is very prominent, e.g. in *Tamburlaine*: M. D. Anderson, *The Medieval Carver*, pp. 71–3, describes how a medieval Empress retained her crown even when she was in disguise! The Mirror for Princes, for Subjects, for London, was a common phrase : Richard takes the old phrase and by using it literally gives a strange depth to the scene. Cf. Hamlet to his mother, III, iv, 19–20.

6. See J. Dover Wilson's edition of the play (Cambridge, 1939), pp. xxxviii–lxxvi and M. W. Black (*AMS*, pp. 199–216), 'The sources of *Richard II*'.

7. Daniel's *Civil Wars* (1595) is generally recognized as one of the sources of *Richard II* and the relevant passages are printed by J. Dover Wilson, ed. cit., pp. 99–106. The popularity of narrative historical poems at this time was very great. Drayton's *Piers Gaveston*, dated 1593–4, is a 'Mirror' poem in which the ghost of Edward II's favourite recounts his career, with, however, very little moral emphasis. It is rather a sensuous celebration of the pleasures of kingly favours, with a few perfunctory moralizings thrown in here and there. The year after the first recorded appearance of *Richard II*, 1596, Drayton issued his *Mortimeriados*, which shows the influence of *Richard II* as well as of Marlowe's *Edward II*, according to Drayton's latest editors (*Works of Drayton*, ed. H. Hebel and K. Tillotson, vol. v, p. 41). All these works on historical characters strongly emphasize what would now be called the human interest at the expense of the dynastic and moral patterns used by the chroniclers, and they appear so closely together (there are other complaints and epistles by both Daniel and Drayton which might be cited) that it seems clear that the years 1594–6 showed a particularly large crop of dramatic and non-dramatic historical poetry.

Brents Stirling

'UP, COUSIN, UP; YOUR HEART IS UP, I KNOW' (1956)

It is common knowledge that the political theme of *Richard II*[1] symbolized threats to Elizabeth's authority and that the deposition scene was censored in certain editions. The disturbing quality of the play could scarcely have arisen, however, from its explicit doctrine, for in the deposition scene Carlisle proclaims that no subject may judge a king and that, should Bolingbroke be crowned, 'The blood of English shall manure the ground,/ And future ages groan for this foul act'. Throughout Shakespeare's cycle of history plays this prophecy is recalled at appropriate stages of the epic story. In *Henry V* the King's prayer at the high point of suspense before Agincourt is 'Not today, Lord,/ O, not today, think not upon the fault/ My father made in compassing the crown!' This is but one of the allusions in the cycle to the usurpation by Bolingbroke of Richard's throne. The deed was viewed by Elizabethan historians as a kind of secular fall of man which tainted generations unborn until England was redeemed from consequent civil war by the Tudor messiah, Henry, Earl of Richmond. The doctrine of *Richard II* and the succeeding plays is thus wholly conventional,[2] and the banning of the deposition scene probably occurred not because the play contained objectionable ideas but because the spectacle of usurpation was too disturbing to be presented even with conservative commentary.

It is likely, moreover, that the provocation found in *Richard II* stemmed partly from Shakespeare's vivid characterization. Without authority from the sources, Richard appears as a royal sentimentalist, a defeatist who resigns the throne as though he preferred acting a role of tragedy to one of governing men. And although the sources show Bolingbroke as a victim of extortion who takes the moribund kingship, Shakespeare magnifies both the extortion and the defunct monarchy. Because of this intensified explanation of Bolingbroke's deed Carlisle's denunciation of the 'foul act' of revolution is easy to interpret as a concession to authority, as a piece of stiff morality almost intrusive in Shakespeare's active world of mixed right and wrong. The only difficulty with such an interpretation is that it is too simple. Plainly it rejects the kind of criticism which would find a moral in Carlisle's prophecy alone, but while rejecting one form of simplicity it substitutes another by assuming that complex motivation in drama denies the presence of clear moral judgment.

The political moral of *Richard II* is clear but it is not simple. It can be described adequately only in terms of the play, which means in part that dramatic structure and development of moral idea are here inseparable. When we understand each in relation to the other, both may appear more effective and more mature than before, and *Richard II* may assume new importance as a landmark in Shakespeare's development as a dramatist.

As resistance against Richard develops at the end of II, i, Northumberland explains the purpose entertained by Bolingbroke's faction :

> If then we shall shake off our slavish yoke,
> Imp out our drooping country's broken wing,
> Redeem from broking pawn the blemished crown,
> Wipe off the dust that hides our sceptre's gilt,
> And make high majesty look like itself. . . .

So far, nothing of deposition; Northumberland's statement is the first of many which stress a goal modestly short of the throne. Two scenes later Bolingbroke's suit is pressed again; the place is Gloucestershire where the insurgent forces encounter old York, regent in Richard's absence. To York's charge of treason 'in braving arms against thy sovereign' the reply by Bolingbroke is that he 'was banish'd Hereford' but returns 'for Lancaster', that he remains a subject of the king, and that having been denied 'attorneys' for lawful redress, he has appeared in person. Before Bolingbroke's assembled power which belies his peaceful aims, and before the claim for Henry's inheritance rights, York stands as the strict constructionist:

> My lords of England, let me tell you this;
> I have had feeling of my cousin's wrongs
> And labour'd all I could to do him right;
> But in this kind to come, in braving arms,
> Be his own carver and cut out his way,
> To find out right with wrong—it may not be.

Thus in a scene of unusual strength the rebels are confronted with clear disposition of their pragmatic morality. Ironically, however, in the lines which follow, York collapses pathetically and almost absurdly:

> But if I could, by Him that gave me life,
> I would attach you all and make you stoop
> Unto the sovereign mercy of the king;
> But since I cannot, be it known to you
> I do remain as neuter.

The luxury of neutrality is denied to York, however, through Bolingbroke's request that he accompany the rebels to Bristol in order to 'weed and pluck away' Bushy and Bagot, the 'caterpillars of the commonwealth'. York, the erstwhile absolutist, cannot even decide this incidental issue: 'It may be I will go with you; but yet I'll pause,/ For I am loath to break our country's laws.' And in any event, 'Things past redress are now with me past care.'

In the first two scenes of Act III Shakespeare now presents Bolingbroke and Richard in characterization which points to the utter difference in temperament between them; then, having shown each individually in parallel scenes, he brings them together for an episode in which the issue of deposition arises naturally and dramatically from conflict between characters. Dramatic structure, characterization, and presentation of idea (the deposition theme) are fused to the extent that none of these qualities can be discussed properly without reference to the others.

Scene i presents Bolingbroke, and in keeping with the character it is short and concentrated. It opens in the midst of events

with Henry's terse 'Bring forth these men'; Bushy and Green
are then presented for his brief but unhurried recitation of the
counts against them : they have misled and 'disfigur'd clean' the
king; they have 'made a divorce betwixt his queen and him'; they
have forced Bolingbroke to taste 'the bitter bread of banishment'
and disinheritance. These deeds condemn them to death. 'My
Lord Northumberland, see them dispatch'd.' Next, the Queen
must be remembered; to York : 'Fairly let her be entreated'. And
lastly Owen Glendower and his forces must be met; unhurried
orders are so given. In a little over forty lines Bolingbroke has
passed a death sentence, attended to the amenities of courtesy,
and has set a campaign in motion.

   Scene ii offers the King and his retinue in a parellel situation,
and its contrast with Bolingbroke's scene lies in the portrayal of
Richard first by soliloquies of self-regard, then by wordy defiance
which collapses as he learns of the Welsh defection, and finally
by near hysteria as Aumerle cautions, 'Comfort my liege; remember who you are.' When Scroop enters with worse news, Richard
proceeds from the false stoicism of anticipated defeat to insults
directed at his absent favorites, and back again to sentimental
despair :

> Let's choose executors and talk of wills;
> And yet not so; for what can we bequeath
> Save our deposed bodies to the ground?
> Our lands, our lives, and all are Bolingbroke's.

The word 'deposed' is repeated as a kind of refrain in the next
few lines as Richard offers to 'sit upon the ground/ And tell sad
stories of the death of kings'. A short speech of defiance as
Carlisle warns against this sitting and wailing of woes, and a final
descent into sentimental resignation as Scroop reports the joining of York with Bolingbroke—these acts complete Richard's
performance in the scene. Lest this account of it end as mere
description, Shakespeare's inventiveness should be stressed; to
the Chronicle version of Richard's misfortune he adds the King's
embracing of deposition far in advance of demand or suggestion,[3]
and in so doing casts him in a self-made martyr's role. The Flint
Castle scene (III, iii) is thus inevitable; figuratively, Richard

will depose himself in an agony of play-acting before the unsentimental Bolingbroke.

The outcome at Flint, however, will be unexpected. Not the realist but the sentimentalist will call the turn, and here Shakespeare will answer ironically our question : *when* did Bolingbroke, after all his protests to the contrary, decide to seize the crown ? One point of the play, it will appear, is that this question has no point.

In a literal reading, Bolingbroke makes no decision prior to Act iv, and there he is scarcely more than at hand to take the throne. This is subject to several interpretations. First, we might decide that prior to the deposition scene there is no stage at which the deviousness of Bolingbroke becomes clear, and that there are obvious lacunae between his early disclaimers of ambition and his sudden coronation in Act iv. In that event *Richard II* is an inferior play, and the fact that Henry's coronation is also sudden in the chronicles does not make it better. Or, secondly, we might conclude that Elizabethan audiences had heard of Bolingbroke's wish to be king,[4] and that a dramatist of the time did not need to explain it. This could scarcely be denied, but the play, at least to us, would still be the worse for it. Nor, in spite of occasional statements to the contrary, is it Shakespeare's custom to allow major characterization to rest upon history which is external to the play. A third explanation of our 'indecisive' Bolingbroke would be that opportunism, of which he becomes the living symbol, is essentially a tacit vice : that although the opportunist is vaguely aware of the ends to which his means commit him, he relies upon events, not upon declarations, to clarify his purposes. On the basis of the scene at Flint and of two prominent episodes which follow it, I believe that the interpretation just expressed is the one which fits the Henry Bolingbroke of Shakespeare's play.

By the time the Flint scene opens we are aware of Richard's impulses toward virtual abdication, but Bolingbroke has never exceeded his demands for simple restitution of rank and estate. Nor have his followers done so. True, York has told him that his very appearance in arms is treason, but Bolingbroke's rejoinder to this has been both disarming and apparently genuine. At the Castle, however, dramatic suggestion begins to take shape. As

Henry's followers hold council, Northumberland lets slip the name 'Richard' unaccompanied by the title of King. York retorts that such brevity once would have seen him shortened by a head's length. Bolingbroke intercedes: 'Mistake not, uncle, further than you should.' To which York answers: 'Take not, cousin, further than you should.' This suggestive colloquy is followed by Bolingbroke's characteristic statement of honest intention: 'Go to . . . the castle . . . and thus deliver: Henry Bolingbroke/ On both his knees does kiss King Richard's hand/ And sends allegiance and true faith of heart/ To his most royal person.' He will lay down his arms if his lands are restored and his banishment repealed. If not, war is the alternative. With dramatic significance, however, Northumberland, who bears this message from a Bolingbroke 'on both his knees', fails himself to kneel before Richard and thus becomes again the medium of suggestive disclosure. Richard, in a rage, sends word back to Henry that 'ere the crown he looks for live in peace,/ Ten thousand bloody crowns of mothers' sons' shall be the price in slaughter. Northumberland's rejoinder is a yet more pious assertion of Bolingbroke's limited aims: 'The King of heaven forbid our lord the King/ Should so with civil and uncivil arms/ Be rush'd upon! Thy thrice noble cousin/ Harry Bolingbroke . . . swears . . . his coming hath no further scope/ Than for his lineal royalties.'

Richard's response is to grant the demands, to render a wish in soliloquy that he be buried where his subjects 'may hourly trample on their sovereign's head', and, when summoned to the 'base court', to make it a further symbol of the rebels' duplicity, to cry out that down, down he comes 'like glist'ring Phaethon,/ Wanting the manage of unruly jades'. He enters the lowly court, and the scene concludes with a wonderful mummery of sovereignty, each participant speaking as a subject to his king.

BOLINGBROKE   Stand all apart,
    And show fair duty to His Majesty. [*He kneels down.*]
    My gracious lord—
RICHARD   Fair Cousin, you debase your princely knee
    To make the base earth proud with kissing it.
    Me rather had my heart might feel your love
    Than my unpleas'd eye see your courtesy.

Up, cousin, up. Your heart is up, I know,
Thus high at least, although your knee be low.
BOLINGBROKE   My gracious lord, I come but for mine own.
RICHARD   Your own is yours, and I am yours, and all.
BOLINGBROKE   So far be mine, my most redoubted lord,
As my true service shall deserve your love.
RICHARD   Well you deserve. They well deserve to have
That know the strong'st and surest way to get. . . .
Cousin, I am too young to be your father,
Though you are old enough to be my heir.
What you will have, I'll give, and willing too;
For do we must what force will have us do.
Set on toward London, cousin, is it so?
BOLINGBROKE   Yea, my good lord.
RICHARD   Then I must not say no.

There is no question of what 'London' means. It is dethronement
for Richard and coronation for Bolingbroke, an implication
which is plain enough here but which Shakespeare underscores
in the next scene where the Gardener, asked by the Queen, 'Why
dost thou say King Richard is deposed?' concludes his answer
with 'Post you to London, and you will find it so.' At Flint,
Bolingbroke's reply to Richard, 'Yea, my good lord', is the aptly
timed climax of the episode, and of the play. With this oblique
admission, coming with great effect immediately after his statement of loyalty and subjection, Henry's purposes become clear,
and the significant fact is that not he but Richard has phrased
his intent. The King's single line, 'Set on toward London, cousin,
is it so?' is the ironic instrument for exposing a long course of
equivocation which the rebels seem to have concealed even from
themselves.[5] And in fact Bolingbroke is still trying to conceal it;
his short answer is the minimum assertion of his motives, an
opportunist's spurious appeal to what 'must be' in order to avoid
a statement of purpose.

This turn in the play rests upon skillful fusion of three elements
—plot construction, disclosure of political moral, and characterization, all of which show parallel irony. In plot unfoldment,
the end of the Flint scene is the point of climax at which Henry's
true purpose is revealed. But the climax is also a studied anticlimax, for the rebels advance upon Flint Castle only, as it were,

to find it abandoned and with the words, 'Come to London', written upon the walls. They, and the audience, had expected not quiet exposure of their aims (the actual climax) but dramatic opportunity for constitutional manifestoes.

As for disclosure of political doctrine, it is during the encounter at Flint that the rebels achieve their most eloquent statement of legality in seeking only a subject's claim to justice from his king. But the luxury of that pretense vanishes at the end of the scene, again with the word 'London'. It becomes suddenly apparent that York's previous judgment was sound, that Bolingbroke's use of force to gain just concessions from his sovereign has committed him to the destruction of sovereignty.

The third factor here is characterization which greatly enhances the complex of ironies. Shakespeare's prior establishment of Bolingbroke's realism, self-containment, and resourcefulness, along with Richard's romantic defeatism, near-hysteria, and pathetic reliance upon others, has furnished a decided pattern for the meeting of the two at Flint. Bolingbroke (with Northumberland) fulfills previously set notes of stability and restraint; Richard repeats the performance he had enacted before his own followers in the preceding scene, and reminds us of a familiar epigram about the protagonist who is spectator at his own tragedy. Full portraiture of Bolingbroke and Richard, both before and during the Castle episode, thus prepares for the paradoxical ending of the scene. There, with Richard's knowing reference to London and Bolingbroke's one-line reply, the shift in characterization materializes. The unstable Richard, who had fled from facts through every form of emotional exaggeration, now drops his sentimental role and points to reality with quiet wit and candor; the plain-dealing Bolingbroke who had offered his demands with such consistency and seeming honesty, now admits his sham of rebellion which was to stop short of rebellion.

The end of Act III, scene iii, is thus pivotal. At this point of multiple effect Bolingbroke's ambiguity is revealed, and it now engages Shakespeare's attention in a pair of episodes which will complete Henry's portrait; the ambiguity will be presented twice again by means of the same dramatic method.

The first of these cumulative parallels to the Flint scene occurs in IV, i (the deposition). Here Richard is again confronted by

the rebels, and again he is by turns both defiant and submissive;
his sentimental display is likewise in dramatic contrast with
Henry's simplicity, forbearance, and directness. And as before,
the paradox comes in the closing lines :

> RICHARD   I'll beg one boon,
> And then be gone and trouble you no more.
> Shall I obtain it?
> BOLINGBROKE   Name it, fair Cousin.
> RICHARD   'Fair Cousin'? I am greater than a king.
> For when I was a king, my flatterers
> Were then but subjects. Being now a subject,
> I have a King here to my flatterer.
> Being so great, I have no need to beg.
> BOLINGBROKE   Yet ask.
> RICHARD   And shall I have?
> BOLINGBROKE   You shall.
> RICHARD   Then give me leave to go.
> BOLINGBROKE   Whither?
> RICHARD   Whither you will, so I were from your sights.
> BOLINGBROKE   Go, some of you convey him to the Tower.

Just as 'London' meant deposition at the end of III, iii, so here
at the end of IV, i the Tower means imprisonment and ultimate
death. Again Richard, who has run his course of theatrical
emotion, becomes pointedly realistic; again Bolingbroke, who has
exhibited every sign of gracious honesty, reveals duplicity in a
concluding line.

The third and final step in Henry's portrayal is analogous in
all essentials to the two scenes we have examined. The fact that
Shakespeare here drew upon the Chronicles might imply that he
found there a suggestion of the shifting taciturnity which Bolingbroke shows in all three episodes. Piers of Exton, in v, iv, ponders
something he has heard. 'Have I no friend will rid me of this
living fear?' Was not that what the new King said? And did he
not repeat it as he 'wishtly look'd on me'? It is enough; Exton
promptly murders Richard and returns with the body. Henry's
lines which conclude the play are well known; he admits desiring
Richard's death but disowns Exton's act and pledges expiation
in a voyage to the Holy Land.

Three times—at the end of III, iii, at the end of the deposition scene, and in the Exton scenes at the end of the play—Henry has taken, if it may be so called, a decisive step. Each time the move he has made has been embodied in a terse statement, and each time someone else has either evoked it from him or stated its implications for him. Never in sixteenth-century drama were motives disclosed with such economy and understatement. The Elizabethan stage character with a moral contradiction usually explains his flaw before, during, and after the event—and at length. Until the short choric 'confession' at the very end of the play, Bolingbroke, however, shows his deviousness in one-line admissions spaced at telling intervals and occurring in contexts which are effectively similar.

And as each of these admissions marks a step in characterization, it indicates a critical stage of plot development : the conflict of forces is resolved with the line on London concluding the Flint Castle scene, for there Richard and Henry reach mutual understanding on the dethronement issue; the falling action becomes defined with the line near the end of the deposition scene which sends Richard to the Tower; the catastrophe is begun by the line to Exton which sends him to death.

Finally, at each of these three points the meaning implicit in the play shows a new clarity. With the reference to London at Flint it becomes apparent that a 'constitutional' show of force against sovereignty leads to the deposition of sovereignty; with the dispatching of Richard to the Tower it appears that deposition of sovereignty requires degradation of the sovereign; and with Henry's line to Exton it becomes plain that murder of sovereignty must be the final outcome.[6]

From his first history to his last tragedy Shakespeare excelled in a poet's expression of Tudor political dogma. But to say this is not enough, for as early as *Richard II* he combined his poet's talent with another difficult art. In this play doctrine, plot, and characterization unfold integrally. With our debt to the English and American revolutions we cannot admire the doctrine, but we can recognize in *Richard II* a stage of Shakespeare's development at which morality and artistry become functionally inseparable.

SOURCE : *Unity in Shakespearian Tragedy* (1956).

NOTES

1. Although one of the 'histories', *Richard II* may be included in a study of Shakespearian tragedy with full propriety under either Elizabethan or modern theory.

2. I refer to the simplified basic doctrine. To say that this is conventional does not mean that Shakespeare treated simply or conventionally the crises of his characters as they attempt to adhere to the doctrine or depart from it.

3. See W. G. Boswell-Stone, *Shakespere's Holinshed* (London, 1896). Holinshed exhibits Richard in an early state of despair, but with no preconception of dethronement (p. 106), and in a mood of willingness to abdicate after arrival in London (p. 113). Shakespeare, however, presents a king determined to abdicate as early as the landing in Wales (III, ii), before Richard has even encountered Bolingbroke; and he continues to portray him in this mood from there onward.

4. Samuel Daniel indicates that in Shakespeare's time Bolingbroke's motives were commonly viewed as suspect. He develops the subject at some length (*Civil Wars*, Book I, stanzas 87–99) and concludes that, in charity, judgment should be suspended.

5. Self-delusion on Bolingbroke's part is a trait clearly suggested by Daniel in his enigmatic passage on Henry's motives (*Civil Wars*, Book I, stanzas 90–1). I mention this only to show that such an interpretation was made at the time *Richard II* was written. The concluding lines of stanza 91 are :

> Men do not know what then themselves will be
> When-as, more than themselves, themselves they see.

For an additional reference to Daniel, as well as for a denial that Bolingbroke is a conscious schemer, see J. Dover Wilson's edition of *Richard II* (Cambridge, 1939), pp. xx and xxi. Mr. Wilson briefly describes Bolingbroke as an opportunist led by Fortune.

6. The Chronicle accounts of Richard's latter days do not provide a suggestion of these cumulative steps. As usual, a play-source comparison emphasizes Shakespeare's artistry both in structure and motivation. Daniel (*Civil Wars*, Books I and II) likewise fails to present Bolingbroke's opportunistic conduct in the telling manner of Shakespeare. He does amply suggest the possibility of 'unconscious' drift toward usurpation but in no way dramatizes this action in successive, cumulative disclosure. . . .

E. H. Kantorowicz

FROM *THE KING'S TWO BODIES* (1957)

> Twin-born with greatness, subject to the breath
> Of every fool, whose sense no more can feel
> But his own wringing. What infinite heart's ease
> Must kings neglect that private men enjoy! . . . .
> What kind of god art thou, that suffer'st more
> Of mortal griefs than do thy worshippers?

Such are, in Shakespeare's play, the meditations of King Henry V on the godhead and manhood of a king.[1] The king is 'twin-born' not only with greatness but also with human nature, hence 'subject to the breath of every fool'.

It was the humanly tragic aspect of royal 'gemination' which Shakespeare outlined and not the legal capacities which English lawyers assembled in the fiction of the King's Two Bodies. However, the legal jargon of the 'two Bodies' scarcely belonged to the arcana of the legal guild alone. That the king 'is a Corporation in himself that liveth ever', was a commonplace found in a simple dictionary of legal terms such as Dr John Cowell's *Interpreter* (1607);[2] and even at an earlier date the gist of the concept of kingship which Plowden's *Reports* reflected,* had passed into the writings of Joseph Kitchin (1580)[3] and Richard Crompton (1594)[4]. Moreover, related notions were carried into public when, in 1603, Francis Bacon suggested for the crowns of England and Scotland, united in James I, the name of 'Great Britain' as an expression of the 'perfect union of bodies, politic as well as natural'.[5] That Plowden's *Reports* were widely known is certainly demonstrated by the phrase 'The case is altered, quoth Plowden', which was used proverbially in England before

*[Editor's Footnote : Edmund Plowden, *Commentaries or Reports* (London, 1816), collected and written under Queen Elizabeth, are discussed in Kantorowicz's previous chapter.]

and after 1600.[6] The suggestion that Shakespeare may have known a case (*Hales* v. *Petit*) reported by Plowden, does not seem far-fetched, and it gains strength on the ground that the anonymous play *Thomas of Woodstock*, of which Shakespeare 'had his head full of echoes' and in which he may even have acted,[7] ends in the pun : 'for I have plodded in Plowden, and can find no law'. Besides, it would have been very strange if Shakespeare, who mastered the lingo of almost every human trade, had been ignorant of the constitutional and judicial talk which went on around him and which the jurists of his days applied so lavishly in court. Shakespeare's familiarity with legal cases of general interest cannot be doubted, and we have other evidence of his association with the students at the Inns and his knowledge of court procedure.

Admittedly, it would make little difference whether or not Shakespeare was familiar with the subtleties of legal speech. The poet's vision of the twin nature of a king is not dependent on constitutional support, since such vision would arise very naturally from a purely human stratum. It therefore may appear futile even to pose the question whether Shakespeare applied any professional idiom of the jurists of his time, or try to determine the die of Shakespeare's coinage. It seems all very trivial and irrelevant, since the image of the twinned nature of a king, or even of man in general, was most genuinely Shakespeare's own and proper vision. Nevertheless, should the poet have chanced upon the legal definitions of kingship, as probably he could not have failed to do when conversing with his friends at the Inns, it will be easily imagined how apropos the simile of the King's Two Bodies would have seemed to him. It was anyhow the live essence of his art to reveal the numerous planes active in any human being, to play them off against each other, to confuse them, or to preserve their equilibrium, depending all upon the pattern of life he bore in mind and wished to create anew. How convenient then to find those ever contending planes, as it were, legalised by the jurists' royal 'christology' and readily served to him !

The legal concept of the King's Two Bodies cannot, for other reasons, be separated from Shakespeare. For if that curious image, which from modern constitutional thought has vanished all but completely, still has a very real and human meaning today, this is largely due to Shakespeare. It is he who has eternalized that metaphor. He has made it not only the symbol, but indeed the very substance and essence of one of his greatest plays: *The Tragedy of King Richard II* is the tragedy of the King's Two Bodies.

Perhaps it is not superfluous to indicate that the Shakespearian Henry V, as he bemoans a king's twofold estate, immediately associates that image with King Richard II. King Henry's soliloquies precede directly that brief intermezzo in which he conjures the spirit of his father's predecessor and to the historic essence of which posterity probably owes that magnificent ex-voto known as the Wilton Diptych.[8]

> Not to-day, O Lord!
> O! not to-day, think not upon the fault
> My father made in encompassing the crown.
> I Richard's body have interr'd anew,
> And on it have bestow'd more contrite tears,
> Than from it issu'd forced drops of blood. (IV, i, 312–17)

Musing over his own royal fate, over the king's two-natured being, Shakespeare's Henry V is disposed to recall Shakespeare's Richard II, who—at least in the poet's concept—appears as the prototype of that 'kind of god that suffers more of mortal griefs than do his worshippers'.

It appears relevant to the general subject of this study, and also otherwise worth our while, to inspect more closely the varieties of royal 'duplications' which Shakespeare has unfolded in the three bewildering central scenes of *Richard II*. The duplications, all one, and all simultaneously active, in Richard —'Thus play I in one person many people' (V, v, 31) are those potentially present in the King, the Fool, and the God. They dissolve, perforce, in the Mirror. Those three prototypes of 'twin-birth' intersect and overlap and interfere with each other continuously. Yet, it may be felt that the 'King' dominates in the scene on the Coast of Wales (III, ii), the 'Fool' at Flint Castle (III, iii), and the 'God' in the Westminster scene (IV, i), with Man's wretchedness as a perpetual companion and antithesis at every stage. Moreover, in each one of those three scenes we encounter the same cascading: from divine kingship to kingship's 'Name', and from the name to the naked misery of man.

Gradually, and only step by step, does the tragedy proper of the King's Two Bodies develop in the scene on the Welsh coast. There is as yet no split in Richard when, on his return from Ireland, he kisses the soil of his kingdom and renders that famous, almost too often quoted, account of the loftiness of his royal estate. What he expounds is, in fact, the indelible character of the king's body politic, god-like or angel-like. The balm of consecration resists the power of the elements, the 'rough rude sea', since

> The breath of worldly man cannot depose
> The deputy elected by the Lord. (III, ii, 54–5)

Man's breath appears to Richard as something inconsistent with kingship. Carlisle, in the Westminster scene, will emphasize once more that God's Anointed cannot be judged 'by inferior breath' (IV, i, 128). It will be Richard himself who 'with his own breath' releases at once kingship and subjects (IV, i, 210), so that finally King Henry V, after the destruction of Richard's divine kingship, could rightly complain that the king is 'subject to the breath of every fool'.[9]

When the scene (III, ii) begins, Richard is, in the most exalted fashion, the 'deputy elected by the Lord' and 'God's substitute . . . anointed in his sight' (I, ii, 37). Still is he the one that in former days gave 'good ear' to the words of his crony, John Busshy, Speaker of the Commons in 1397, who, when addressing the king, 'did not attribute to him titles of honour, due and accustomed, but invented unused termes and such strange names, as were rather agreeable to the divine maiestie of God, than to any earthly potentate'.[10] He still appears the one said to have asserted that the 'Laws are in the King's mouth, or sometimes in his breast', and to have demanded that 'if he looked at anyone, that person had to bend the knee'. He still is sure of himself, of his dignity, and even of the help of the celestial hosts, which are at his disposal.

> For every man that Bolingbroke hath press'd . . . ,
> God for his Richard hath in heavenly pay
> A glorious angel. (III, ii, 58, 60–1)

This glorious image of kingship 'By the Grace of God' does not last. It slowly fades, as the bad tidings trickle in. A curious change in Richard's attitude—as it were, a metamorphosis from 'Realism' to 'Nominalism'—now takes place. The Universal called 'Kingship' begins to disintegrate; its transcendental 'Reality', its objective truth and god-like existence, so brilliant shortly before, pales into a nothing, a *nomen*. And the remaining half-reality resembles a state of amnesia or of sleep.

> I had forgot myself, am I not king?
> Awake thou coward majesty! thou sleepest,
> Is not the king's name twenty thousand names?
> *Arm, arm, my name!* A puny subject strikes
> At thy great glory. (III, ii, 83–7)

This state of half-reality, of royal oblivion and slumber, adumbrates the royal 'Fool' of Flint Castle. And similarly the divine prototype of gemination, the God-man, begins to announce its presence, as Richard alludes to Judas' treason :

> Snakes, in my heart-blood warm'd, that sting my heart!
> Three Judases, each one thrice worse than Judas! (III, ii, 131–2)

It is as though it has dawned upon Richard that his vicariate of the God Christ might imply also a vicariate of the man Jesus, and that he, the royal 'deputy elected by the Lord', might have to follow his divine Master also in his human humiliation and take the cross.

However, neither the twin-born Fool nor the twin-born God are dominant in that scene. Only their nearness is forecast, while to the fore there steps the body natural and mortal of the king :

> Let's talk of graves, of worms and epitaphs . . . (III, ii, 145ff)

Not only does the king's manhood prevail over the godhead of the Crown, and mortality over immortality; but, worse than that, kingship itself seems to have changed its essence. Instead of being unaffected 'by Nonage or Old Age and other natural Defects and Imbecilities', kingship itself comes to mean Death, and nothing but Death. And the long procession of tortured kings passing in review before Richard's eyes is proof of that change :

> For God's sake let us sit upon the ground,
> And tell sad stories of the death of kings—
> How some have been deposed, some slain in war,
> Some haunted by the ghosts they have deposed,
> Some poisoned by their wives, some sleeping killed;
> *All murdered*—for within the hollow crown
> That rounds the mortal temples of a king,
> Keeps Death his court, and there the antic sits
> Scoffing his state and grinning at his pomp,
> Allowing him a breath, a little scene,
> To monarchize, be feared, and kill with looks,
> Infusing him with self and vain conceit,
> As if the flesh which walls about our life,
> Were brass impregnable : and humoured thus,
> Comes at the last, and with a little pin
> Bores through his castle wall, and farewell king ! (III, ii, 155–70)

The king that 'never dies' here has been replaced by the king that always dies and suffers death more cruelly than other mortals. Gone is the oneness of the body natural with the immortal body politic, 'this double Body, to which no Body is equal'. Gone also is the fiction of royal prerogatives of any kind, and all that remains is the feeble human nature of a king :

> mock not flesh and blood
> With solemn reverence, throw away respect,
> Tradition, form, and ceremonious duty,
> For you have but mistook me all this while :
> I live with bread like you, feel want,
> Taste grief, need friends—subjected thus,
> How can you say to me, I am a king? (III, ii, 171–7)

The fiction of the oneness of the double body breaks apart. Godhead and manhood of the King's Two Bodies, both clearly outlined with a few strokes, stand in contrast to each other. A first low is reached. The scene now shifts to Flint Castle.

The structure of the second great scene (III, iii) resembles the first. Richard's kingship, his body politic, has been hopelessly shaken, it is true; but still there remains, though hollowed out, the semblance of kingship. At least this might be saved. 'Yet looks he like a king', states York at Flint Castle (III, iii, 68); and in Richard's temper there dominates, at first, the consciousness of his royal dignity. He had made up his mind beforehand to appear a king at the Castle :

> A king, woe's slave, shall kingly woe obey. (III, iii, 210)

He acts accordingly; he snorts at Northumberland who has omitted the vassal's and subject's customary genuflection before his liege lord and the deputy of God :

> We are amazed, and thus long have we stood
> To watch the fearful bending of thy knee,
> Because we thought ourself thy lawful king :
> And if we be, how dare thy joints forget
> To pay their awful duty to our presence? (III, iii, 72–7)

The 'cascades' then begin to fall as they did in the first scene. The celestial hosts are called upon once more, this time avenging angels and 'armies of pestilence', which God is said to muster in his clouds—'on our behalf' (III, iii, 85f). Again the 'Name' of kingship plays its part :

> O, that I were as great
> As is my grief, or lesser than my *name* ! (III, iii, 136–7)

> Must [the king] lose
> The *name* of king? a God's *name*, let it go. (III, iii, 145–6)

From the shadowy name of kingship there leads, once more, the path to new disintegration. No longer does Richard impersonate the mystic body of his subjects and the nation. It is a lonely man's miserable and mortal nature that replaces the king as King :

> I'll give my jewels for a set of beads :
> My gorgeous palace for a hermitage :
> My gay apparel for an almsman's gown :
> My figured goblets for a dish of wood :
> My sceptre for a palmer's walking-staff :
> My subjects for a pair of carved saints,
> And my large kingdom for a little grave,
> A little little grave, an obscure grave. (III, iii, 147–54)

The shiver of those anaphoric clauses is followed by a profusion of gruesome images of High-Gothic *macabresse*. However, the second scene—different from the first—does not end in those outbursts of self-pity which recall, not a Dance of Death, but a dance around one's own grave. There follows a state of even greater abjectness.

The new note, indicating a change for the worse, is struck when Northumberland demands that the king come down into the base court of the castle to meet Bolingbroke, and when Richard, whose personal badge was the 'Sun emerging from a cloud', retorts in a language of confusing brightness and terrifying puns :

> Down, down I come like glist'ring Phaethon :
> Wanting the manage of unruly jades. . . .
> In the base court? Base court, where kings grow base,
> To come at traitors' calls, and do them grace.
> In the base court? Come down? Down court! down king!
> For night-owls shriek where mounting larks should sing.
>
> (III, iii, 178–83)

It has been noticed at different times how prominent a place is held in *Richard II* by the symbolism of the Sun, and occasionally a passage reads like the description of a Roman *Oriens Augusti* coin (III, ii, 36–53).[11] The Sun imagery, as interwoven in Richard's answer, reflects the 'splendour of the catastrophe' in a manner remindful of Brueghel's *Icarus* and Lucifer's fall from the empyrean, reflecting also those 'shreds of glow. . . . That round the limbs of fallen angels hover'. On the other hand, the 'traitors' calls' may be reminiscent of the 'three Judases' in the foregoing scene. In general, however, biblical imagery is unimportant at Flint Castle : it is saved for the Westminster scene. At Flint, there is another vision which, along with foolish Phaethons and Icari, the poet now produces.

> I talk but idly, and you laugh at me,

remarks Richard (III, iii, 171), growing self-conscious and embarrassed. The sudden awkwardness is noticed by Northumberland, too :

> Sorrow and grief of heart
> Makes him speak fondly like a frantic man. (III, iii, 185)

Shakespeare, in that scene, conjures up the image of another human being, the Fool, who is two-in-one and whom the poet otherwise introduces so often as counter-type of lords and kings. Richard II plays now the roles of both : fool of his royal self and fool of kingship. Therewith, he becomes somewhat less than merely 'man' or (as on the Beach) 'king body natural'. However, only in that new role of Fool—a fool playing king, and a king playing fool—is Richard capable of greeting his victorious cousin and of playing to the end, with Bolingbroke in genuflection before him, the comedy of his brittle and dubious kingship. Again he escapes into 'speaking fondly', that is, into puns :

> Fair cousin, you debase your princely knee,
> To make the base earth proud with kissing it. . . .
> Up, cousin, up—your heart is up, I know,
> Thus high (*touching his own head*) at least, although your
> knee be low. (III, iii, 190–1, 194–5)

The jurists had claimed that the king's body politic is utterly void of 'natural Defects and Imbecilities'. Here, however, 'Imbecility' seems to hold sway. And yet, the very bottom has not been reached. Each scene, progressively, designates a new low. 'King body natural' in the first scene, and 'Kingly Fool' in the second : with those two twin-born beings there is associated, in the half-sacramental abdication scene, the twin-born deity as an even lower estate. For the 'Fool' marks the transition from 'King' to 'God', and nothing could be more miserable, it seems, than the God in the wretchedness of man.

As the third scene (IV, i) opens, there prevails again—now for the third time—the image of sacramental kingship. On the Beach of Wales, Richard himself had been the herald of the loftiness of kingship by right divine; at Flint Castle, he had made it his 'program' to save at least the face of a king and to justify the 'Name', although the title no longer fitted his condition; at Westminster, he is incapable of expounding his kingship himself. Another person will speak for him and interpret the image of God-established royalty; and very fittingly, a bishop. The Bishop of Carlisle now plays the *logothetes*; he constrains, once more, the *rex imago Dei* to appear :

> What subject can give sentence on his king?
> And who sits here that is not Richard's subject? . . .
> And shall the figure of God's majesty,
> His captain, steward, deputy-elect,
> Anointed, crowned, planted many years,
> Be judged by subject and inferior breath,
> And he himself not present? O, forfend it, God,
> That in a Christian climate souls refined
> Should show so heinous, black, obscene a deed !
>
> 　　　　　　　　　　　　　　(IV, i, 121-2, 125-31)

Those are, in good mediaeval fashion, the features of the *vicarius Dei*. And it likewise agrees with mediaeval tradition that the Bishop of Carlisle views the present against the background of the Biblical past. True, he leaves it to Richard to draw the final conclusions and to make manifest the resemblance of the humbled king with the humbled Christ. Yet, it is the Bishop who, as it were, prepares the Biblical climate by prophesying future horrors and foretelling England's Golgotha :

> Disorder, horror, fear, and mutiny
> Shall here inhabit, and this land be called
> The field of Golgotha and dead men's skulls. (IV, i, 142-4)

The Bishop, for his bold speech, was promptly arrested; but into the atmosphere prepared by him there enters King Richard.

When led into Westminster Hall, he strikes the same chords as the Bishop, those of Biblicism. He points to the hostile assembly, to the lords surrounding Bolingbroke :

> Did they not sometimes cry 'all hail' to me?
> So Judas did to Christ : But He, in twelve,
> Found truth in all, but one : I in twelve thousand, none.
>
> 　　　　　　　　　　　　　　(IV, i, 169-71)

For the third time the name of Judas is cited to stigmatize the foes of Richard. Soon the name of Pilate will follow and make the implied parallel unequivocal. But before being delivered up to his judges and his cross, King Richard has to 'un-king' himself.

The scene in which Richard 'undoes his kingship' and releases his body politic into thin air, leaves the spectator breathless. It is a scene of sacramental solemnity, since the ecclesiastical ritual of undoing the effects of consecration is no less solemn or of less weight than the ritual which has built up the sacramental dignity. Not to mention the rigid punctilio which was observed at the ousting of a Knight of the Garter or the Golden Fleece,[12] there had been set a famous precedent by Pope Celestine V who, in the Castel Nuovo at Naples, had 'undone' himself by stripping off from his body, with his own hands, the insignia of the dignity which he resigned—ring, tiara, and purple. But whereas Pope Celestine resigned his dignity to his electors, the College of Cardinals, Richard, the hereditary king, resigned his office to God— *Deo ius suum resignavit.* The Shakespearian scene in which Richard 'undoes himself with hierophantic solemnity', has attracted the attention of many a critic, and Walter Pater has called it very correctly an inverted rite, a rite of degradation and a long agonizing ceremony in which the order of coronation is reversed.[13] Since none is entitled to lay finger on the Anointed of God and royal bearer of a *character indelibilis*, King Richard, when defrocking himself, appears as his own celebrant:

> Am I both priest and clerk? well then, amen. (IV, i, 173)

Bit by bit he deprives his body politic of the symbols of its dignity and exposes his poor body natural to the eyes of the spectators:

> Now mark me how I will undo myself:
> I give this heavy weight from off my head,
> And this unwieldy sceptre from my hand,
> The pride of kingly sway from out my heart;
> With mine own tears I wash away my balm,
> With mine own hands I give away my crown,
> With mine own tongue deny my sacred state,
> With mine own breath release all duteous oaths:
> All pomp and majesty do I foreswear. . . . (IV, i, 203–11)

Self-deprived of all his former glories, Richard seems to fly back to his old trick of Flint Castle, to the role of Fool, as he renders to his 'successor' some double-edged acclamations. This time, however, the fool's cap is of no avail. Richard declines to 'ravel out his weaved-up follies', which his cold-efficient foe Northumberland demands him to read aloud. Nor can he shield himself behind his 'Name'. This, too, is gone irrevocably:

> I have no name....
> And know not now what name to call myself. (IV, i, 254ff)

In a new flash of inventiveness, he tries to hide behind another screen. He creates a new split, a chink for his former glory through which to escape and thus to survive. Over against his lost outward kingship he sets an inner kingship, makes his true kingship to retire to inner man, to soul and mind and 'regal thoughts':

> You may my glories and my state depose,
> But not my griefs, still am I king of those. (IV, i, 192–3)

Invisible his kingship, and relegated to within: visible his flesh, and exposed to contempt and derision or to pity and mockery—there remains but one parallel to his miserable self: the derided Son of man. Not only Northumberland, so Richard exclaims, will be found 'damned in the book of heaven', but others as well:

> Nay, all of you, that stand and look upon me,
> Whilst that my wretchedness doth bait myself,
> Though some of you, with Pilate, wash your hands,
> Showing an outward pity; yet you Pilates
> Have here delivered me to my sour cross,
> And water cannot wash away your sin. (IV, i, 237)

It is not at random that Shakespeare introduces here, as antitype of Richard, the image of Christ before Pilate, mocked as King of the Jews and delivered to the cross. Shakespeare's sources, contemporary with the events, had transmitted that scene in a similar light.

At this hour did he (Bolingbroke) remind me of Pilate, who caused our Lord Jesus Christ to be scourged at the stake, and afterwards had him brought before the multitude of the Jews, saying, 'Fair Sirs, behold your king!' who replied, 'Let him be crucified!' Then

Pilate washed his hands of it, saying, 'I am innocent of the just blood.' And so he delivered our Lord unto them. Much in the like manner did Duke Henry, when he gave up his rightful lord to the rabble of London, in order that, if they should put him to death, he might say, 'I am innocent of this deed.'[14]

The parallel of Bolingbroke–Richard and Pilate–Christ reflects a widespread feeling among the anti-Lancastrian groups. Such feeling was revived, to some extent, in Tudor times. But this is not important here; for Shakespeare, when using the biblical comparison, integrates it into the entire development of Richard's misery, of which the nadir has as yet not been reached. The Son of man, despite his humiliation and the mocking, remained the *deus absconditus*, remained the 'concealed God' with regard to inner man, just as Shakespeare's Richard would trust for a moment's length in his concealed inner kingship. This inner kingship, however, dissolved too. For of a sudden Richard realizes that he, when facing his Lancastrian Pilate, is not at all like Christ, but that he himself, Richard, has his place among the Pilates and Judases, because he is no less a traitor than the others, or is even worse than they are : he is a traitor to his own immortal body politic and to kingship such as it had been to his day :

> Mine eyes are full of tears, I cannot see. . . .
> But they can see a sort of traitors here.
> Nay, if I turn mine eyes upon myself,
> I find myself a traitor with the rest :
> For I have given here my soul's consent
> T'undeck the pompous body of a king. . . .
>   (IV, i, 244, 246–50)

That is, the king body natural becomes a traitor to the king body politic, to the 'pompous body of a king'. It is as though Richard's self-indictment of treason anticipated the charge of 1649, the charge of high treason committed by the *k*ing against the *K*ing.

This cleavage is not yet the climax of Richard's duplications, since the splitting of his personality will be continued without mercy. Once more does there emerge that metaphor of 'Sun-kingship'. It appears, however, in the reverse order, when Richard breaks into that comparison of singular imagination :

> O, that I were a mockery king of snow,
> Standing before the sun of Bolingbroke,
> To melt myself away in water-drops! (iv, i, 260–2)

But it is not before that new Sun—symbol of divine majesty throughout the play—that Richard 'melts himself away', and together with his self also the image of kingship in the early liturgical sense; it is before his own ordinary face that there dissolves both his bankrupt majesty and his nameless manhood.

The mirror scene is the climax of that tragedy of dual personality. The looking-glass has the effects of a magic mirror, and Richard himself is the wizard who, comparable to the trapped and cornered wizard in the fairy tales, is forced to set his magic art to work against himself. The physical face which the mirror reflects, no longer is one with Richard's inner experience, his outer appearance, no longer identical with inner man. 'Was this the face?' The treble question and the answers to it reflect once more the three main facets of the double nature—King, God (Sun), and Fool:

> Was this the face
> That every day under his household roof
> Did keep ten thousand men?
> Was this the face
> That, like the sun, did make beholders wink?
> Was this the face, that faced so many follies,
> And was at last outfaced by Bolingbroke? (iv, i, 281–6)

When finally, at the 'brittle glory' of his face, Richard dashes the mirror to the ground, there shatters not only Richard's past and present, but every aspect of a super-world. His catoptromancy has ended. The features as reflected by the looking-glass betray that he is stripped of every possibility of a second or super-body —of the pompous body politic of king, of the God-likeness of the Lord's deputy elect, of the follies of the fool, and even of the most human griefs residing in inner man. The splintering mirror means, or is, the breaking apart of any possible duality. All those facets are reduced to one: to the banal face and insignificant *physis* of a miserable man, a *physis* now void of any metaphysis whatsoever. It is both less and more than Death. It is the *demise* of Richard, and the rise of a new body natural.

BOLINGBROKE   Go, some of you, convey him to the Tower.
RICHARD   O, good! convey? conveyors are you all,
    That rise thus nimbly by a great king's fall. (IV, i, 316f)

PLOWDEN   Demise is a word, signifying that there is a Separation
    of the two Bodies; and that the Body politic is conveyed over
    from the Body natural, now dead or removed from the Dignity
    royal, to another Body natural.[15]

The Tragedy of King Richard II has always been felt to be a
political play. The deposition scene, though performed scores of
times after the first performance in 1595, was not printed, or not
allowed to be printed, until after the death of Queen Elizabeth.
Historical plays in general attracted the English people, especially
in the years following the destruction of the Armada; but
Richard II attracted more than the usual attention. Not to speak
of other causes, the conflict between Elizabeth and Essex
appeared to Shakespeare's contemporaries in the light of the conflict between Richard and Bolingbroke. It is well known that in
1601, on the eve of his unsuccessful rebellion against the Queen,
the Earl of Essex ordered a special performance of *Richard II*
to be played in the Globe Theatre before his supporters and the
people of London. In the course of the state trial against Essex
that performance was discussed at some length by the royal
judges—among them the two greatest lawyers of that age, Coke
and Bacon—who could not fail to recognize the allusions to the
present which the performance of that play intended. It is likewise well known that Elizabeth looked upon that tragedy with
most unfavorable feelings. At the time of Essex' execution she
complained that 'this tragedy had been played 40 times in open
streets and houses', and she carried her self-identification with
the title character so far as to exclaim : 'I am Richard II, know
ye not that?'
Richard II remained a political play. It was suppressed under
Charles II in the 1680s. The play illustrated perhaps too overtly
the latest events of England's revolutionary history, the 'Day of
the Martyrdom of the Blessed King Charles I' as commemorated
in those years in the Book of Common Prayer.[16] The Restoration
avoided these and other recollections and had no liking for that
tragedy which centered, not only on the concept of a Christ-like

martyr king, but also on that most unpleasant idea of a violent separation of the King's Two Bodies.

It would not be surprising at all had Charles I himself thought of his tragic fate in terms of Shakespeare's *Richard II* and of the king's twin-born being. In some copies of the *Eikon Basilike* there is printed a lament, a long poem otherwise called *Majesty in Misery*, which is ascribed to Charles I and in which the unfortunate king, if really he was the poet, quite obviously alluded to the King's Two Bodies:

> With my own power my majesty they wound,
> In the King's name the king himself uncrowned.
> So does the dust destroy the diamond.[17]

SOURCE : *The King's Two Bodies* (1957).

NOTES

32 footnoes in the original are here shortened to 17.

1. *King Henry V*, IV, i, 254ff.
2. Dr. John Cowell, *The Interpreter or Booke Containing the Signification of Words* (Cambridge, 1607), s.v. 'King (*Rex*)', also s.v. 'Prerogative', where Plowden is actually quoted.
3. Joseph Kitchin, *Le Court Leete et Court Baron* (London, 1580), fol. 1r-v, referring to the case of the Duchy of Lancaster.
4. Richard Crompton, *L'Authoritie et Jurisdiction des Courts de la Maiestie de la Roygne* (London, 1954), fol. 134r-v, reproducing on the basis of Plowden the theory about the Two Bodies in connection with the Lancaster case.
5. See Bacon's *Brief Discourse Touching the Happy Union of the Kingdoms of England and Scotland*, in J. Spedding, *Letters and Life of Francis Bacon* (London, 1861–74), III, 90ff.
6. A. P. Rossiter, *Woodstock* (London, 1946), p. 238.
7. *Woodstock*, v, vi, 34f, ed. Rossiter, p. 169.
8. V. H. Galbraith, 'A New Life of Richard II', *History*, XXVI (1942), p. 237ff.
9. See also *King John*, III, iii, 147–8 :

> What earthly name to interrogatories
> Can task the free breath of a sacred king?

10. This is reported only by Holinshed; see W. G. Boswell-Stone, *Shakespeare's Holinshed* (London, 1896), p. 130; Wilson, 'Introduction', p. lii. The *Rotuli Parliamentorum* do not refer to the speech of John Busshy, in 1397.

11. For Richard's symbol of the 'Rising Sun', see Paul Reyher, 'Le symbole du soleil dans la tragédie de Richard II', *Revue de l'enseignement des langues vivantes*, XI (1923), pp. 254–60. The 'sunne arysing out of the clouds' was actually the banner borne by the Black Prince; Richard II had a sun shining carried by a white hart, whereas his standard was sprinkled with ten suns 'in splendor' with a white hart lodged; see Lord Howard de Walden, *Banners, Standards, and Badges from a Tudor Manuscript in the College of Arms* (De Walden Library, 1904), figs. 4, 5, 71.

12. The ecclesiastical *Forma degradationis* was, on the whole, faithfully observed; see the Pontifical of William Durandus (ca. 1293–5), III, c.7, §§21–24, ed. M. Andrieu, *Le pontifical romain au moyen-âge* (Studi e testi, LXXXVIII, Rome, 1940), III, 607f and Appendix IV, pp. 68of. The person to be degraded has to appear in full pontificals, then the places of his chrismation are rubbed with some acid; finally 'seriatim et sigillatim detrahit [episcopus] illi omnia insignia, sive sacra ornamenta, que in ordinum susceptione recepit, et demum exuit illum habitu clericali. . . .'

13. See p. 58 above.

14. The passage is found in the *Chronique de la Traïson et Mort de Richard II*, ed. B. Williams, *English Historical Society*, 1846, and in Creton's French metrical *History of the Deposition of Richard II*, ed. J. Webb, *Royal Society of the Antiquaries* (London, 1819). A fifteenth-century English version, which has been rendered here, was edited by J. Webb, in *Archaeologia*, XX (1824), 179. See, on those sources, Wilson, 'Introduction', lviii, cf. xvi f and 211. The crime of treason would naturally evoke the comparison with Judas. The comparison with Pilate was likewise quite common (see, e.g., Dante, *Purg.*, XX, 91), though his role was not always purely negative.

15. Plowden, *Reports*, 233a.

16. See *Richard II*, xvii, edited by John Dover Wilson, and *The Stage History of* Richard II, lxxix, by Harold Child, both in the Cambridge *Works of Shakespeare* (Cambridge, 1939).

17. According to Rosemary Freeman, *English Emblem Books* (London, 1948), 162, n. 1, the poem was first printed in the *Eikon Basilike*, edition of 1648.

J. A. Bryant Jr

THE LINKED ANALOGIES OF
RICHARD II (1957)

However one looks at it now, *Richard II* seems to mark a kind of transition in Shakespeare's development as a dramatic poet. To his contemporaries it may very well have seemed a relatively tame performance after the exciting combination of historical material and Senecan villainy in *Richard III* and the lyrical movement of his sophisticated *Romeo and Juliet*. For us, it is perhaps easier to see that Shakespeare had reached a terminus of sorts in both of these early plays. *Romeo and Juliet* is something that we should not willingly part with, but we should be reluctant to acquire many more like it. For that matter, a play surpassing *Romeo and Juliet* in its kind almost defies the imagination. Of possible plays like *Richard III*, also perfect in its way, one specimen is quite enough. And so it is with plays like *Comedy of Errors*, *Love's Labour's Lost*, and *Titus Andronicus*. Shakespeare, by the time he came to write *Richard II*, had proved that he was capable of achieving as much perfection as was desirable in several of the more important dramatic forms that his predecessors had sketched out for him. It remained for him to show that he had something new to offer, either by producing a startling innovation in form or by offering a new idea of drama. We can be grateful that he left the first of these alternatives to his younger contemporary Ben Jonson, whose surer sense of structure enabled him to produce innovations that found few imitators mainly because he himself did all that could conceivably be done with them. Shakespeare's great contribution was the rediscovery of an ancient and all but forgotten path for drama. That he too had few followers is regrettable, but hardly his fault. Even now we come stumblingly to a definition of what it was he found. Tragedy, since Bradley, looms large in our eye, and we still tend to define Shakespeare's achievement in relation to that. The value of *Richard II*, we are sometimes tempted to say, lies in its anticipations of characterizations yet to come, Brutus, Hamlet, and Macbeth. So it does, but not exclusively there. What really sets this remarkable play sharply apart from Shakespeare's own earlier work and the work of all his contemporaries is an approach—demonstrable in most of his later work quite without regard to formal classification—which reveals Shakespeare clearly as a poet with a metaphysical turn of mind, capable of seeing the particular event both as something unique and as something participating in a universal web of analogy. We find next to nothing of this in the *Henry VI* plays, in *Comedy of Errors*, in *Love's Labour's Lost*, in *Romeo and Juliet*, or in *Richard III*, which, for all its slick dramaturgy, remains a play about Richard III, at its farthest conceivable extension a warning to would-be usurpers and tyrants. It is in *Richard II*, a play popularly and rightly famous for one passage in glorification of England, that Shakespeare manages for the first time to extend his field of reference to include everybody.

The kind of seeing which this new approach to material requires is illustrated in that scene in Act II in which the Queen betrays an inclination to see more in Richard's going to Ireland than a mere separation. Bushy, with more common sense than foresight, tries to persuade the lady that simple sorrow has distorted her judgment and made her look upon perfectly normal situations as if they were ingenious *trompes-l'oeil*,

> . . . perspectives, which rightly gaz'd upon
> Show nothing but confusion, ey'd awry
> Distinguish form; so your sweet Majesty,
> Looking awry upon your lord's departure,
> Find shapes of grief, more than himself, to wail;
> Which, look'd on as it tis, is nought but shadows
> Of what it is not. (II, ii, 18–24)

Bushy would have her look squarely at the event and accept it at face value. The Queen, however, is not easily comforted. 'It may be so,' she replies; 'but yet my inward soul/ Persuades me it is otherwise.' She happens to be right, of course; history makes her right. But Shakespeare gives her kind of vision at least as much vindication as history does. If we may believe some of the critics who have written about it, *Richard II* contains much that is un-assimilated, contradictory, and without especial significance. That is, if we look at the play 'rightly', in Bushy's sense, we see in it at least a partial failure to achieve complete control over the historical materials. Perhaps this is so. Nevertheless, if we take a hint from Richard's Queen and eye the play awry (as, for example, in our recollection of it), it has a way of subtly distin-guishing a form that tends to pull all the seemingly irrelevant parts together and make the whole meaningful as no chronicle before it, dramatic or nondramatic, had ever been.

Some writers have attributed this 'informed quality' of *Richard II* to Shakespeare's conscious or unconscious depend-ence upon an analogy with ritual. Among those who have acknowledged the importance of ceremony and ritual in the play is E. M. W. Tillyard, who devotes several illuminating pages of his *Shakespeare's History Plays* (see pp. 131–51 above) to the matter; but Tillyard sees ceremony only as part of the data of the play, an attribute of Richard and his medieval kingship, which Bolingbroke is about to destroy. One might say that Tillyard looks at the play 'rightly', in Bushy's sense. J. Dover Wilson, on the other hand, following some remarks by Walter Pater, has observed in his edition that *Richard II* stands so remarkably close to the Catholic service of the Mass that it ought to be played throughout as ritual. Hardier critics than Wilson have gone still further and made out cases for relating the play to ancient fertility rites, some of which, like their Christian counter-parts, present remarkably close analogies with this play. For example, of the four types of fertility ritual in which F. M. Cornford found a significant tendency toward drama (*The Origin of Attic Comedy*, London, 1914, p. 53 ff.), three show a resemblance to the action of this play which is too striking to be ignored. In one of these, which Cornford calls 'The Carrying Out of Death', the sin of a whole kingdom is symbolically purged with the death of a single victim. In another, 'The Fight of Summer and Winter', winter personified as an evil antagonist is defeated by the representative of summer. In a third, perhaps the most suggestive of all, the old king, or old year, having grown evil through decay, is deposed and replaced by the new.

Suggestive as all these examples of ritual are, however, they have only the most doubtful kind of connection with plays of the Elizabethan theater; for as far as responsible investigators have been able to tell, the theater which Shakespeare inherited was a lineal descendant of neither folk rite nor Christian ritual. It is much more sensible to explain whatever ritual movement we find in *Richard II* as something Shakespeare himself achieved— partly by analogy with existing ritual perhaps, but achieved by himself—in the process of shaping a particular event from chronicle history into a living poetic symbol. In that sense, it may be said that he imported into English drama something that it had not inherited legitimately—or, to revert to our first meta- phor, he rediscovered for drama an almost forgotten path, impossible for most but vastly rewarding for those few capable of using it. The question to be asked and answered is, how did he happen to stumble upon it? One cannot answer such a question with finality. Shakespeare's own profound sense of analogy must, of course, provide nine tenths of any answer anyone might suggest; and the presence in England of a powerful Christian ritual, revitalized by half a century of intermittently vigorous opposition, certainly had something to do with it. But in addition to these aspects of Shakespeare's achievement, one other, related to both and yet isolable in its own right, commands attention; and that is his persistent use of Biblical story as analogue for his secular fable. In *Richard II* this aspect confronts us from begin- ning to end.

The most obvious manifestation of it is the identification of Richard with Christ, which happens to be an historical one. Shakespeare makes explicit use of it first in Act III, when he makes Richard refer to Bushy, Bagot, and Green as 'Three Judases, each one thrice worse than Judas!' (III, ii, 132). In Act IV, of course, there is considerably more of this sort of thing. There the Bishop of Carlisle warns that if Bolingbroke ascends the throne, England shall be called 'The field of Golgotha and dead men's skulls' (IV, i, 144). And Richard observes of Boling- broke's supporters :

> ... I well remember
> The favours of these men. Were they not mine?

> Did they not sometime cry, 'All hail !' to me?
> So Judas did to Christ; but He, in twelve,
> Found truth in all but one; I, in twelve thousand, none.
>   (IV, i, 167–71)

A bit farther on he calls his enemies by another name :

> . . . some of you with Pilate wash your hands
> Showing an outward pity; yet you Pilates
> Have here deliver'd me to my sour cross,
> And water cannot wash away your sin. (IV, i, 239–42)

This set of allusions, familiar even to casual students of the play,
serves admirably to point up Richard's own view of the situation
and also to underline effectively the official Elizabethan view that
(in the language of the *Homilies*) 'The violence and injury that
is committed against aucthoritie is committed against God. . . .'
A second set of allusions, equally familiar, begins with Gaunt's
reference to 'This other Eden, demi-paradise', which gets its
proper qualification somewhat later in the Garden scene of Act
III, when the Gardener's man describes England as a 'sea-
walled garden' choked with weeds and the Gardener himself
receives the Queen's rebuke for presuming to accuse Richard of
negligence :

> Thou, old Adam's likeness, set to dress this garden,
> How dares thy harsh rude tongue sound this unpleasing news?
> What Eve, what serpent, hath suggested thee
> To make a second fall of cursed man? (III, iv, 73–6)

Here with these allusions a second attitude, not exclusively
Elizabethan, is underscored : viz., that the king, as himself man,
is responsible to God for the right use of sovereignty, both by
defending true religion and the honest subject and by punishing
the wicked.

Taken together these two sets of allusions give us a double
image of Richard—Richard *microchristus* and Richard *micro-
cosmos*, Richard the Lord's Anointed and Richard Everyman.
This, of course, is simply the conventional Elizabethan double
image of kingship and would not of itself be particularly startling
were it not for the additional suggestion of a pattern that unfolds

as the play proceeds. The Golgotha of which Carlisle speaks does indeed come to pass. Richard rides to London with many to throw dust upon his head but none to cry, 'God save him!' Despised and rejected, he languishes at Pomfret, only to face his executioners with such a manifestation of regality in death that Exton, like the centurion at the foot of the cross (who said of Jesus, 'Truly this man was the Son of God.'—cf. *Matt.* 27 :54; *Mark* 15 : 39), is compelled to acknowledge it :

> As full of valour as of royal blood !
> Both have I spill'd; O would the deed were good !
> For now the devil, that told me I did well,
> Says that this deed is chronicled in hell. (v, v, 114–17)

Even Bolingbroke, to whom Richard alive was a 'living fear', is moved to say :

> Though I did wish him dead,
> I hate the murder, love him murdered. (v, vi, 39–40)

Perhaps some Elizabethans, long accustomed to hearing and seeing typological interpretations of Scripture, saw in this combination of allusion and historical fable a kind of significance that we are likely to overlook. What Shakespeare was giving them in this presentation of Richard as a sort of Adam–Christ was nothing less than a typological interpretation of history. In Scripture the fall and death of the First Adam is corrected and atoned for by the sacrificial death of the Second (see *Romans* 5 : 12–21). That is, Adam's disobedience and death is an anticipatory realization of a pattern that achieved its complete historical realization only in the perfect obedience and death of Jesus of Nazareth, with whose resurrection a way was cleared for Adam (and all those who had sinned in Adam) to escape the full consequence of death. From the typologist's point of view this pattern, perfectly symbolized by one Adam's atonement for the other's sin, is the eternal principle of which all history is in one way or another but the spelling out. Whether he realized it or not at the time, Shakespeare, in laying the outlines of such a complex and richly suggestive symbol against the surface of his chronicle material, had given to secular fable a significance that it had achieved only rarely in drama since the days of Aeschylus and

Sophocles. To paraphrase Dryden, he had affected the metaphysical in his treatment of it. Moreover, having underscored
that revolutionary affectation by utilizing ceremonial in his play,
by presenting ceremonially much that was not strictly ceremony,
and by freqently alluding to the symbolic substance of analogous pagan ritual (sun and ice, summer and winter, etc.), he
had also produced a work which 'eyed awry' strongly suggests
an analogy with ritual.

Seeing a ritualistic aspect in a play, however, is not the same
as identifying it with ritual or attempting to play it as ritual. To
see Richard as a ritual type of Adam–Christ is certainly
warranted by Shakespeare's text, but to see him exclusively as
that is to see Bolingbroke exclusively as Satan–Judas; and this
is certainly *not* warranted by the text. The leading question of
the play is not simply 'What is true kingship?' but 'What is the
true king? What is the Lord's Anointed?' Mere ritual is power-
less to answer this question, and history and the *Homilies* do
little better. Shakespeare could expect his audience to know the
report of history that both Richard and the Lancastrian usurper
in their turns possessed the title of 'Lord's Anointed' and could
expect them accordingly to stand with Gaunt when he says rue-
fully near the beginning of the play :

> God's is the quarrel; for God's substitute,
> His deputy anointed in His sight,
> Hath caus'd his death; the which if wrongfully,
> Let Heaven revenge.... (I, ii, 37–40)

He could assume that the judgment of York on Bolingbroke in
Act II would be accepted as appropriate by loyal Englishmen
everywhere :

> My lords of England, let me tell you this :
> I have had feeling of my cousin's wrongs
> And labour'd all I could to do him right;
> But in this kind to come, in braving arms,
> Be his own carver and cut out his way,
> To find our right with wrong—it may not be;
> And you that do abet him in this kind
> Cherish rebellion and are rebels all. (II, iii, 140–7)

Similarly, he could let York's pained acquiescence in Bolingbroke's accession to the throne serve as an appropriate public
moral for the play as a whole : '. . . Heaven hath a hand in these
events,/ To whose high will we bow our calm contents' (v, ii,
37–8). Yet there is something less than a martyr's acquiescence
in Richard's famous metaphor for the historic turnabout :

> Now is this golden crown like a deep well
> That owes two buckets, filling one another,
> The emptier ever dancing in the air,
> The other down, unseen, and full of water.
> That bucket down and full of tears am I,
> Drinking my griefs, whilst you mount up on high. (iv, i, 184–9)

The conclusion startles Bolingbroke into saying, 'I thought you
had been willing to resign.' And Richard replies with three lines
that would be uncomfortably out of place in a play reduced to
the level of ritual :

> My crown I am; but still my griefs are mine.
> You may my glories and my state depose,
> But not my griefs; still am I king of those.

Here Richard is undoubtedly already thinking of himself as a
betrayed and repudiated Christ, moving ahead to a sour cross
while the Pilates stand about washing their hands. The role
evidently delights him, and he plays it well. Nevertheless, we
should notice that the role is one he has himself discovered, not
one that has come looking for him. We should also notice that
Shakespeare cast Richard initially in quite another role, which
he plays equally well, in spite of himself, and which temporarily
at least disqualifies him as a spotless victim.

The Richard that Shakespeare sets before us at the beginning
of the play is not only God's Anointed but a man guilty, ultimately if not directly, of his uncle's death. He knows that no one
has proved his guilt, and he thinks that no one, except Aumerle
of course, knows exactly what the details of Woodstock's death
were. Yet Bolingbroke, in the very first scene, pronounces the
murdered man Abel and his murderer by implication Cain :

> . . . like a traitor coward,
> Sluic'd out his innocent soul through streams of blood;
> Which blood, like sacrificing Abel's, cries,
> Even from the tongueless caverns of the earth,
> To me for justice and rough chastisement;
> And, by the glorious worth of my descent,
> This arm shall do it, or this life be spent. (I, i, 102-8)

What Bolingbroke does not realize is that his condemnation and threat of revenge, hurled at the innocent Mowbray, are applicable only to Richard. The Cain he really seeks, however unwittingly, sits on the throne before him and wears the robes of the Lord's Anointed. And ironic as this situation is, it becomes even more ironic when we think of the ancient identification of Abel with Christ and of Cain with the disbelieving Jews who slew him. In Shakespeare's time there was nothing particularly esoteric about such an identification. The New Testament provides ample authority for it (*Matt.* 23:25 and *Heb.* 11:4; 12–24); there is a reference to it in the Canon of the Mass; and frequent use of it is made in the writings of the Church Fathers. Among Shakespeare's audience there must have been at least a few who had encountered it in contemporary exegetical works and a great many who knew about it from pictorial representations in the familiar *Biblia Pauperum.* Yet even if the identification of Richard–Christ with Richard–Cain escaped the audience entirely, the primary application of Bolingbroke's allusion to the story of Cain and Abel could hardly have escaped them. They all knew well enough what had happened to Woodstock and who was directly responsible for it, and they could not have missed the implication that Richard secretly bore the curse of Cain. A second allusion to the murder of Woodstock, however, completes the identification. It is Gaunt who makes this one:

> O, spare me not, my brother Edward's son,
> For that I was his father Edward's son.
> That blood already, like the pelican,
> Hast thou tapp'd out and drunkenly carous'd. (II, i, 124-7)

Here we have one of our oldest symbols for the Savior, the pelican mother who feeds the young with her own blood, inverted by Gaunt to make an accusation against the young king. That is, Richard, who should have been the parent pelican of the figure, prepared to nourish his brood with his own life if need be, is here accused of having caroused on the blood of another (Woodstock), leaving his young to fare for themselves. Perhaps Shakespeare's audience missed this allusion too. No one can say for sure about that. The important point is that Shakespeare put it there; and with it the chain of analogies, as Shakespeare conceived it, seems complete : Richard–Christ–antichrist–Cain, all are linked as one.

But what of Bolingbroke, who also assumes the role of the Lord's Anointed before the play is complete? After Cain had killed his brother, God put his mark on the fugitive murderer and decreed that no vengeance be taken upon him. The traditional Christian explanation for God's prohibition against revenge in this case was that satisfaction for Abel's blood was to be expected only with the advent of 'Jesus, the mediator of the new covenant, and . . . the blood of sprinkling, that speaketh better things than that of Abel' (*Hebrews* 12 : 24). Bolingbroke, in proclaiming himself the avenger of a murdered Abel, was using a figure of speech, to be sure, but he was nevertheless presuming to make right in his own way something that mere man can never make right. In other words, he was presuming to do something that even as *microchristus* he could not expect to accomplish without committing the same sin he would avenge. The place of Bolingbroke in the action of the play is perhaps clear enough without the use of Biblical allusion, but such allusion can help us state it : Bolingbroke's story is that of a man who sets out to slay the murderer Cain and does so, only to find that he has the blood of Abel on his hands.

Richard II, then, if it is to be compared to ritual, must be compared to some of the pagan rituals we know, and not to any Christian ritual. The allusions point to a clear, unambiguous analogy with Christ for neither of the principals. Each is a *microchristus* with a specifically human blind spot, a failure to see that kingship, like human nature generally, involves both a crown and a potential Cain who wears the crown. Each discovers, among other things, that the crown is never enough to make the wearer immune to the consequences of being human, but each finds in his turn that the crown can be an eloquent teacher. The crown is a well of instruction, and Richard gets his in the process of descending. From the moment he sets foot on English soil after his return from Ireland, he alternately gropes for and rejects the knowledge which he fully possesses only in the hour of his death at Pomfret. There, breeding thoughts, setting Scripture against Scripture, and imaginatively assuming and repudiating all sorts and conditions of mankind, he comes at last to the flat truth,

> Nor I nor any man that but man is
> With nothing shall be pleas'd, till he be eas'd
> With being nothing. (v, v, 39–41)

At this moment, ironically, he achieves his most kingly stature and in physical weakness poses his greatest threat to Bolingbroke, who at almost the same time receives a similar enlightenment on the way up. Up to the moment of his coronation Bolingbroke has never once thought of the terrifying efficacy that regal power confers upon human impulses. As Bolingbroke he could wish Richard dead and bury the guilt of the wish in his own soul. As Henry he must learn that even a whispered wish is a powerful command. That he wished Richard dead is now enough to make Richard dead, and the blood of Richard is upon him. Turning upon Pierce of Exton, who held the actual dagger, he condemns him in the words of innocent Mowbray:

> With Cain go wander through the shades of night,
> And never show thy head by day nor light. (v, vi, 43–4)

But the Mowbray who once left England 'To dwell in solemn shades of endless night' (i, iii, 177) now rests in Abraham's bosom and was never Cain. The two lines that follow are at once sober and plaintive:

> Lords, I protest, my soul is full of woe
> That blood should sprinkle me to make me grow.

And with these lines we come full circle. The great Biblical-metaphysical framework of allusion that began with Bolingbroke's reference to the murder of Abel has encompassed the fable and returned to its starting point. We can now state the questions of the play in terms of the analogies that define them : Who is the Cain? Who, the Christ? Can one avenge Abel with becoming Cain? Can Cain dwell with Christ in the same golden well?

Such questions as these inevitably arise whenever a great dramatic poet lays the relatively clear-cut distinctions of mythic pattern against the disorderly flux of human affairs. It makes little difference whether the poet particularizes his myth and so brings it to the status of history (as the Greeks frequently did) or brings to the particularity of chronicle history the outlines of a more ancient imitation. The result is the same. In either case we find good and evil, innocence and guilt, so inextricably mixed that human ingenuity cannot say for sure where the dividing line is. As in the ancient fertility rites and in the Christian mass, we tend to find slayer and slain, old king and new king, Cain and Christ, united in one human frame. There is no other solution in purely human terms. And the bewildered protagonist who suddenly sees the unresolvable paradox in his human situation can only cry out, as Bolingbroke does :

> Lords, I protest my soul is full of woe
> That blood should sprinkle me to make me grow.

SOURCE : *Sewanee Review*, 65 (1957).

M. M. Mahood

WORDPLAY IN *RICHARD II* (1957)

When Dogberry, briefing his Watch in the third act of *Much Ado*, commands them to 'bid any man stand in the Princes name', he is met by the disconcerting question 'How if a will not stand?' The same problem, in a historic instead of a comic context, confronts the Duke of York at Bolingbroke's return from banishment, and like Dogberry he has to let the invader pass when the magic of the royal name fails to work. The King's power which lies in York's 'loyal bosom' is only verbal authority, not material strength. Shakespeare's plays have many characters who, like Harry Hereford and the watchman of Messina, question the power of words; if the sixteenth century as a whole preserved a medieval faith in verbal magic, it had also its Sancho Panzas who knew that fine words buttered no parsnips, its Hotspurs who could call up spirits from the vasty deep but took leave to doubt if they would come when so called. It was to be expected that Hotspur, a verbal sceptic, would also be a political rebel. For ultimately, in a process that took some two centuries, the question 'What's in a name?' was to destroy Authority. To doubt the real relationship between name and nominee, between a word and the thing it signified, was to shake the whole structure of Elizabethan thought and society.[1]

Richard II is a play about the efficacy of a king's words. Shakespeare here sets 'the word against the word' : the words of a poet against the words of a politician. Richard is a poet, but not, of course, for the reason that as a character in a poetic drama he speaks verse which is magnificent in its imagery and cadence. If the whole play were in prose, he would still be a poet by virtue of his faith in words; his loss of this faith and his consequent self-discovery that for all the wordy flattery of others he is not agueproof, constitute Richard's tragedy. Bolingbroke, on the

other hand, knows words have no inherent potency of meaning,
but by strength of character and force of arms he is able to make
them mean what he wants them to mean. The historical, as distinct from the tragic, action of the play lies in Bolingbroke's
perilous contravention of the divine decree which made Richard
king; and this historical action is not self-contained but belongs
to the whole sequence of the mature Histories.

These two themes are supported and often impelled by the
play's verbal ambiguities which nearly all have to do with language. The words most often played upon include *breath* in the
meaning of 'respiration', 'life', 'time for breathing', 'utterance'
and 'will expressed in words';[2] *title* in meanings ranging from
'legal right', through 'appellation of honour' to 'a label'; *name*
either as a superficial labelling or as inherent reputation; *honour*
in a range of meanings to be further developed when Falstaff
answers his own question: 'What is honour? a word!'; *tongue*
as the mere organ that makes sounds or as the whole complex
organisation of a language; *sentence* meaning 'a unit of speech',
'judgment', 'an apophthegm' or 'significance'; and the word
word itself, signifying on the one hand 'an element of speech'
and on the other, 'contention', 'command', 'promise', 'apophthegm' or 'divine utterance'. The almost polar extremes of meaning in many of these words contribute to the rigid symmetry of
the play's action, the descent of Richard and rise of Bolingbroke
like buckets in a well. At the same time, the most delicate nuances
of meaning between these extremes are used to give a poetic
subtlety which can only be suggested here in a brief survey of the
play's development.

I

Shakespeare uses his favorite device of a play-within-a-play at
the very beginning of *Richard II*. As soon as the playhouse
trumpet has sounded and the actors are entered Richard, with
his own triple blast of resonant language, stages a miniature
drama between Bolingbroke and Mowbray, which he promises
himself shall be a good show :

> Then call them to our presence face to face,
> And frowning brow to brow our selues will heare,
> The accuser and the accused freely speake.[3] (I, i, 15–17)

The poet is never more a maker than when he enacts the very semblance of life in a play; and the poet Richard combines the work of producer and chief actor when he attempts to stage, by royal command, a drama of quarrel and reconciliation in which he himself will play the controlling part of *deus ex machina*. But Bolingbroke and Mowbray, for all the splendour of their rhetoric, are not content with words. They are in such haste to make their accusations good by their deeds, that the words themselves take on the nature of action: Bolingbroke stuffs the name of traitor down Mowbray's throat; Mowbray, as he spits out his counter-challenge, retaliates by cramming these terms of abuse *doubled* down Bolingbroke's. Each detail of Bolingbroke's charge is prefaced by his resolve to verify his words with deeds:

> Looke what I speake, my life shall proue it true . . .
>
> Besides I say, and will in battle proue . . .
>
> Further I say and further will maintaine . . . (87, 92, 98)

His last accusation, that Mowbray complotted in the murder of the Duke of Gloucester, whose blood

> like sacrificing Abels cries,
> Euen from tounglesse Cauernes of the earth, (104–5)

lends ironic support to Bolingbroke's belief that deeds speak louder than words. Shakespeare's audience, whether or not they had seen *Thomas of Woodstock*, would know that Richard was implicated in Gloucester's death and that Richard's own murder was a proof of the belief that blood would have blood; but as the instigator of Richard's death, Bolingbroke calls upon himself that curse of Cain which he pronounces against Exton at the end of the play.[4]

The king has no wish to see Mowbray's guilt exposed by a trial of arms, and he attempts to end this scene of quarrel by his own trite epilogue on the theme of 'Forget, forgive'. But neither contestant will swallow his words. Mowbray's 'fair *name*' is more to him than an appellation: it is his reputation, the dearest part of him—'Mine honour is my life, both grow in one.' Bolingbroke will not be *crestfallen*: unless he can prove his words in battle, he has no right to the armorial bearings which signify his nobility.

The words of both are pitted against the king's words, and by force of character they carry the day. The king who was 'not borne to sue, but to commaund' must wait until the meeting at Coventry for his decree in Council to carry the authority which his own words lack.

A dancing tattoo of language accompanies the flourishes and fanfares of trumpets at the Coventry lists. There is a gaiety of rhythm and image in the farewell speeches of Mowbray and Bolingbroke; both speak of the approaching fight as a feast, both are savouring this chance to prove by action the truth of their words. But the King asserts the authority of his word in Council, the fight is called off and the champions banished the kingdom. At this point Mowbray, not an important character in the plot, is given a significant speech full of puns upon *breath*, *sentence* and *tongue*—words which shuttle back and forth to weave the elaborate verbal fabric of the play. In contrast to the 'golden vncontrould enfranchisment' promised by the contest, he now faces an enforced inactivity among people whose language he cannot speak. The irony of this becomes clear in the fourth act, when a noisy and abortive war of words between the nobles is silenced by Carlisle's account of how Mowbray in fact led a life of honourable action after his banishment:

> Manie a time hath banisht Norffolke fought,
> For Iesu Christ in glorious Christian feild,
> Streaming the ensigne of the Christian Crosse,
> Against black Pagans, Turkes, and Saracens,
> And toild with workes of warre, retird him selfe
> To Italie, and there at Venice gaue
> His bodie to that pleasant Countries earth,
> And his pure soule vnto his Captaine Christ,
> Vnder whose coulours he had fought so long. (iv, i, 92–100)

Placed as they are in the play, these lines strengthen its symmetry of action. As Bolingbroke's star rises, he himself declines in our estimation; as the fortunes of Richard and his friends deteriorate they win new regard and sympathy from the audience. When this praise of Mowbray's 'pure soul' is spoken, Bolingbroke is king, and this gives the words a further ironic value. Throughout his reign Bolingbroke will long to expiate his usurpation in a crusade, but that hope is destroyed when he fulfils a quibbling prophecy by dying in 'Jerusalem'—the Jerusalem Chamber at Westminster.

The first climax of the play is reached at Coventry. The King plays with the power of the royal word by changing the years of Bolingbroke's banishment from ten to six. It is a dramatic instant, the moment when, with Richard at the height of his power and Bolingbroke at the lowest reach of his fortunes, the buckets begin to move; for Bolingbroke seems suddenly to comprehend and covet the efficacy of a king's words:

> How long a time lies in one little *word*,
> Foure lagging winters and foure wanton springes,
> End in a *word*, such is the *breath* of Kinges. (I, iii, 213–15)

By Elizabethan analogy the breath of the king should be a life-giving force, a human imitation of the Divine Spirit; but whereas Bolingbroke's reaction to the king's words is the envious acknowledgment of their god-like power, Gaunt sees only the king's human limitations and speaks of them in words which echo Bolingbroke's, but with subtle differences of meaning:

> Thou canst helpe time to furrow me with age,
> But stoppe no wrinckle in his pilgrimage :
> Thy *word* is currant with him for my death,
> But dead, thy kingdome cannot buy my *breath*. (229–32)

The court leaves. Gaunt tries to console Bolingbroke with empty words that bear no relation to his real thoughts, while his son cannot find words that are adequate to his grief,

> When the tongues office should be prodigall
> To breathe the aboundant *dolor* of the heart. (256–7)

The pun is less trivial than it seems; Bolingbroke will be found to be much concerned with the *value* of words, which for him lies only in the actuality of the things they signify. Words for him can never make or obscure facts. When Gaunt bids him call his exile 'a *trauaile* that thou takst for pleasure' and a '*foyle* wherein thou art to set, The pretious Iewell of thy home returne', Bolingbroke takes up *travel* in its harsher sense of 'travail' and *foil* in the meaning 'frustration, obstacle' to fashion the bitter word-play of his reply :

> Must I not serue a long apprentishood,
> To forreine passages, and in the end,
> Hauing my freedome, boast of nothing else,
> But that I was a *iourneyman* to griefe. (271–4)

At the end of the scene, the contrast between the outlooks of father and son is formalised into two rhetorical speeches. Gaunt sententiously proclaims that there is no virtue but necessity, and Bolingbroke, who knows the real meaning of Richard's sentence, cries out against such deceptive verbiage :

> Oh who can hold a fier in his hand,
> By thinking on the frosty Caucasus? (294–5)

This is just what Richard, who has always been deceived by the seeming power of words, will strive to do when his fortunes turn. Bolingbroke, although he is not to be so deceived, uses the conceptual power of words to snare others; and Richard implies this when he describes his cousin's departure after his banishment :

> Our self and Bushie,
> Obserued his *courtship* to the common people,
> How he did seeme to diue into their harts,
> With humble and familiar *courtesie*,
> What *reuerence* he did throw away on slaues,
> Wooing poore craftsmen with the *craft* of smiles
> And patient *vnder-bearing* of his fortune
> As twere to *banish their affects* with him. (i, iv, 23–30)

Bolingbroke's double-dealing is implicit in the choice of words here. *Courtship* may be a serious attempt to gain affection, or mere bowing and scraping; *courtesy* can be an innate virtue, *la politesse du cœur*, or a formal curtsey ('Me rather had my hart might feele your loue, Then my vnpleased eie see your curtesie' Richard says to Bolingbroke at Flint Castle); *reverence* is likewise either the deepest regard or the outward sign of a respect which may or may not exist; and *craft* can be either the craftsman's admirable skill or a deplorable cunning. The last two lines can be interpreted in two ways. Either they mean 'making so

light of his troubles that he seemed not to want people to worry
about him'—the superficial appearance of Bolingbroke's behaviour—or they mean 'supporting great sorrow so bravely that he
has taken their love into exile with him'—the actuality of the
scene for both Bolingbroke and the populace. All the dangerous
power of Bolingbroke's 'candied courtesy' is here made vivid in
a few words.[5]

At Coventry, Gaunt protested that the King's words which
should, in the nature of things, give life to their country, could
deal only death; and at the beginning of Act II Gaunt himself
dies, uttering with his last breath words which would be life to
both King and kingdom if only Richard would heed them. We
are made aware of the depth and weight of the language in this
scene by the way Shakespeare has framed it between two pieces
of dialogue in which words are identified with life : the opening
quibbles on *breath* and *breathe* :

GAUNT   Wil the King come that I may *breathe* my last?
        In holsome counsell to his vnstaied youth.
YORKE   Vex not your selfe, nor striue not with your *breath*,
        For all in vaine comes counsell to his eare.
GAUNT   Oh but they say, the tongues of dying men,
        Inforce attention like deepe harmony :
        Where words are scarce they are seldome spent in vaine,
        For they breathe truth that breathe their wordes in paine,
                                                        (II, i, 1–8)

and the announcement of Gaunt's death :

NORTHUMBERLAND   My liege, old Gaunt commends him to your
        Maiestie.
KING   What saies he?
NORTHUMBERLAND   Nay nothing, all is said :
        His tongue is now a stringlesse instrument,
        Words, life, and al, old Lancaster hath spent. (147–51)

The Sceptred Isle speech has a much richer meaning within this
sharply-defined context than when it is extracted for a patriotic
set piece, and it is worth seeing what are the elements that go to
its composition. 'This earth of maiestie, this seate of Mars' fits in
with the garden theme which is a *motif* of the play from its first

hints in the opening scenes (Gaunt's pun about 'unstaied youth'
—giddy, or unpropped—at the beginning of the present scene
being one) to its full statement in Act III, scene iv. Here the
garden is that of Eden[6] symbolic of security ('this fortresse built
by Nature') and of fertility ('this happy breede . . . this teeming
wombe of royall Kings'). But we do not expect to find Mars in
Eden; and this same line—'This earth of maiestie, this seate of
Mars' operates in another way by introducing a string of paradoxes and oxymora. *Earth* can be mere soil or the great globe
itself,[7] *seat* is any stool till Mars makes it a throne, *stone* would
be any pebble if the restrictive adjective did not make it a jewel.
The effect is of something which might appear without value but
is in fact of untold value, and 'this *dear dear* land' sharpens the
paradox : what is dear in the sense that it is loved cannot be dear
in the sense that it is priced for sale. By this time a third element
has been introduced : England's rulers are

> Renowned for theyr deeds as far from home,
> For christian seruice, and true chiualry,
> As is the sepulchre in stubburne Iewry,
> Of the worlds ransome blessed Maries sonne. (53–6)

Gaunt may mean that some of England's kings have won fame
fighting to regain Jerusalem, the kind of fame which his son will
crave throughout his reign. But the grammatical ambiguity of
the passage also yields the meaning that their virtues have made
the English kings as famous as the sepulchre of Christ. Then,
after the point at which most quotations end (short of a main
verb), this King–Christ parallel, the garden-of-Paradise image
and the paradoxes upon the theme of value are all brought
together in a powerful climax :

> This land of such deare soules, this deere deere land,
> Deare for her reputation through the world,
> Is now leasde out ; I dye pronouncing it,
> Like to a tenement or pelting Farme. (57–60)

What is beyond all value has been valued and leased. The king,
whose relation to his kingdom should be that of God to Paradise,
who ought to 'regain the happy seat' has, instead of redeeming
it (and here I suspect some Herbertish wordplay on the legal

sense of *redemption*[8]), jeopardised its security and fertility by farming it out. The God–King analogy is a real one to Gaunt who has already been shown, in the second scene of the play, to have such belief in the divine right of kings that he 'may neuer lift An angry arme against his minister'. Yet he knows how little there is of the godlike in Richard's nature, and his bitter awareness of this gap between the ideal and the actual passes to the audience and later conditions our response to Richard's 'dear earth' speech over the land he has farmed out, or to his identification of himself with the betrayed and condemned Christ at a further stage of the drama.

From the profound wordplay of this speech to Gaunt's quibbles on his own name may seem a sharp descent; but the 'Gaunt as a grave' puns have a force which the king acknowledges when he asks 'Can sicke men play so *nicely* with their names?' *Nicely* means 'subtly' as well as 'trivially'. Gaunt's pun is not only true to the trivial preoccupations of the dying; it also reminds us of the play's dominant theme, the relationship between names and their bearers. Gaunt is saying in effect: 'I am true to my name, Gaunt, but you are not true to the name you bear of King'. Besides this, *gaunt* in the sense of 'wasted' prepares us for his long speech of remonstrance, in which wordplay underlines that relationship between the spiritual health of the king and the well-being of his kingdom which was a living concept for the Elizabethans, and which has been revived for us in the writings of modern anthropologists. Here the most telling puns are upon *possessed* and *verge*. If the king had attained self-government, were in possession of his kingdom of the mind, he would possess and not squander his wider inheritance; but the disorder of his mind within the verge (or rim) of his crown matches the external disorder that reigns through the *verge*— that part of the country, within a twelve-mile radius of the king himself, which fell immediately under the royal jurisdiction.

This by no means exhausts the puns with which Gaunt endeavours to pack the most meaning into the few words left for him to utter. But his efforts are in vain. Richard seizes Bolingbroke's estates and leaves for Ireland. Northumberland, Ross and Willoughby remain to sound each other's feelings from behind the cover of verbal ambiguities: 'My heart is *great* but it

must *breake* with silence' says Ross, and the other lords take this
in its oblique sense that his courage is high and he needs must
speak his thoughts. Soon they are sure enough of each other to
appreciate Northumberland's

> We see the wind sit sore vpon our sailes,
> And yet we *strike* not, but securely perish, (266–7)

and the scene ends with their resolve to

> Wipe off the dust that hides our Scepters *guilt*,
> And make high Maiestie looke like it selfe, (294–5)

which could be either a promise to reclaim Richard or a threat
to overthrow him. It depends how we read *gilt*—and it is a pun
which Shakespeare is seldom able to resist.

II

The scenes of Bolingbroke's progress through Gloucestershire
and of Richard's landing in Wales balance each other in the
play's symmetrical action. This is the point at which the two
buckets in a well pass each other. From Northumberland's ful-
some praise, we gather that Bolingbroke has beguiled the tedium
of their journey by the same charm of tongue that he exercised
upon the citizens at his departure. His reply to this flattery is,
however, short and meaningful: 'Of much lesse value is my
company, Then your good wordes.' Unlike Richard, who
believes in the extensional power of words and that the bearer
of them will really be paid on demand, Bolingbroke knows his
words of promise to his supporters to be pure speculation. There
is nothing in the bank, but if the speculation succeeds it will
bring him in a wealth of power and authority :

> all my treasury
> Is yet but vnfelt thanks, which more inricht,
> Shal be your loue and labours recompence.
> ROSSE Your presence[9] makes vs rich, most noble Lord.
> WILLOUGHBY And far surmounts our labour to attaine it.
> BULLINGBROOKE Euermore thanke's the exchequer of the poore.
> Which till my infant fortune comes to yeares,
> Stands for my bounty. (ii, iii, 60–7)

York's wordy rejection of his nephew's courtesies—

grace me no grace, nor vnckle me no vnckle,
I am no traitors Vnckle, and that word Grace
In an vngratious mouth is but prophane (87–9)

—implies what *Henry IV* confirms: that Bolingbroke's words
are in fact as blank as Richard's charters. Bolingbroke has, however, enough military strength to carry York along with him on
the tide of rebellion; and by the time Bristol Castle is taken,
Bolingbroke's fair words have won him the power to speak with
regal authority in his sentence upon Bushy and Green. His words,
unlike those of Richard, are no sooner said than done. The terse
'See them *dispatcht*' means 'Send them away, see they are
executed and hurry up about it'. Such is the breath of kings—but
such death-dealing is not the breath of a true king; and the Pilate
image with which Bolingbroke washes his hands of the two
minions' blood shifts our sympathy towards Richard even while
our admiration mounts for Bolingbroke.

Meanwhile Richard has landed on the Welsh coast, unconscious of the fact that his glory is falling 'like a shooting star' and
confident in the belief that

Not all the water in the rough rude sea,
Can wash the balme off from an annointed King,
The breath of *worldly* men cannot depose,
The deputy elected by the Lord,
For euery man that Bullingbrooke hath *prest*,
To lifte shrewd steele against our golden *crowne*,
God for his Ric : hath in heauenly pay,
A glorious *Angell*; then if *Angels* fight
Weake men must fall, for heauen still gardes the right.
(III, ii, 54–62)

The secondary meaning of *worldly*—'mercenary'—provokes a
shock of dissent with Richard's trust in his divine right. Worldly
men like Bolingbroke, who offer rewards, and worldly men like
Northumberland, who are hungry to be rewarded, can easily
depose the Lord's annointed. The monetary senses of *crown* and
angel, which are prompted by the sub-meaning of 'minted' for
pressed, sustain this threat that might, bought by the promise to
pay, is going to make short work of even divine right.

As the King's real power melts away in the disastrous news
brought by Salisbury and Scroop, he clings hard to the illusory

power of words : first to the power of his name :

> Is not the Kings name twenty thousand names?
> Arme arme, my name a puny subiect strikes,
> At thy great glorie; (III, ii, 85–7)

then to the worn consolations of philosophy, the trite 'sentences'
so fiercely rejected by Bolingbroke in his misfortunes :

> Say, is my kingdome lost? why twas my care,
> And what losse is it to be rid of care? (95–6)

and then to the power of curses against those who have deserted
him :

> Would they make peace? terrible hel,
> Make war vpon their spotted soules for this. (133–4)

Even these words are as futile as the Queen's vain curse upon
the gardener's plants, for Bushy and Green were not traitors.
Words cannot blow out facts, and finally, in a great speech,
Richard acknowledges this. When he sits to tell sad stories of the
deaths of kings he is no longer camouflaging hard truths with
verbal fictions. He is admitting the discovery that the word and
its referent are two things, the self-discovery that he is not all he
has been called; although like the self-discovery of most of
Shakespeare's tragic heroes this comes too late for disaster to be
averted. This is Richard's real abdication. It is also in a sense his
coronation, for he is made a king of griefs by a vision of human
insignificance which carries him far beyond the discovery that
the king is a man as other men are. Like Peer Gynt unpeeling the
onion, Richard goes further than the man beneath the crown,
to find the skull beneath the skin :

> within the hollow *crowne*
> That roundes the *mortall temples* of a king,
> Keepes death his *court*, and there the *antique* sits,
> Scoffing his state and grinning at his pompe,
> Allowing him a *breath*, a litle sceane,
> To monarchise be feard, and kil with lookes,
> Infusing him with selfe and vaine conceit,
> As if this flesh which wals about our life,
> Were brasse impregnable : and humord thus,
> Comes at the last, and with a little pin
> Boares thorough his Castle wall, and farewell King. (160–70)

Crown is both coronet and head, *temples* suggests the king's person (as in 'the Lord's annointed temple') as well as forehead; death is present not only as an external threat of disaster but as the inner inevitability. A further meaning of *temple* introduces the image of death presiding over a *court* of law as well as a royal court. There is an echo here of the verge image in Gaunt's reproaches to the King in Act II, and perhaps also a further echo of Marlowe's 'Death Keeping his circuit' in *Tamburlaine*, for Marlowe's metaphors are fresh in Shakespeare's memory when he is writing *Richard II*. The double meaning of *antic*, a clown as well as a gargoyle or death's head, leads to a further metaphor; the showman Richard finds life reduced to play-acting, a little scene, and that he too is a shadow in this kind. Death appears, as in the morality plays, with mops and mows that parody the king's *mortal* authority. *Mortal* means 'subject to death' as well as 'deadly', and at the last the king's power is shown to be itself a parody and his life a mere breathing-space in the dance of death. The final image takes us back to the Sceptred Isle speech. England, bound in with the triumphant sea, is not impregnable against traitors; no divinity can hedge a king's person from the commonest enemy.

Wordplay and imagery here combine to give a poetic depth, rivalled only by the verse of *Macbeth*, to Richard's discovery that life has lost its meaning. The cliché implies, if we pause to ask what meaning here means, a philosophical experience of the first importance. Richard has discovered that words express only desires and not facts, that to call a man friend does not ensure the reality of friendship, that the name King, despite the sacramental nature of a coronation, does not imbue a man with kingly authority. If Richard were of the stature of Hamlet or Lear this tragic insight would remain clear even at the expense of his sanity, but his temperament cannot bear the sight of such bleak reality for long. He soon begins to draw round it the rags and shreds of appearance, to act the regal role once more—with this difference, that now he knows himself to be acting and that his words carry no effective weight. York's lines, spoken as Richard appears on the battlements of Flint Castle, help to emphasise this element of play-acting in the king's bearing :

Yet lookes he like a King, beholde his eye,
As bright as is the Eagles, lightens forth
Controlling maiestie; alack alacke for woe,
That any harme should staine so faire a *shew*. (III, iii, 68–71)

The King is playing a part throughout the scene at Flint Castle, whether the role is that of offended majesty calling down vengeance upon those who dare to question his sovereignty or the role of a man disillusioned with pomp and power, willing to be buried in the king's highway. The elaborate verbal fancies—'I talke but idlely, and you laugh at me'—reveal that these speeches are not the real humility of Lear. They represent rather Richard's efforts to conceal his revelation from himself as well as others. His true feelings are exposed only for an instant in his cry to Aumerle :

Oh that I were as *great*
As is my griefe, or lesser than my name! (136–7)

A greater character could bear the reality he has glimpsed and now tries to obscure with words; a character less great in the material sense, in authority and reputation, would never have suffered from the illusion that Richard has lost.

The deposition scene, for all its brilliance, adds very little to the total effect of the play. If *Richard II* was ever acted in the mutilated text represented by the first and second Quartos—and the long and rather irrelevant 'gage' scene which precedes the deposition reads like the padding to an abbreviated text—the loss, though serious, cannot have been structural, for the deposition only repeats the contrast, made in the scene at Flint Castle, between the reality of Richard's inward grief and its sham appearance in a profusion of words. From Richard's speech on entry—'Yet I well remember The *fauors* of these men' all the wordplay in the scene serves to intensify the theme of appearance and reality. 'Are you contented to resigne the Crowne?' Bolingbroke asks. Richard's reply :

I, no; *no, I* : for *I* must nothing bee :
Therefore *no, no*, for *I* resigne to thee, (IV, i, 201–2)

besides suggesting in one meaning (Aye, no; no, aye) his tormenting indecision, and in another (Aye—no; no I) the overwrought mind that finds an outlet in punning, also represents

in the meaning 'I know no I' Richard's pathetic play-acting, his
attempt to conjure with a magic he no longer believes. Can he
exist if he no longer bears his right name of King? The mirror
shows him the question is rhetorical but he dashes it to the
ground, only to have Bolingbroke expose the self-deception of
this histrionic gesture :

> The shadow of your Sorrow hath destroy'd
> The shadow of your Face. (292–3)

It is true that the ritual of abdication invented by Richard, his
rhetorical outbursts to Northumberland, the pantomime of the
mirror, are all the shadows of his sorrow. In these speeches,
Richard behaves as if words had value and effective meaning;
whereas the substance of his sorrow is the unseen grief—unseen
because undemonstrable—that no meaning is left in words.
Bolingbroke has acted upon this knowledge ever since his
banishment; and Richard's quibbles before the mirror weigh his
own disastrous self-deception against Bolingbroke's politic decep-
tion of others :

> Is this the Face, which *fac'd* so many follyes,
> That was at last *out-fac'd* by Bullingbrooke? (285–6)

The long duel ends here in a curious sort of truce; both king and
usurper now know there is no way of crossing the gulf between
the world of words and the world of things. The knowledge has
won the throne for Bolingbroke. It has also gained for Richard a
kingly dignity he did not possess as king :

> You may my Glories and my State depose,
> But not my Griefes; still am I King of those. (192–3)

Richard retains this crown till the end of the play. The
Elizabethan belief in the sanctity of kingship is not the only
reason why the callow and capricious figure of the first acts is
shown to die with the dignity of a martyr. Disaster has held up a
mirror to Richard and in it he has glimpsed 'the truth of what
we are'. He himself goes on playing with words, even alone at
Pomfret; but at the motionless centre of this coloured wheel of
language is the still and inescapable knowledge that it is all a
play :

Thus play I in one person many people,
And none contented; sometimes am I King,
Then treasons make me wish my selfe a beggar,
And so I am : then crushing penurie
Perswades me I was better when a king,
Then am I kingd againe, and by and by,
Thinke that I am vnkingd by Bullingbrooke,
And strait am nothing. But what ere I be,
Nor I, nor any man, that but man is,
With nothing shall be pleasde, till he be easde,
With being nothing. (v, v, 31–41)

SOURCE : *Shakespeare's Wordplay* (1957).

NOTES

1. See *Shakespeare's Wordplay*, Chapter VIII, for a fuller discussion of this.
2. The *O.E.D.* gives an illustration from Burns which is apposite here : 'Princes and lords are but the breath of kings'.
3. The quotations from the play in this chapter are from the First Quarto, 1597 (Griggs Facsimile, 1890), except those from the abdication episode in Act IV, for which the Folio text has been used.
4. With Cayne go wander through shades of night,
   And neuer shew thy head by day nor light.
Pace Dr Wilson, this framing of the play's action between two occurrences of the same image almost proves these lines to be Shakespeare's. 'By day nor light' is lame, but not 'merely nonsense' (New Cambridge edn., p. lxx), since it could presumably mean 'by real or artificial light'.
5. If the lines are also taken to refer to Bolingbroke's conduct generally, and not only his leavetaking, 'underbearing of his fortune' can mean 'modest behaviour in spite of his high status'.
6. Milton twice calls Paradise a happy seat.
7. See a valuable article by Richard Altick : 'Symphonic Imagery in *Richard II*', pp. 101–30 above, which gives a full analysis of the play's images and shows how closely they are connected with its wordplay.
8. It would be a concealed pun, but not the only one in the play. See J. Dover Wilson's note on v, i, 13–15.
9. Ross plays insidiously on the commonplace and royal meanings of *presence*.

A. P. Rossiter

UNCONFORMITY IN *RICHARD II* (1961)

The ancients had a thrifty habit of scrubbing parchments and using them again : these written-over documents are called palimpsests. It is a pity that frugal Elizabethan dramatists did not use parchments for play-books : we should not then need to rely on the hazardous ultra-violet of interpretative criticism or the infra-red of critical bibliography, to decide whether to treat a play as a palimpsest or some other kind of problem, such as lack of coherence in its author's mind, divided aims, and the like We only want to know things like this where immediate or considered subjective reaction makes us feel some kind of discontinuity, or inconsistency, in the *stuff* (a vague term, used deliberately : ultimately, the arrangements of words and their effects).

Over *Richard II* most critics have felt this. Pater is an exception : for him it does possess 'like a musical composition . . . a certain concentration of all its parts, a simple continuity, an evenness in execution, which are rare in the great dramatist'.[1] Dover Wilson echoes this; but elsewhere excludes the Fifth Act, which he wants blamed on to one of his 'old plays' : the lucubrations of that Master William Hypothesis, energetic researcher but no poet, who 'assembled' Shakespeare's plots. Other commentators are bothered by inconsistencies or discontinuities; and I share their view. Whether you approach *Richard II* from the angle of the texture of the verse, the verse-styles, character, plot or theme, you encounter what geologists call 'unconformities' :

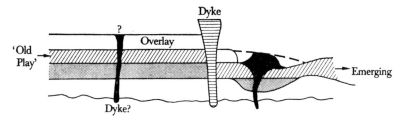

The strata right of the 'dyke' are said to be 'unconformable'; and as geology has an overriding time-scheme, the dykes and upper layers are 'later' than the rest. Applied to a play, it is only a rough analogy; although 'old play' and 'revisionist' theories will accept it as descriptively diagrammatic. I only use it to clarify the word 'unconformable': implying 'the whole *may* be consistent; but only if we have a theory of derangements or interruptions'.

If ours is the character-approach, we find a lack of continuity between the Richard of Acts I and II and the melancholy introvert re-imported from Ireland. Those who praise the play as character-piece most highly, seem to *begin* their reading with Act III; and to 'explain' the autocratic, capricious Richard of the first two acts as an imperious adolescent play-acting. This does not cover up the *lack of inside* in the early Richard; and when Coleridge remarks on 'a constant flow of emotions from a total incapability of controlling them . . . a waste of that energy which should have been reserved for action', he as clearly labels the *second* Richard as he misses the *first*, who shows uncontrolled *action* and a lack of *feeling*. He makes him a Hamlet of the sentiments: i.e. what Coleridge thought 'thought' was to Hamlet, he made emotion to Richard.

Dowden, in a study mainly very sound in what it points to, leaves him as sentimentalist, dreamer and dilettante; with a wistful charm, but condemned morally for want of what Newman called 'seriousness of the intellect: the adult mind'. That at any rate gives a firm line. There is something in Richard which calls out the latent homosexuality of critics; and I am gratified to find Dowden resisting it. Pater is all the other way: Richard is 'an exquisite poet . . . from first to last, in light and gloom alike, able to see all things poetically, to give a poetic turn to his conduct of them' (and so on, to be softly echoed in a dozen school editions). 'What a garden of words!' as Pater says. Others take the diametrically opposite view of exactly the same matter: plainly more from moral than dramatic reasons. And for all but the stern moralists, Richard's physical beauty is almost a main characteristic. You can dodge all contradictions by taking Aristotle's ὁμαλῶς ἀνώμαλον[2]; but, despite Aristotle, I think that such a character cannot be tragic: it surely lacks the perspicuity which makes logic of the tragic action.

About the other characters the critics are fairly agreed. Boling-broke is an outline—a strong one; Gaunt is made rather too much of, considering he is gone by Act III; the Favourites are zeros; York 'an incomparable, an incredible, an unintelligible and a monstrous nullity' (Swinburne) or (G. M. Young) 'the first civil servant in our literature'.[3] (I do not offer these as synonyms.) In short, they are mainly orchestra: Gaunt, the wood-wind Queen, Messengers, marches and noises-off.

If we consider the play's themes, we find that although politi-cal approaches—making the play historical–epical–moral—do something to smooth-in the Duchess of Gloucester (I, ii), the omens, the Gardener and the substance of Gaunt, they cannot make the beginning unragged, nor the rumpus in Westminster Hall (the second Quarrel-scene) clearly relevant; nor do any-thing to put the York–Aumerle scenes into any sort of order or 'degree'. To generalize, most commentators direct attention to parts of the play which they *can* manage, and tacitly divert it from 'misfits' they cannot; and in this there is no great critical difference between 'character' and 'thematic' approaches. Both do vaguely agree in taking measures to smooth over a kind of 'fold' between Acts II and III; and both, in different ways, have difficulties over Shakespeare's not very pellucid method of pre-senting some of the essentials of the story, over the awkward way in which he leaves us to guess here and there, mainly in, or as a result of, Acts I and II. This also applies to his artistic intentions. The view of the play as 'ceremonial'; Dover Wilson's contention that 'it ought to be played throughout as ritual . . . it stands far closer to the Catholic service of the Mass than to Ibsen's *Brand* or . . . *St. Joan*'; the lyrical-tragedy view;[4] the poet-king view: all show a similar smoothing-over of unconformities, once taken back to the text.

If we look at the verse, it is a crude discrimination to say there are three styles: rhyme (mainly couplets) and two sorts of blank verse—that of the Deposition, say, and an 'earlier' kind. The 'early' type in fact ranges from a flattish competence (Act I, or Bolingbroke at v, iii, 1–12, 'Can no man tell me of my unthrifty son? . . .') to a jumbled incompetence, aptly described by York's comment on the state of England at II, ii, 121–2 :

> All is uneven,
> And everything is left at six and seven.

The couplets vary as much, although this is less striking, as Shakespeare wrote within a convention that did not *hear* bad couplets as we hear them; and in Acts I and II especially they pop in and out most disconcertingly. The worst in both kinds, rhyme and blank verse, is distressingly or comically bad. As a *formal* type of play in what Dover Wilson[5] calls 'deliberately patterned speech', it contrasts strikingly with the operatic consistency of *Richard III*.

Examine the texture of the verse, and Eliot's 'patterned speech' *is* there; mainly in the 'early' type of verse, but also in some of the other. It is easiest seen where not very good: where it represents the heavily over-written Elizabethan High-Renaissance manner, over-ingenious with a mainly *verbal* wit, and obtrusive. It is obtrusive, I mean, in Keats's sense: 'Poetry should be great and *unobtrusive*, a thing which enters into one's soul and does not startle or amaze it with itself, but with its subject.'

> e.g. The setting sun, and music at the close,
>   As the last taste of sweets, is sweetest last,
>   Writ in remembrance more than things long past. (II, i, 12–14)

There is a marked degree of what Keats would call 'obtrusiveness' in such writing. Frigid ingenuities accompany it, such as this from Northumberland:

> And hope to joy, is little less in joy
> Than hope enjoy'd. (II, iii, 15)

or the Queen's tortuous lines where she has conceived a grief, and wrenches her imagination to find out what has caused it:

> BUSHY 'Tis nothing but conceit, my gracious lady.
> QUEEN 'Tis nothing less : conceit is still deriv'd
>   From some forefather grief; mine is not so,
>   For nothing hath begot my something grief,
>   Or something hath the nothing that I grieve;
>   'Tis in reversion that I do possess—
>   But what it is that is not yet known what,
>   I cannot name; 'tis nameless woe, I wot. (II, ii, 33–40)

That is really far worse than York's simple Kyd-pattern :

> Grace me no grace, nor uncle me no uncle.
> I am no traitor's uncle; and that word 'grace'
> In an ungracious mouth is but profane. (II, iii, 87–9)

lines all right as patterned, although what follows—'Why have those banish'd and forbidden legs . . .'—is not easily taken seriously.[6]

It is not only that there is more wit in the word-connections than in the thought (and the 'wit', even when called 'metaphysical', is always rather shallow); it is that these 'formal' tricks, like the eruptions of couplets, upset and confuse the *tone* both for reader and actor. Take, for instance, Bolingbroke's lines in III, i, 'Bring forth these men . . .': blank verse in neither the 'early' nor the 'more mature' style, but extremely fluent, very competent, totally without flourish. He has a statement of a heart-felt grievance to make, and he makes it : with force, clarity and cool dignity. Look back at Bolingbroke's lines in Act I, and you see at once how difficult two such disparate manners are for the best of actors.

The result tends to be recitation in a pageant, where dress and décor are everything (bar, of course, Richard). Once again, there is a kind of fold (or 'fault') in the play; Acts I and II are on one side of it, III and IV on the other; and in Act V something comes up to the surface which one is very strongly tempted to call 'half-revised Old Play'. I cannot pretend that the division in verse-texture is as sharp as all that; but the view of the play as 'ceremonial' rests heavily on the Quarrel, the Lists and the 'patriotic' oration of Gaunt; and in Act III there does come a marked change. Richard's

> Well you deserve. They well deserve to have
> That know the strong'st and surest way to get (III, iii, 200–1)

has, for example, in context, a sinewy force, an essential *unobtrusive* poetry, which is totally absent in Acts I and II (say what you will of Gaunt's melodious lamentation on England gone to the dogs).

It is on the assumption of that unconformity of Acts I and II that I shall rest my further examination of the play : accepting, that is, a discontinuity in character; some marked incoherences and dubieties in the story; a related uncertainty in the theme (tragic or political); and more than one kind of inconsistency in the texture of the verse. In so doing, I shall seem to be quarrelling with the 'political' view of the play : that here we have the fall of a rightful king, brought about by wilful rebellion, the lifting of 'an angry arm against God's minister', his Deputy; and that the curse that this brings on Lancaster and England is the uniting theme of an English dramatic-epic, in Shakespeare's peculiar double tetralogy. I am not really refuting the political pattern, although it has been given too much emphasis, and also, I think, made too *simple*. What I really question is the *unity*, the integral quality of the sequence.

Richard II, as the first play, seems to me to have no real beginning; a coherent middle; and a ragged, muddled end, only some of which can be explained as a Shakespearian parallel to the famous 'end-links' of Chaucer. Taken by itself, if we stand back far enough, it does look like the Aristotelean 'simple' tragedy : the sort he thought inferior, having neither *peripeteia* nor any real *anagnorisis*. Richard seems to slip steadily into calamity, mainly through 'force of circumstances'; and his *hamartia* (unless we accept all the Bradleyan critics tell us) is a fatal step, a *blunder*, the mishandling of a quarrel between two violent noblemen. But go near enough to grasp the *action*, sticking tight to the text, and you will find that this alleged first term in a coherently planned series is thoroughly uncertain about its own start, and uncertain at the simplest level of the story, as well as on the major matter of essential (or political) rights and wrongs.

From now on, I shall dogmatize : state my case, and leave it to your verdicts.

Richard II's value as first term in an epic-historical series is seriously flawed by its peculiar dependence on *Woodstock* :[7] peculiar since Shakespeare not only took items from it, but also *left behind* in it explanations badly needed in his play, items taken for granted, or as read, which produce puzzles that cannot be cleared up without reference to the earlier play. To some extent, then, *Richard II* as a play does not contain within itself the reason why it is thus and not otherwise. If so, the alleged epic

scheme is faulty, since the 'beginning' is not a beginning.
Richard II is about the fall and deposition of a King. The fall
results from two events: (*a*) the quarrel of Bolingbroke and
Mowbray, which Shakespeare invites us to focus down to the
pin-point *hamartia* of throwing down the warder in the lists (see
Mowbray's son in *2 Henry IV*, IV, i, 25–9); and (*b*) the falling-
away of York, and all England, on Bolingbroke's landing. This
second event has to do with Richard's failings as monarch: with
'the state of England', which some critics make a main theme,
although (Gaunt's reproaches apart) there is very little about it
in the text. Ross (at II, i, 246) says, 'The commons hath he
pill'd with grievous taxes', but that, as it happens, is a direct
echo from *Woodstock* (I, iii, 112),[8] where 'Plain Thomas', being
mocked about his homespun frieze, says: 'did some here wear
that fashion,/ They would not tax and pill the commons so.' In
short, the connection between favourites and extravagance,
extravagance and exaction, exactions and Richard's loss of
power, is crystal-clear in *Woodstock* and nowhere else. In
Richard II Willoughby takes up Ross with a mention of 'daily
new exactions', 'As blanks, benevolences, and I wot not what';
and we wot not what neither. *Editors* tell us; but the fact is,
there is precious little in Holinshed about 'blanks'; nothing
about 'benevolences' (devised by Edward IV!); and one sentence about a *rumour* 'that the King had set to farme the realme
of England unto sir Wm. Scroope earle of Wiltshire . . . to Sir
Jno. Bushie, sir Jno. Bagot, and sir Hy. Greene knights' (iii, 496,
col. i *ad fin.*). If we look at *Richard II*, taking it as it comes (as
an audience *must*), we find: (1) *Before* Gaunt's accusations,
only one inexplicit line by Richard, 'We are enforc'd to farm our
royal realm' (I, iv, 45); a bit more on blank charters following
it, but no connecting of either with the evil influence of
favourites. (2) It is only 190 lines *after* Gaunt's 'Bound in with
. . . inky blots and rotten parchment bonds', that Ross growls,
'The Earl of Wiltshire hath the realm in farm' (II, i, 256).
(3) *Between* these references lie Gaunt's two nearly-unintelligible
charges: 'rotten parchment bonds' and 'Thy state of law is bond-
slave to the law' (II, i, 64 and 114). The Arden edition notes
show these *are* obscurities: both notes are nonsense.
    Now these things are perfectly clear and straightforward to

anyone who reads *Woodstock*, Acts ii, iii and iv of which are
concerned with the rise to power of the favourites, headed by the
villainous Lord Chief Justice Tresilian; their financial iniquities
when *in* power (iii and iv); and what 'blanks' meant to the
Commons (iv, iii). I can make but one point: the author of
Woodstock scrambles and hashes history to make Richard's
extortions a matter of *legal* iniquity: slavery to bonds, regal
servitude to the law of contract.[9] And he therefore *stages* Richard
presented with a legal instrument (a bond or lease), giving the
favourites full command of the Exchequer and all the royal
estates etc. in exchange for a monthly stipend of £7,000. That
is what Gaunt is alluding to; and the whole difficulty of the
financial wickedness of both Richard and the favourites in
Richard II is simply that Shakespeare *alludes* and never explains.
Nor is that all. Gaunt's accusations are not only explained by
Woodstock: his terms of reproach derive from that text. England
is

> now leas'd out . . .
> Like to a tenement or pelting farm;

and later:

> Landlord of England art thou now, not King.
> Thy state of law is bondslave to the law. (ii, i, 59–60, 113–14)

In *Woodstock*, iv, i, where Richard is presented with the bond,
later read by Tresilian in full, and before the flattering Greene
twists him round to it, Richard has a (cancelled) speech of
apprehension or self-reproach: 'We shall be censured strangely
. . .' (when people think of the Black Prince)

> . . . And we his son, to ease our wanton youth
> Become a landlord to this warlike realm,
> Rent out our kingdom like a pelting farm,
> That erst was held, as fair as Babylon,
> The maiden conqueress to all the world (iv, i, 146)

The term 'landlord' is applied to Richard four times in this play:
inter alia by the Ghost of Edward III:

> Richard of Bordeaux, my accursed grandchild . . .
> Becomes a landlord to my kingly titles,
> Rents out my crown's revenues . . . (v, i, 86 ff);

and by Gaunt himself :

> England now laments . . .
> Her royalties are lost : her state made base;
> And thou no king, but landlord now become
> To this great state that terrored christendom (v, iii, 104 ff)

The emphasis of iteration and the word 'lease' (not in Holinshed) show how Shakespeare's Gaunt has, so to speak, his past
political experience in mind—in a play much rather than a
Chronicle. This is not simply a source-hunter's game : it affects
the whole moral complexion of Richard in Acts I and II, and
alters both the colour of the theme and Shakespeare's reading of
history.

It also bears on what we make of the *personae*, as 'characters'
or as 'symbols' : especially the favourites, but, by repercussion
Gaunt too. In *Richard II* the blank-charter iniquity is less
skimped; but only in *Woodstock* does the wickedness of income-
tax returns signed 'blank' (leaving the collector to invent the
income) receive the emphasis we can call 'normal'. Nor, in
Richard, is the dressy extravagance of favourites and Court
made a clear cause. Shakespeare's Bushy, Greene and Bagot are
nearly 'blank-charters' themselves : once again because they are
taken as *seen* (in their bad habits as they lived—on the stage)
and 'recognised' as shadows of vanity, flattery and contempt of
good counsel, opposed symbolically and morally to what Gaunt
stands for (which is identical with what he and York and
Thomas of Woodstock stood for in *Woodstock* : in flat defiance
of Chronicle and truth). Shakespeare's play leaves us wondering
what vices they had; for apart from Bolingbroke's accusations of
homosexuality (refuted by the Queen's behaviour throughout)
they do not get beyond being a *1066 and All That* 'bad thing'.

Their real evil, which Shakespeare presents only by allusion
is that they *were* the political and moral opposites to Richard's
'good old uncles', all of whom, in both plays, are economy
retrenchment, conservatism, public service and plain-Englishry
A phrase here points incontrovertibly to *Woodstock*. Gaunt's
'My brother Gloucester, plain well-meaning soul' (II, i, 128)
refers solely to the other play. 'Plain homespun Thomas', who
wears frieze at Court and is comically mistaken for a groom by

an overdressed popinjay (III, ii), is, historically, a male Mrs Harris. In Chronicle there is no such person : he is purely a *dramatis persona*, partly modelled on the good Duke Humphrey of *2 Henry VI* and with comparable moral functions. Against Dover Wilson's attempt to extract a 'good' Gaunt from Froissart, I find that Shakespeare's Gaunt is the same 'form' (or 'shadow' in an allegory of State) as Thomas. By this I do not mean that either lacks 'character' : only that moral function, not history, determines their forms.

The most unquestionably historical thing that Woodstock does is to get murdered; and here the events of *Woodstock*, assumed to be known, have their most important bearing on the moral structure of Shakespeare's play : on the character of Richard, the mechanism of his fall, and the essential rights and wrongs behind the quarrel. No one can read *Richard II* and not encounter the problem, 'Who killed Woodstock?' Bolingbroke accuses Mowbray of it; Gaunt tells the Duchess of Gloucester that Richard was responsible; Bagot and Fitzwater say it was Aumerle : they imply, moreover, that the murder took place *after* Bolingbroke was banished, and add that Mowbray said so (IV, i, 80). To say they are all liars is no more than they all say to one another. The whole thing makes sense, and makes the plot of Acts I and II far more coherent, as soon as we know that Woodstock was (1) kidnapped in a masque, with Richard and his favourites present; (2) conveyed to Calais, the Governor of which is called Lapoole in the play, but *was* Thomas Mowbray; and (3) there put to death (in a stirring scene) not by the Governor, but rather against his will, and by two experts in tidy murder sent from England.

Thus in the quarrel, Mowbray knows that Richard knows the truth, and that Bolingbroke knows most of it. Hence Richard's desire to quiet the pair, and his saying *he* will calm Norfolk, while Gaunt calms Bolingbroke. Hence his 'How high a pitch his resolution soars!' (I, i, 109), when Bolingbroke has said that Gloucester's blood cries 'to me for justice and rough chastisement'. Hence, too, the riddling lines where Mowbray says :

... For Gloucester's death—
I slew him not, but to my own disgrace
Neglected my sworn duty in that case. (I, i, 132-4)

Reference to *Woodstock* suggests at once that the allusion is to Act v, i, where Woodstock appeals to Lapoole 'by virtue of nobility' and 'on that allegiance/ Thou ow'st the offspring of King Edward's house' (v, i, 145 f.), when he fears murder. The lines in Shakespeare mean, then, that Mowbray admits he was Governor (which is known to everyone), and that he failed in his sworn duty to protect the blood royal (which again is obvious). But simultaneously he reminds Richard of *why* he failed (Richard threatened his life if Woodstock was not killed), while giving nothing away. For 'I slew him not' is perfectly true of Lapoole himself : Woodstock was killed by agents, and all Lapoole–Mowbray did was not to prevent them.[10]

This criminal collusion with Mowbray *could* supply the motive for the stopping of the single-combat at Coventry. The principle of trial-by-arms is that it gives 'the judgement of God'; and we may plausibly make the induction that Richard is afraid that God will give the right verdict. But it is only a reasonable *induction*, for Shakespeare gives no hint of Richard's motives. Character-critics are content to see here only an exhibition of Richard's exhibitionism : his self-regarding theatricality in the kingly role—even, perhaps, the actor-manager's vanity, in dramatically focusing all eyes on himself and dragging them away from the combatants (like a film-star at a prize-fight). That is there, no doubt : the Deposition-scene supports it, with Richard in a complex pageant of vanity, as the Middle Ages regarded it : stripping himself of kingly vanities, the pomps and glories of temporal rule; gazing in the glass of vanity; and yet, vanity of vanities, still making himself the focus of a dramatic contemplation of the essential human vanity, persistent though the robe is stripped, the mirror shivered.

But this act of throwing down the warder is of fatal consequence : fatal and fateful. From that one act a strict logic of events throws down Plantagenet and, inside ninety years, throws up Tudor. The logic of the eight-play series *and* the exact apprehension of the 'tragedy' demand that we should know if it was *guilt* (and guilt of royal blood) which started this momentous sequence. If not, where is the beginning of the epic-drama? Further back. Then it has no unity. And in this case we cannot delve into *Woodstock* for the answer and come out certain.

We must be satisfied with a fair degree of probability and the absence of final certainty. The explanation of the King's desertion by England is writ large in *Woodstock* : favourites, vanities, extravagances, taxation, extortion, antipathy to sound counsel : all these are kingly vices. The explanation of the quarrel is there too : briefly, 'Woodstock's blood', the wanton murder of a royal prince, epitome of the right-mindedness and political and social responsibility which are expressed in Gaunt. Integrate the causes of Richard's fall, and his confused actions throughout Acts I and II derive from a guilt, or guilts, out of which there is no clear path. Shakespeare knows this—indeed too well : he slips into the lecturer's commonest fault, of assuming that everybody must know what, as it happens, many do *not*. But this applies mainly to the first two acts alone. It explains Richard as he there appears, and explains too why a different Richard arrives from Ireland in Act III. It also suggests why Bolingbroke's intentions about the crown are left rather obscure. I believe that the *historic* fact is that there was a well-contrived conspiracy, leading to a well-timed landing. But Shakespeare took Halle's hint that Bolingbroke had no glimmer of what fate had in store for him : that chance would have him King (as we should say), and so chance crowned him. It is, after all, what he tells Warwick before his death :

> . . . God knows, I had no such intent,
> But that necessity so bow'd the state
> That I and greatness were compell'd to kiss.
> > (2 *Henry IV*, III, i, 72–4)

If, though, we accept the many hints in *Richard II* that Richard was a guilty *King*—and it is the guilt of the King, much rather than the innate wickedness of the man, that *Woodstock* emphasizes—then Bolingbroke's walk-in to kingship is itself one more instance of that process of retributive reaction which is the really *tragic* element in the History plays (the judgement of God in the process of history, as I suppose Professor Butterfield would call it). This retributive reaction, as a divinity that shapes the ends of England, is a principle which makes sense and logic of Bolingbroke's incredibly easy usurpation. Richard is *wrong*, but Bolingbroke's coronation is *not right*; and Richard's murder

converts it to the blackest wrong. This greatly reduces the possibility of regarding Richard as a 'royal martyr' or 'sacrificial-
king'. It should also prevent our making Shakespeare a kind of
sentimental conservative, looking nostalgically back, like Walter
Scott, to the 'great age' of Chivalry and showing us 'the waning
of the Middle Ages'.

It implies a conception, or apprehension, of *history*. If the ills
of England do not begin with Richard's deposition, then there
is a dreary endlessness in this long sample of human affairs,
sometimes cyclical, but always a conspectus of half-blinded
actions and unpremeditated reactions, apparently with neither
end nor beginning. Thus Shakespeare *'ends'* with the triumph of
Henry V, pointing straight to Henry VI and all *that*: 'Another
Troy will rise and rot, another lineage feed the crow.' The effect
is to present the 'historical process' as *obscure tragedy*, in which
men are compelled, constrained, baffled and bent by circumstances in which their actions do *not* express their characters.
Even in *Richard II* there are many light touches of irony, mainly
the irony of frustration: for what makes such tragedy 'obscure'
is a kind of *stupidity* in events (in men and things), something
far more confused and uncertain than Fate or Destiny. Hence
the weariness of both Richard ('Learn, good soul,/ To think our
former state a happy dream': v, i, 17 f.) and King Henry (his
invocation of sleep: 2 *Henry IV*, III, i). The times are always
out of joint: and the weak men, strong men, good men and bad
men who try to re-articulate them, are *all* fumblers, or so com-
promised that their very skill is vain. As Pater said, 'No!
Shakespeare's kings are not, nor are meant to be, great men.'

But if we turn to *Hamlet*, is not that, too, in a different sense,
an 'obscure tragedy'? Obscure, in the sense that *Othello* is not,
nor *Coriolanus*, nor *Antony and Cleopatra*. And though 'the
mystery of things' is heavy enough within *Macbeth* and *Lear*,
they bear the mind beyond that iron curtain which shuts about
the 'History' world. *Hamlet* stands between: and its two worlds
of action and sensibility have their somewhat shadowy counter-
parts in *Richard II*. It is not a dream of 'sensibility' in any way
like Hamlet's: rather, of sentiments, of the sentimentalist, as
defined in Meredith's aphorism, quoted by Stephen Dedalus to
Malachi Mulligan: 'The sentimentalist is he who would enjoy

without incurring the immense debtorship for a thing done.'

The central experience in *Richard II* is its *middle*, the substance of Acts III and IV. The ceremonial or ritual scenes and
styles do matter: although only six scenes out of nineteen can be
called 'ritualistic' or formalized. They matter because of what
they *contrast* with; for in that contrast there is a tonal and visual
rendering of the contrast of Richard and his group and Bolingbroke and his, but more as *Weltanschauungen* or aspects of
human experience than as just 'characters'.

However and whenever *Richard II* is played, the pageant-
element is important (as much for 1955 as for 1595). But this
element is double, not single. After the lists, etc., a new tone
begins to emerge at the end of II, i, in the huddle of sullen earls
plotting together after the fops have gone. Northumberland
emerges there; and a grim meaning is given him at once in :

> Not so; even through the hollow eyes of death
> I spy life peering . . . (II, i, 270)

That is more than 'character'. When Bolingbroke lands,
Northumberland is there beside him; and in III, i and III, iii I
am sure that the *visual* contrast between these armed cam-
paigners and the toy warfare of the lists, the brilliant and vapid
refinement of the Court, are part of the play as images. Elizabethan eyes saw iron as we see khaki battle-dress and camouflage.
And, significantly, Richard's words in banishing Bolingbroke
foreshadow this very change : he would *avoid* the

> . . . harsh-resounding trumpets' dreadful bray,
> And grating shock of wrathful iron arms. . . . (I, iii, 135–6)

But the iron comes; and with it a touch of iron in the verse : as
witness Bolingbroke's opening lines in the scenes before and after
Richard's speech on landing in Wales, 'Dear earth, I do salute
thee with my hand. . . .' The answer to that is the efficient staff-
officer's : 'So that by this intelligence we learn/ The Welshmen
are dispers'd.' (III, iii, 1). It is more than character-contrast :
the verse, backed by the hardening of the human exteriors, the
steel-framed faces, jars two worlds together. The same jar is in
the Deposition-scene. It gives the play its meaning and experi-

ence, as a kind of tragic drama : the obscure tragedy, unclear, interesting, rather disheartening, of 'Shakespearian history'.

The nature of the jar—the nature of those two worlds— makes Richard less than the fully tragic hero. One is the half-fantasy world of the Court, where Richard's half-dream kingship reigns, with angels at his beck and serpents for his foes; the other is that other dream, of action, will and curt-worded decision, in which he is nothing, or a passive sufferer, a king of woes (or merely a king of words). In the mirror-episode the two dreams doubly confront each other. This it is that makes the Arden editor, following Pater, tell us Richard's nature is 'that of the poet who has unfortunately had kingship thrust upon him'. One need not reply, 'If so, surely a very *bad* poet'; for the answer is in Dowden, or in what Dowden quotes from Kreyssig : '. . . he affords us the shocking spectacle of an absolute bankruptcy, mental and spiritual no less than in the world of outward affairs, caused by one condition only : that nature has given him the character of a Dilettante, and called him to a position which, more than any other, demands the Artist.'[11]

SOURCE : *Angel with Horns* (1961).

NOTES

1. See p. 61 above.

2. 'consistently inconsistent'.

3. In a private letter to Dover Wilson quoted in the *New Cambridge* edn. of *Richard II*, p. iv.

4. If this is what Dover Wilson's relation of it to *Love's Labour's Lost* means (ibid., p. xi).

5. Ibid., p. xii.

6. York's lines embarrass most Yorks; and so much of him is a fussy, incompetent old gentleman, that I wonder whether he always *was* a bit of a joke : a mild one, and perhaps poorly and misguidedly imitated from the comical side of Woodstock.

7. Egerton MS. 1944, ed. Frijlinck (M.S.R., 1929); A. P. Rossiter, *Woodstock: A Moral History* (Chatto & Windus, 1946).

8. References are to Rossiter's edition.

9. He shifts back the fiscal tyranny from 1498 to a mythical date before 1488 (when Tresilian was hanged). Why does he do this?

Because he was a Common-Law man, writing a moral history against the King's-Law men (i.e. Bacon as *versus* Coke). Hence the contradiction between his play and Shakespeare's on kingly right, as stated by Gaunt in *Richard II*, i, ii.

10. Before dismissing *Woodstock*, let me remark that several of Dover Wilson's notes on *Richard II* (*New Cambridge* edn.) are unreliable, mainly because of his predisposition to lay a non-Shakespearian 'old play' behind Shakespeare's, written by a wide-reading historian who potted many recondite chronicles. But the puzzle he makes of Bagot (who loses his head *en route* for Ireland and then apparently comes back to life again) vanishes if *Woodstock* is consulted; York's reference to 'nor my own disgrace' (II, i, 168) is not a loose end, but alludes to the same Duke's 'Disgraced our names and thrust us from his court' (*Woodstock*, III, ii, 4; and his attempts to make the phrase 'upon pain of life' (I, iii, 140 and 153) a link with Froissart ('I have not found the phrase in any of the sources except Froissart . . .') fails completely, as it is used in *Woodstock*, IV, iii, 171.

11. Kreyssig, *Vorlesungen über Shakespeare* (ed. 1874), i, p. 189, quoted (in original) by Dowden, *Shakspere: His Mind and Art* (ed. 1892), p. 195.

Nicholas Brooke

DIVINE SUBSTITUTES AND STREAMS OF BLOOD (1968)

[Section I is largely concerned with matters more fully discussed in the *Introduction* to this volume.]

II

The conception of Richard as a wilting poet is completely out of place in Act I, which opens in terms of high rhetorical splendour :

> Old John of Gaunt, time-honoured Lancaster,
> Hast thou according to thy oath and band
> Brought hither Henry Herford thy bold son . . . (I, i, 1–3)

This pitch is sustained throughout the court scenes, i and iii. It is, of course, possible to make Richard bleat these lines in feeble imitation of royal utterance, but only in defiance of the strong rhetorical rhythm they obviously have. That this is often done points to a general contempt for Shakespeare's use of words in his early plays : but the controlled variety of utterance which I have noted should give us more confidence in accepting his rhythms here, and we shall find the same variations of tone in this play as in its predecessors. Richard, here, is every inch a king : his reply to the first greetings of Bolingbroke and Mowbray suggests authority :

> We thank you both, yet one but flatters us,
> As well appeareth by the cause you come,
> Namely, to appeal each other of high treason. (25–7)

The logic is questionable, but that does not diminish the shrewdness and confidence of the royal pomp; and these qualities are still apparent in Richard's speech at the end of the scene :

> We were not born to sue, but to command. (196)

And the commands he then issues are obeyed.

The main substance of the scene is in the vaunting speeches of Bolingbroke and Mowbray which seem to me rather strange. They accuse each other, indeed, of high treason, but mostly only in the form of abuse : the only real charges are Bolingbroke's, of Mowbray's misappropriation of cash, and his responsibility for the murder of Gloucester (Woodstock), and these Mowbray answers with some dignity (124–51). It is true that in both defences the king is implicated, but very obscurely, and the point is not taken up. Richard's response—and it is Gaunt's too—is to treat the matter as a personal quarrel, taking virtually no notice of the charges themselves :

> Wrath-kindled gentlemen, be rul'd by me ...
> Forget, forgive, conclude and be agreed. (152, 156)

There is no suggestion that Richard is 'huddling it aside' because he is implicated. The complexities of historical detail are submerged in the general stress on wrath-kindled gentlemen, the threat they offer to civil peace, and Richard's efforts to calm them :

> Let's purge this choler without letting blood. (153)

The main development is of the choleric utterance, and the imagery of blood. The first is stressed in Richard's comment before Bolingbroke and Mowbray appear :

> High-stomach'd are they both and full of ire,
> In rage, deaf as the sea, hasty as fire. (18–19)

The tone is Marlowan, the heroic note of Tamburlaine, which is clearly heard in Mowbray's

> ... I would allow him odds,
> And meet him were I tied to run afoot
> Even to the frozen ridges of the Alps. (62–4)

And Richard remarks of Bolingbroke :

> How high a pitch his resolution soars! (109)

It does indeed, in the startling image with which Bolingbroke follows up his charges :

> That he did plot the Duke of Gloucester's death,
> Suggest his soon-believing adversaries,
> And consequently, like a traitor coward,
> Sluic'd out his innocent soul through streams of blood,
> Which blood, like sacrificing Abel's, cries
> Even from the tongueless caverns of the earth
> To me for justice and rough chastisement. (100–6)

The streams of blood may seem to take us straight into the world of *Titus Andronicus*, and so does much else in this scene. But, in fact, though there is far more blood on the stage in *Titus*, there is more in the poetry of *Richard II*. Blood in this scene refers to the choleric humour, the nobility of high blood, and the tie of kinship, as well as the spilt blood of fratricide (or civil war). This is developed more formally in scene ii, and extended later when the sun itself becomes bloody. But here it is associated with the significant reference to Abel's murder, the offence against God himself. Biblical allusion is at least as prominent here as Ovidian in *Titus Andronicus*, and it serves a similar interpretative function. Judas, Pilate, and Christ himself are all invoked in later scenes, and the play ends with a return to the guilt of Cain, in Bolingbroke's curse on Exton :

> With Cain go wander thorough shades of night,
> And never show thy head by day nor light. (v, vi, 43–4)

The crimes of men in this play are very directly related to the divine scheme of things; and the problem of man as anointed king develops into a tragic dilemma which neither Richard nor Bolingbroke can solve. The Marlowan afflatus in the verse of this Act sets the play on a very high heroic plane indeed; when, later, a more flexible and human utterance emerges, it is not so much a maturing of Shakespeare's way of writing as the assertion of a humanity that cannot fulfil the divine image. In this respect *Richard II* differs from *Richard III*, for no character here seeks independence by repudiating the divine order, though there are several points at which the play itself (apparently supremely orthodox) could be accused of blasphemy.

The consistent impress of this opening scene, then, is of the heroic pitch of choler; the soaring resolution of the contestants (in renaissance, not medieval, form) and the supreme status of the king who rules them under, but only just under, God. All these things are related to the blood image, in the significant circumstances of the first murder. The historical-political situation is given, but, as it seems to me, suppressed for the time being to permit the establishing of a blood tragedy, and of a Richard who *is* a King. Similarly, his badness as a ruler and his weakness as a man are held back for subsequent revelation : no hint of either has been given yet.

III

The blood image is fully defined in scene ii, where Gaunt and the Duchess of Gloucester develop a series of formal emblems in a manner which might reasonably be called 'choric' : the scene has something of the air of a prologue postponed till the initial tableau has been presented. But the hieratic tone is varied by reference to the violent actions of men, in a fashion reminiscent of Act I of *Titus* : Gloucester is said to have been 'hack'd down' by 'butcher Mowbray'. The apparent concern of the scene is with Gloucester's murder and his widow's desire for revenge; but the handling of this is again rather odd, as though the audience already knew of it, rather than had to be told. On the other hand, it is very explicit in elaboration of the blood relationship in which the central figures are involved :

> Edward's seven sons, whereof thyself art one,
> Were as seven vials of his sacred blood,
> Or seven fair branches springing from one root.
> Some of those seven are dried by nature's course,
> Some of those branches by the Destinies cut;
> But Thomas my dear lord, my life, my Gloucester,
> One vial full of Edward's sacred blood,
> One flourishing branch of his most royal root,
> Is crack'd, and all the precious liquor spilt,
> Is hack'd down, and his summer leaves all faded,
> By envy's hand, and murder's bloody axe. (I, ii, 11–21)

The Duchess sustains her double emblem, of tree and blood vessels, at great length : it is at once a compulsion to unity, and to revenge; an emblem of family unity, and of what distinguishes princes from lesser men :

> That which in mean men we intitle patience
> Is pale cold cowardice in noble breasts. (33–4)

Gaunt, like Marcus Andronicus, resists the impulsion to human revenge : 'God's is the quarrel'; and instead of descending into bestial insanity, he proceeds to elaborate the divine order and the rule of law :

> for God's substitute,
> His deputy anointed in His sight,
> Hath caus'd his death; the which if wrongfully,
> Let heaven revenge, for I may never lift
> An angry arm against His minister. (37–41)

Gaunt implies, once more, Richard's guilt, but sets the actions of men against the divine appointment of kings, and thus establishes the dilemma of the play. The Duchess sustains her plea for revenge, but never against Richard :

> Be Mowbray's sins so heavy in his bosom
> That they may break his foaming courser's back . . . (50–1)

The spirited courser recurs as an image of spirited humanity : Shakespeare had presented it at length in *Venus and Adonis* in the stallion who can nothing lack 'Save a proud rider on so proud a back' (300), and he reverts to it at key points in this play. Richard, in III, iii, comes down to the base court 'like glist'ring Phaeton, Wanting the manage of unruly jades'; and in the last Act there is a strange interlude with the groom, discussing the faithlessness of roan Barbary :

> RICHARD   Rode he on Barbary? Tell me, gentle friend,
> How went he under him?
> GROOM   So proudly as if he disdain'd the ground.
> RICHARD   So proud that Bolingbroke was on his back!
> That jade hath eat bread from my royal hand;
> This hand hath made him proud with clapping him.

Would he not stumble? would he not fall down,
Since pride must have a fall, and break the neck
Of that proud man that did usurp his back? (v, v, 81–9)

Richard is divorced from both his divine anointment and his animal spirits in the end, the links in the chain of being broken at both ends, God and roan Barbary seeming equally indifferent.

Here in I, ii, the old Duchess, deprived of her passionate hope of revenge, loses the will to live and waits bloodless with her companion Grief for death to visit her

empty lodgings and unfurnish'd walls,
Unpeopled offices, untrodden stones . . . (I, ii, 68–9)

The scene establishes, then, an elaborate and vivid sequence of emblems: the living tree, rooted in the earth but associated with the vials of human blood; the threatening figures of Envy and Murder, and the noble spiritedness of violent action, contrasted with the bloodless figure of Grief pouring watery tears on untrodden stones. All these recur in pointed echoes till they are reassembled at the end of the play. They serve here to interpret the heroic terms of the opening scene, the conflict of an anointed King with high-blooded subjects. That is established *first*; other facets develop subsequently: of a criminal Richard we have had hints (no more); of a weak man, so far none at all.

IV

I, iii sustains the heroic pitch: the full panoply of royalty in the elaborate staging of the joust. It proceeds in much the same tone as scene i until the sudden anticlimax of Richard's intervention: the audience's disappointment is as intense as the combatants', for we are deprived of a promised spectacle. But the effect of this is not to affirm Richard's uncertainty so much as to shift the play to a more sophisticated plane than armed combat. Richard's speech links the emblems already noted to a stress only implicit before, but now explicit, on the realm of England. The tree and blood collocation reappears as:

our kingdom's earth should not be soil'd
With that dear blood which it hath fostered. (I, iii, 125–6)

Bolingbroke and Mowbray threaten civil war with their

> eagle-winged pride
> Of sky-aspiring and ambitious thoughts. (129–30)

Their 'greatness' will 'make us wade even in our kindred's blood'. The independence of the eagle is contrasted with the organic structure of earth–tree–sky: an opposition of the will of man to the order of nature and the divine will. The sentence of banishment provokes contrasting reactions: Bolingbroke's stoical acceptance—

> That sun that warms you here, shall shine on me (145)

includes a sense of organic unity preserved, and is set against Mowbray's sense of tragic deprivation in being cut off from his roots, his source of life:

> What is thy sentence then but speechless death . . .
> Then thus I turn me from my country's light,
> To dwell in solemn shades of endless night. (172, 176–7)

Gaunt has a similar vision:

> My oil-dried lamp and time-bewasted light
> Shall be extinct with age and endless night. (221–2)

The crushing of ambitious pride provokes for them, as lack of revenge did for the Duchess, death and endless night, and Bolingbroke's reflections on the soul wandering in the air:

> Banish'd this frail sepulchre of our flesh,
> As now our flesh is banish'd from this land. (196–7)

The place of man in the organic structure of nature and heavens is felt to be curiously insecure.

The insecurity is brought to bear on Richard himself: he has acted with divine right, and his clemency in reducing Bolingbroke's sentence by four years may also seem divine; but it provokes the response:

> Four lagging winters and four wanton springs
> End in a word: such is the breath of kings. (214–15)

The irony is completed ten lines later :

RICHARD   Why, uncle, thou hast many years to live.
GAUNT   But not a minute, king, that thou canst give . . .
    Thy word is current with him for my death,
    But dead, thy kingdom cannot buy my breath. (225–32)

Richard's authority is still unquestioned, but he is brought sharply within the confines of mortality; Bolingbroke, on the other hand, appropriates the organic images to himself :

> Then, England's ground, farewell; sweet soil, adieu,
> My mother and my nurse that bears me yet ! (306–7)

Out of this he can achieve the final development into excruciating patriotism that establishes him clearly as a growing branch :

> Where'er I wander boast of this I can,
> Though banish'd, yet a true-born Englishman. (308–9)

These opening scenes have developed a series of related conflicts : of human self-sufficient pride against dependence on a superior will; of the force of individual will against a determined pattern; of violence against the process of continuous growth. All these characteristic themes are imaginatively realized in the splendour of the staging and the utterance, and unified in the all-pervading blood imagery. All this has been applied (by both Richard and Bolingbroke) to political questions of order or chaos in government; but so far the highly formal rhetoric, and the formalized verse patterns, have resisted any considerable shift of attention from the cosmic scale.

v

The next two scenes (I, iv and II, i) provide a series of shocks, reinforced by abrupt changes of tone. The heroic, the grandiose, and the universal is suddenly presented in a different light. Aumerle's account of his farewell to Bolingbroke has an offensive levity :

> I brought high Herford, if you call him so,
> But to the next highway, and there I left him. (I, iv, 3–4)

Richard does not immediately imitate this tone (nor reprove it), but he does turn to questions of political expediency: Bolingbroke's wooing of the people—'What reverence he did throw away on slaves'—and from the suspicion that Bolingbroke will end in rebellion he turns to the economic problems of the Irish war:

> We are inforc'd to farm our royal realm ...
>   If that come short,
> Our substitutes at home shall have blank charters,
> Whereto, when they shall know what men are rich,
> They shall subscribe them for large sums of gold. (45–50)

The climax of this movement comes with Bushy's announcement of Gaunt's illness:

> RICHARD   Now put it, God, in the physician's mind
> To help him to his grave immediately!
> The lining of his coffers shall make coats
> To deck our soldiers for these Irish wars.
> Come, gentlemen, let's all go visit him,
> Pray God we may make haste and come too late! (59–64)

The offensive levity of Aumerle and the plain falsity of Richard's economics are conflated in this blasphemous wit. The puissant and glorious Monarch is presented suddenly as a cold politician with atheistic tendencies. The figure of the Machiavel is remotely discernible here; but without the ambitious mastery of Richard III or Marlowe's Guise, it is merely distasteful. The more so, because this emerges as Richard's personality, cheap however witty; but still confident, he is not yet hesitant or weak.

The material for this scene is largely drawn from the anonymous *Woodstock*,[1] and the comparison serves to indicate differences in Shakespeare's stress. *Woodstock* is very largely concerned with economics: it goes into great detail with statistics showing the 'farming' and 'blank-chartering' in action round the country. Shakespeare suppresses a great deal, and brings in what he does use only incidentally, by no means as a central issue in his play. Further, his Richard is a radically different figure, even here: in *Woodstock*, the king is a 'rude boy' who derives his nasty schemes from his flatterers; and he wants the money chiefly for lavish spending :

> At Westminster shalt see my sumptuous hall,
> My royal tables richly furnished
> Where every day I feast ten thousand men :
> To furnish out which feast I daily spend
> Thirty fat oxen and three hundred sheep,
> With fish and fowl in numbers numberless. (III, i, 83–8)

(The statistical tendency is clear enough.) This Richard is a feeble-minded luxur : Shakespeare's king has at least the ability to evolve his own nasty schemes, and he wants the cash to supply his Irish wars. He is, in short, still a king in action as well as name; the nastiness that is personal is also political, in him it springs from the problems of government. We have as yet no sign of feebleness.

The ideas and responses suggested by setting this scene against its predecessors are worked out in II, i (I have suggested that the Act division is misplaced here). Gaunt's famous prophetic speech sets

> This royal throne of kings, this scept'red isle (II, i, 40)

modulating through a long series of images to

> Is now leas'd out—I die pronouncing it—
> Like to a tenement or pelting farm. (59–60)

Richard's entry is preluded by York's warning,

> deal mildly with his youth,
> For young hot colts being rag'd do rage the more (69–70)

which introduces a further discovery of his private character, whose limitations are clearly indicated in the contrast between the Queen's greeting :

> How fares our noble uncle, Lancaster? (71)

and his own :

> What comfort, man? how is't with aged Gaunt? (72)

It is very poetical with aged Gaunt, as Richard (not yet a poet-king, or in the least flower-like) remarks :

> Can sick men play so nicely with their names? (84)

Gaunt proceeds nevertheless to utter his criticism :

> A thousand flatterers sit within thy crown,
> Whose compass is no bigger than thy head . . .
> O, had thy grandsire with a prophet's eye
> Seen how his son's son should destroy his sons . . .

through to :

> Landlord of England art thou now, not king. (100–13)

Richard's temper blazes as York had anticipated :

> A lunatic lean-witted fool,
> Presuming on an ague's privilege. (115–16)

York is right : Richard is a hot colt, and his tone is obviously inappropriate. But Gaunt is not altogether right : Richard is still a king :

> Now by my seat's right royal majesty,
> Wert thou not brother to great Edward's son,
> This tongue that runs so roundly in thy head
> Should run thy head from thy unreverent shoulders. (120–3)

It is therefore Richard himself who leads Gaunt back to his major theme, the blood and plant emblems :

> O, spare me not, my brother Edward's son,
> For that I was his father Edward's son;
> That blood already, like the pelican,
> Hast thou tapp'd out and drunkenly carous'd :
> My brother Gloucester, plain well-meaning soul,
> Whom fair befall in heaven 'mongst happy souls,
> May be a president and witness good
> That thou respect'st not spilling Edward's blood.
> Join with the present sickness that I have,
> And thy unkindness be like crooked age,
> To crop at once a too long withered flower. (124–34)

That is the climax of Gaunt's scene; the sequel is the specific crime that upsets the unstable equilibrium of the realm: Richard's illegal seizure of Gaunt's property (still for the purpose of fighting in Ireland), which sets York off again on Edward's sons, comparing Richard to his father:

> His face thou hast, for even so look'd he,
> Accomplish'd with the number of thy hours. (176–7)

York prophesies rebellion; but Richard goes no further in offence than to stick to his point, makes York regent, and exits to make merry with his Queen.

The first movement ends with Northumberland's news of Bolingbroke's imminent landing, and the plotting of rebellion. It has proceeded from the majestic royalty of I, i, through a series of discoveries to this final indication of disaster. In this it resembles, structurally, the first Act of *Titus Andronicus*, with its succession of prepared revelations; and as in *Titus* the emergence of human qualities that betray the royal image is revealed in striking contrasts of tone. It is the gap between the two which constitutes the tragic foundation of the play. On the one hand, Richard as king fulfils, in utterance and appearance, the panoply of royalty, the theme of blood as linking man and man, spilt in destruction, related to the family tree of Edward's progeny which grows out of the fertile soil of England. On the other, within this grandiose framework, Richard is a hot colt, whose misrule provokes rebellion. In the heroic frame, Richard is King, Bolingbroke a sky-aspiring rebel, whose doom in blood and guilt is evident; in the second, Richard is a bad governor whose downfall in rebellion is foretold, and Bolingbroke the necessary substitute. This distinction is lost entirely if it is assumed that the rhetoric of the opening scenes is merely a conventional dramatic mode without a specific function in this play, or if the actor attempts to reveal Richard's faults before Shakespeare exposes them in I, iv. The blood tragedy, in its largest terms, is established first; the political in a narrow sense, only secondarily. Whereas *Woodstock* sees the affairs of man in terms of a purely social environment, Shakespeare sets these against a cosmic continuum, represented by 'England' and symbolized by the generative soil. Economics is so much less Shakespeare's concern than *Wood-*

stock's that it hardly becomes a major stress at all; it is used only to establish a particular local effect. The splendour of man is fulfilment as king, the sun shining on his kingdom; his tragedy is in his humanity, that he is beneath the sun, no less mortal than his subjects.

[Section VI discusses the second movement of the play, from II, ii to III, iii.]

VII

These two major scenes [III, ii and IV, i] are distanced from each other by the Queen's interlude with her gardeners, of which the function is very obviously choric. The tears and growing earth emblems are given a final extension in the lecture demonstration on good husbandry. The scene is embarrassing nowadays, and can never have been very lively; but if the rhetorical structure was allowed its full development, this brief commentary would seem more in place than it does in productions struggling to invest the play with a false naturalism. The scene is important to revive the political theme, which has been obscured by the more personal stress in IV, iii. England the sea-walled garden continues to grow in spite of weeping queens, but needs a gardener; it needs in fact the specialty. not of majesty, but of rule. In Richard's fall his Queen imagines a second loss of Eden :

> What Eve, what serpent, hath suggested thee
> To make a second fall of cursed man? (III, iv, 75–6)

The allusion ties in with the Biblical reference of the play; but the gardener's retort is bluntly matter-of-fact :

> King Richard he is in the mighty hold
> Of Bolingbroke. Their fortunes both are weigh'd;
> In your lord's scale is nothing but himself,
> And some few vanities that make him light. (83–6)

The need for Bolingbroke is plainly stated, and the inevitability of Richard's fall. To this view, the whole edifice of rhetorical and imaginative splendour has no validity; the play is momentarily stripped of all its larger forms. But only for a moment : if government needs Bolingbroke, Bolingbroke needs majesty, as the opening of Act IV plainly demonstrates.

The first part consists of a quarrel over responsibility for Gloucester's murder. The crime which should be the central item of the indictment against Richard only leads to a vulgar brawl from which we can never learn who really was guilty. The situation of I, i is recapitulated, but without the splendour; and Bolingbroke now has less power to control the squabbling lords than Richard had then. He tries to restore the tone by announcing the repeal of Mowbray; but the gesture is nullified by Carlisle's news of his death. The fates, obscurely here but clearly in a moment, are spoiling Bolingbroke's triumph.

The second part of the scene follows York's announcement that Richard will abdicate. Bolingbroke ascends the throne without ceremony, which produces a startling peripeteia in Carlisle's prompt and magnificent attack. Richard's crime has just been dissolved in doubt and argument; Bolingbroke's is before us, the stage setting the emblem of usurpation as he sits on Richard's throne. The scene is set for Carlisle's denunciation :

> The blood of English shall manure the ground,
> And future ages groan for this foul act. (IV, i, 137-8)

The heroic memory of Mowbray fighting crusades

> For Jesu Christ in glorious Christian field,
> Streaming the ensign of the Christian cross
> Against black Pagans, Turks, and Saracens (93-5)

is transposed into

> Peace shall go sleep with Turks and infidels. (139)

And, finally, Carlisle translates the established blood emblems into the supreme sacrifice :

> Disorder, horror, fear, and mutiny,
> Shall here inhabit, and this land be call'd
> The field of Golgotha and dead men's skulls. (142-4)

The name of Christ echoes through the rest of the scene.
Richard takes it up on his entry:

> So Judas did to Christ. But he, in twelve,
> Found truth in all but one; I, in twelve thousand, none. (170-1)

Against this image, Bolingbroke's rational intention ('so we shall
proceed without suspicion') becomes ironical; and Richard does
not spare him. This, I take it, is the effect of the famous speech in
which Richard goes through the coronation rites in reverse:

> With mine own tears I wash away my balm,
> With mine own hands I give away my crown,
> With mine own tongue deny my sacred state,
> With mine own breath release all duteous oaths. (207-10)

The image of Christ leads us to this ritual solemnity; and at the
same time Bolingbroke on the throne is in a conspicuously false
position. Richard presses home his advantage:

> Though some of you, with Pilate, wash your hands,
> Showing an outward pity—yet you Pilates
> Have here deliver'd me to my sour cross,
> And water cannot wash away your sin. (239-42)

Bolingbroke has no reply: Shakespeare interpolates the cruder
figure of Northumberland to resist the imaginative power with
blunt insensitivity; Northumberland who can (in v, i) dispose of
guilt with a brusqueness in marked contrast to Bolingbroke:

> My guilt be on my head, and there an end. (v, i, 69)

Northumberland's bluntness, however, cannot dispose of the
power that Richard has invoked, and Bolingbroke has to restrain
him:

> Urge it no more, my Lord Northumberland. (271)

This preludes the 'mirror scene', which is too often under-
estimated. Richard has been descanting on the proposition that,
deprived of the throne to which he was born, he has no identity:

> No, not that name was given me at the font. (256)

He develops this theme into the mirror-image :

> That it may show me what a face I have
> Since it is bankrupt of his majesty. (266–7)

What he sees when the looking-glass is brought derives its numerals from Holinshed, but its verbal form from Marlowe's *Faustus* :[2]

> Was this face the face
> .That every day under his household roof
> Did keep ten thousand men? (281–3)

The echo of Faustus, the man who was thrust forever from the sight of Christ, is curious here; and more remarkable since there are two other echoes of Faustus within the previous twenty lines :

> O that I were a mockery king of snow,
> Standing before the sun of Bolingbroke,
> To melt myself away in water-drops (260–2)

and,

> Fiend, thou torments me ere I come to hell. (270)

The words are addressed to Northumberland, but their force is strange : Richard has represented himself as Christ; but he is now the damned Faustus on his way to hell, seeking oblivion. So that when he speaks of

> the unseen grief
> That swells with silence in the tortur'd soul (297–8)

he is expressly referring to his own guilt; a guilt which is reflected on Bolingbroke, who, seated on the throne, is another 'mirror' of Richard's predicament :

> Mark, silent king, the moral of this sport—
> How soon my sorrow hath destroy'd my face. (290–1)

Bolingbroke's silent figure adds to its emblematic connotations that of 'silence in the tortur'd soul'. Their guilts reflect each other : men who, like Marlowe's heroes, presume to the sweet fruition of an earthly crown, and are damned for it. The peculiar twist here is that Richard was born to it; but his sense of damnation is no less strong than his divinity. Bolingbroke's immediate implication in all this is too often overlooked, because his silent presence, so impressive on the stage, is invisible to the reader.

The problem that drove Richard to look in the glass is by no means a purely fanciful one. To Tudor orthodoxy, the *man* who was *king* was an exceptional mortal, possessed of peculiar virtú, and by this fitted for his role so that he could fill no lesser one. Richard 'looks like a king' but is not one. Shakespeare does not here (it is different in *Henry IV*) make a simple distinction between the man and the office : the office is the necessary concomitant of the man.

Richard has involved Bolingbroke in this emblematic reflection of greatness and guilt; he leaves him with impressive scorn :

> Then give me leave to go.
> BOLINGBROKE Whither?
> RICHARD Whither you will, so I were from your sights. (313–15)

It is Richard who is dominant here, not as a weeping Narcissus, but as a man conscious of moral victory. Our final impression cannot be of his weakness alone. The question in fact is, how far should we (freed from traditional prejudice) feel his weakness in this scene? I am somewhat uncertain. By concentrating on the imaginative power of the emblem-images, I have seen a tragic splendour, as I think it should be seen, moving between man and divine appointment, heaven and hell. The other view of the scene derives from noting that it is Richard who says all this, that it is his romantic vision of himself. It is, however, obviously more than this : it was Carlisle, not Richard, who invoked the figure of Christ on the field of Golgotha, and the only challenge to these terms comes from Northumberland who rather serves to test the strength of the imaginative power than to countervale it. A hint of criticism can be heard in Bolingbroke's shrewd retort—

> The shadow of your sorrow hath destroy'd
> The shadow of your face— (292–3)

but Richard's come-back is strong enough to embarrass Bolingbroke more than himself. The abruptness with which Bolingbroke turns from Richard's exit to announce his own coronation is ambiguous in effect: one may take it as the reticence of guilt, or as efficiency released from patient endurance of a long and embarrassing exhibition. Efficiency predominates in Bolingbroke's performance in the opening of Act v; but the burden of guilt returns to him at the end of the play.

One cannot simplify this: we are to feel simultaneously the force of all Richard's utterance, and yet to see the weakness implicit in the fact that *he* is uttering it. It is partly the dilemma evident in all these early plays, of a form of poetic statement derived from narrative verse, where it would be unequivocal (Richard not seeming weak unless the narrator called him so) becoming equivocal by the mere fact of being delivered by an actor on the stage. But here, I think, Shakespeare is partly taking advantage of that ambiguity: Richard's character is the least important aspect of the scene, but it is allowed to be felt; and the same is (even more ambiguously) true of Bolingbroke. The resultant complexity of effect is impressive, but somewhat distracting, because it is not handled with the assurance of Shakespeare's later technique (when, for instance, Othello speaks of his own splendour, the double sense is far more sharply defined).

[Sections viii and ix are concerned with the last movement of the play, Act v.]

SOURCE: from *Shakespeare's Early Tragedies* (1968).

NOTES

1. *Woodstock: A Moral History*, ed. A. P. Rossiter, 1946, pp. 47–53. The relationship with Shakespeare's play is fully discussed in Rossiter's Introduction (and see above, pp. 214–29).

2. P. Ure, *Richard II* (1956), note on line 283.

SELECT BIBLIOGRAPHY

EDITIONS

(including introductory essays on the play, and in some cases stage history)

J. Dover Wilson, ed., New Cambridge Shakespeare (Cambridge, England, 1939). (Stage History by Harold Child.)
M. Black, ed., New Variorum Edition (Philadelphia & London, 1955).
M. Black, ed., Pelican Shakespeare (Baltimore, 1957).
P. Ure, ed., New Arden Shakespeare (London & Cambridge, Mass., 1956).
K. Muir, ed., Signet Classic Shakespeare (New York, 1963).
S. Wells, ed., New Penguin Shakespeare (London, 1969).

BOOKS

A. C. Sprague, *Shakespeare's Histories* (London, 1964). Chapter III is devoted largely to a valuable review of the play on the stage in England and America in the nineteenth and twentieth centuries.

A. R. Humphreys, *Shakespeare: Richard II* (Studies in English Literature, 31, London, 1967). The fullest study of the play to date.

ARTICLES

Travis Bogard, 'Shakespeare's Second Richard', in *PMLA*, 70 (1955) 192–209. Contrasts the technique of character presentation with Richard's cruder namesake in *Richard III*.

M. Quinn, ' "The King is Not Himself" : the Personal Tragedy of Richard II', *Studies in Philology*, 56 (1959) 169–86. This essay like Peter Ure's in his Arden edition, views the play primarily as a tragedy rather than the first part of a historical tetralogy.

S. K. Heninger Jr., 'The Sun-King Analogy in *Richard II*', *Shakespeare Quarterly*, 11 (1960) 319–27.

P. G. Phialas, 'The Medieval in *Richard II*', *Shakespeare Quarterly*, 12 (1961) 305–10.

D. C. Hockey, 'A World of Rhetoric in *Richard II*', *Shakespeare Quarterly*, 15 (1964) 179–91.

These three essays move in different directions from criticisms of Tillyard's influential study reprinted in this volume.

John R. Elliott Jr., 'History and Tragedy in *Richard II*', *Studies in English Literature*, 8 (1968) 253–71. Discusses the structural influence of different interests in the play.

Terence Hawkes, 'The Word Against the Word: the role of language in *Richard II*', *Language and Style*, 2 (1969) 296–322. Proposes the role of the spoken word should be of reciprocity, and that this is essentially violated by Richard, and subsequently by Bolingbroke.

Michel Grivelet, 'Shakespeare's "War with Time" : The *Sonnets* and *Richard II*', *Shakespeare Survey*, 23 (1970) 69–78. Discusses a common theme in the poems and the play.

NOTES ON CONTRIBUTORS

RICHARD D. ALTICK : Professor of English at Ohio State University. His books include *Scholar Adventurers* and *The Art of Literary Research*.

M. C. BRADBROOK: formerly Professor of English Literature at the University of Cambridge and Mistress of Girton College. Her numerous books include *Themes and Conventions of Elizabethan Tragedy, Ibsen the Norwegian, T. S. Eliot, Shakespeare and Elizabethan Poetry, The Growth and Structure of Elizabethan Comedy, The Rise of the Common Player*.

NICHOLAS BROOKE : Professor of English Literature, University of East Anglia, Norwich. His books include *Shakespeare: King Lear* and *Shakespeare's Early Tragedies*.

JOHN RUSSELL BROWN : Professor of English at the University of Sussex and Associate Director, National Theatre, London. He has edited and directed plays by Shakespeare, Webster, etc. His books include *Shakespeare's Plays in Performance, Effective Theatre, Shakespeare's Dramatic Style*.

J. A. BRYANT JR : Professor of English at Syracuse University, New York. His main interests have been in Renaissance drama; publications include *Hyppolita's View: Some Christian Aspects of Shakespeare's plays*.

SIR JOHN GIELGUD : He has been, for many years now, the finest of English actors; there can be few, if any, of the leading Shakespearian roles which he has not played. He has published two volumes of memoirs, *Early Stages* and *Stage Directions*.

E. H. KANTOROWICZ : Medieval historian whose work ranges over history of ideas, art history, liturgical and legal history. He left

Germany before the war; in 1951 he was appointed Professor at the Institute for Advanced Study, Princeton.

M. M. MAHOOD: Professor of English and American Literature at the University of Kent at Canterbury. She was formerly at the University of Ibadan, Nigeria. In addition to *Shakespeare's Wordplay* she has published *Poetry and Humanism*, and *Joyce Cary's Africa*.

A. P. ROSSITER: Fellow of Jesus College, Cambridge, from 1945 to his death in 1957, and was University Lecturer in Cambridge University. His publications include *English Drama from Early Times to the Elizabethans*; *Angel with Horns* was edited posthumously from notes of lectures delivered in Cambridge and at Stratford-on-Avon.

BRENTS STIRLING: formerly Professor of English at the University of Washington. His main interests have been in sixteenth-century English literature; in addition to *Unity in Shakespearian Tragedy* he has published *The Populace in Shakespeare*.

E. M. W. TILLYARD: Master of Jesus College, Cambridge, 1945–59, and a leading scholar in both Shakespeare and Milton studies. His books include *Shakespeare's History Plays*, *The Elizabethan World Picture* and *The Epic Strain in the English Novel*. He died in 1962.

INDEX

References to Richard II and to Bolingbroke (Hereford, Henry IV) are so numerous that they are not entered in this index.